"Alessandra and O'Connor have hit a real home run with *People Smart*. It's the best thing I've ever seen written in this area! It is a must read for anyone who wants to learn more about themselves and others—easy to read, but powerful in content. *People Smart* will make you more aware and more effective from the moment you finish reading it."

Kenneth Blanchard, Ph.D.
Co-author, *The One Minute Manager*

People Smart

Powerful Techniques for Turning Every Encounter into a Mutual Win

Tony Alessandra, Ph.D.
and
Michael J. O'Connor, Ph.D.
with
Janice VanDyke

KEYNOTE
PUBLISHING
COMPANY
La Jolla, California

First Printing 1990   Sixth Printing 1993
Second Printing 1990   Seventh Printing 1993
Third Printing 1991   Eighth Printing 1995
Fourth Printing 1992
Fifth Printing 1992

Library of Congress Cataloging-in-Publication Data
Alessandra, Anthony J.
  People Smart : powerful techniques for turning every encounter into a mutual win / Tony Alessandra and Michael O'Connor with Janice VanDyke
    p.   cm.
  ISBN 0-9625161-1-2
  1. Inspirational relations.   I. O'Connor, Michael J.
II. VanDyke, Janice.   III. Title.
HM132.A354   1990
302-dc20   89-71069
                                                    CIP

Dedications

From Tony:

To my children, Justin and Jessica

From Michael:

To Mary Ann, my loving wife and my greatest teacher, and to my children Kevin and Kara, for their patience, tolerance, and appreciation of my life's work

Acknowledgments

Writing this book has become more and more a team effort as we have progressed from one stage to the next. Some people contributed content, either directly or indirectly; others gave helpful comments about the manuscript; some recharged our batteries when the going got rough; and some reached seemingly unreachable deadlines to keep the project going on time.

With this in mind, the authors would like to thank Carl Jung, David Merrill, Larry Wilson, and Myers and Briggs for their pioneering research and observations. Those who gave valuable feedback on the manuscript include Rick Barrera, Sheila Murray-Bethel, Don Cipriano, Judy Zitzloff, Marcia Feener, Charles Boyd and Jay Lewis.

Many others contributed input on their particular personality types—Ron Friedman, Holli Olson, Paula Cathcart, Danny Colleran, Colleen Alessandra, John Lee, Catherine Carpenter, Mary Faith Reading, Stan and Melody Leopard, Mikala Limbrecht, Seymour Myers, and Jessica and Justin Alessandra. Their insights especially enlivened the chapters on romance and family.

Thanks to Gary Alessandra for his tireless dedication in getting several days of copy ready today, Linda Brown and Lynda London for transforming text into graphics, and Melody Leopard for making the format "reader friendly." Dee Jones and Catherine Carpenter made sure everything was organized and sent off to the right people at the right time.

Additionally, the authors wish to thank and acknowledge Carlson Learning Company and its Performax Network Division for their support in supplying information on the needs model of behavior (DISC). For further information on their learning instruments and related materials, please write or call Carlson Learning Company; Carlson Parkway; P.O. Box 59159; Minneapolis, MN 55459-8247; (612) 449-2856.

Contents

Introduction

Everybody is interested in finding out more about themselves—and how to deal with others more effectively. If you're like most people, you want to improve your interactions with others. This book shows you a simple, yet proven, way to positively influence others.

The purpose of *People Smart* is threefold: to give you a conscious awareness of what people do, to help you predict what people are likely to do and why they do it, and to accept yourself and others as worthwhile so you can adapt and successfully relate.

Managers want to know how to maximize productivity and efficiency from their staff, salespeople need to build better rapport with customers, employees want to get along with their peers and managers. It's natural for people to aspire to success in business organizations. Those in helping professions want to provide better care for their patients and clients.

Entertainers seek to reach a larger audience and more effectual agents, while speakers want to leave their audiences with something to grow on. Engineers want to fit into their workplace as they turn out more quality products. Diplomats and public officials desire to influence varying groups so they can improve communication—whether internationally, nationally, or locally. And, of course, it's important for parents to relate well with their children—and vice versa. In short, virtually everyone is fascinated with making their working and living relationships better.

People Smart will not only help you become a better you, it will help you behave more maturely and productively by teaching you how to focus on your goals instead of your fears. Then you can develop and use more of your natural strengths, while recognizing, improving upon, and modifying your weaknesses. This book does not deal with values or judgments. Instead, we concentrate on individuals' needs and fears—our natural tendencies that cause us to do the things we do.

Every person has his or her own special way of doing things and an identifiable and predictable behavioral type. Behavioral type is a pattern, or group of recurring habits, resulting from the way you typically do things—the way you deal with people and situations. It's your comfortable method of behaving, most of the time, when you relax and just *act yourself*.

Often, when we do what comes naturally we alienate others without realizing it. Why? Because that same behavior may not be natural for them. If we want to get along with our colleagues, employees, bosses, friends, and families, it's essential we become aware of our natural tendencies—and their natural preferences! Then we can defuse extreme behaviors before we sabotage ourselves. We do this by temporarily using behavioral modification to change only our own behavior so the other person feels comfortable. When this happens, tension lessens and cooperation zooms.

Your technique of interacting with people succeeds when you receive and heed their external signals; it fails when you ignore and cross them. Of course, everyone experiences the same basic human needs, but each of us ranks some needs higher than others.

When you understand something about your own habitual style and how it differs from others' styles, you can modify your approach to get on the same wavelength with them. The ideas you present don't change. But you can change the way you present those ideas. And people will teach you how to treat them if you're willing to discover their unique signals.

For example, one type of person measures his success by results. He heads for the finished product and the bottom line.

He'll do whatever it takes, within reason, to get the job done. In fact, his natural response to what he views as other people's lack of accomplishment is, "Don't just sit around wasting time! Get busy!" He needs achievements.

Another type places high value on recognition and measures success by the amount of acknowledgment and praise she receives. Consequently, she typically follows that route to attention and applause. She gravitates toward friendliness and enjoyment, popularity and prestige—while consciously avoiding rejection, negativism, and arguments.

Then we have the steady, cooperative type of person who needs close relationships. He places a high value on sharing and trust, but bases his feelings about people and things on concrete evidence. He wants the security and predictability found in daily routine—so he resists sudden, unplanned changes and needs stable, predictable environments. He thrives on the familiar. Changes or surprises make him uncomfortable.

The last type concerns herself more with content than with congratulations. She wants to know how things work so she can evaluate how correctly they function. At the extreme, this tendency toward perfectionism can result in *paralysis by analysis*. Because she needs to be right, she prefers checking processes herself. Concerned with appearances, she focuses on the process—how to perform a task—while complying with established rules and regulations. As the most cerebral of the four types (in terms of how they deal with people and situations, not I.Q.), tasks win over people and a slow pace prevails.

People Smart will help you connect with people in the workplace and in your personal life. For example, Part One, "Understanding People Smarts," helps you to identify and better deal with virtually everyone. In "The Platinum Rule," we show you more about treating others the way they want to be treated, not the way you want to be treated—without being phony or underhanded. In "I Know Who You Are, But What Am I?", we describe each behavioral style and help you determine which one you are. Next, we assist you to identify other people's natural styles. The Adaptability chapter includes both versatility and flexibility characteristics and helps you to determine how adaptable you are in life's varying situations.

Part Two deals with "Workplace Applications." The chapters here help you identify and appropriately respond to the four basic types in a work environment. And we show how the different types typically lead and want to be managed. The sales and service chapter covers how the four types prefer to sell—and be sold.

"Personal Applications" is the thrust of Part Three. "The Social Scene" depicts each type behaving with friends and acquaintances, while the family chapter describes the four types at home with spouse and children. And the romance chapter portrays each type in dating situations.

In Part Four, we delve into more specific behaviors, combination patterns that more accurately describe you and others. Then we summarize all 15 commonly combined patterns and show you what they specifically want, need, and fear.

This is a reader-friendly book, with lots of charts and graphs to summarize and explain the text. The reader can use and reuse it as a constant companion for dealing with difficult people and stressful situations. *People Smart* shows clearly how to understand both your own unique strengths and inherent shortcomings and those of others. It gives you the tools to get what you want in various life situations. This reference equips you with the power and knowledge to cash in on these insights through more positive and productive exchanges with others. You can realistically take charge of improving all your relationships and this book shows how.

Part One

Understanding People Smarts

Chapter 1
The Platinum Rule

Personality clash or instant rapport?

In your dealings with others, have you ever experienced a personality conflict? (If you haven't, check to see if you're still breathing like the rest of us mortals.) No matter how much you may try, your teeth clench and your adrenalin pumps faster when you're with this difficult character. Whatever you may want to call the process, you clash. You're not tuned in on the same wavelength.

When we clash with someone, we often move towards the extreme of avoiding that person, no matter what. Or the other extreme of telling him exactly what we think of his unacceptable behavior. Or we may tell everyone else how distasteful we find him. Or just grit our teeth and tolerate him. Whatever our initial reaction, we feel uncomfortable because we have a personality conflict.

On the other hand, we'll bet you can think of somebody you liked immediately. You had instant rapport, immediate chemistry. "Ann is so down-to-earth, I feel as though I've known her for years." After ten minutes you felt like you'd known Mr. or Ms. Wonderful for half a lifetime. Here was a soul mate who clicked with you from word one. Her personality *felt right* and you also felt good about yourself when you were near her. You felt relaxed and comfortable with this person. Chemistry prevailed, and Ann made your Top Ten list of favorites.

What could possibly account for these two extreme variations in the human species? Certainly, our unique sets of experiences coupled with the genes passed down by Mom and Dad ensure we're all different. Everyone's idea of a person to avoid versus a best friend varies. Given these subjective differences, the way people communicate can result in conflict or chemistry. So how do you go about interacting with all those fascinatingly diverse, sometimes difficult, people out there?

How to deal with difficult people

This book will teach you how to treat people in a way which allows them to feel comfortable with you, so there'll be less tension between you. When tension goes down, positive outcomes—trust, credibility, creativity, cooperation, respect, commitment, and productivity—go up. How do you get results with people? By communicating with them on their level so they're at ease. Because challenging relationships are a fact of life, we'd like to show you how to:

— *understand* your own style, its strengths and weaknesses, and how your behaviors communicate that style to others.
— *identify* someone else's style by quick, easily learned techniques so you'll know how to *read people* and treat them the way they'd like to be treated.
— *adjust* your behavior to make all kinds of people more at ease with you, and you with them!

Bending the Golden Rule

We contend that you can create much more chemistry and far less conflict in all your relationships—work, social, dating, and family—based on how well you practice the Golden Rule. If you exercise the Golden Rule appropriately, you'll create much more relationship chemistry. But if you fail to understand the true spirit of the Golden Rule, you'll create many more personality conflicts. Just to make sure you have the proper perspective, what is the Golden Rule?

It's simply, "Do unto others as you would have them do unto you." Not the managerial version—"The person with the gold makes the rules,"—or the skeptical interpretation—"Do unto others before they do unto you."

"So," you say? "How could people get in trouble if they practiced that truth? Living by the Golden Rule should result in more harmonious relationships, not create conflict!" You're right. The problem lies with practicing the Golden Rule verbatim and not understanding its true intent. When you misapply it, you stand a much greater chance of triggering conflict over chemistry.

Let's explain. When you treat others as you want to be treated, you can end up offending others who have different needs, wants, and expectations from you. So when you apply the Golden Rule verbatim, there's a much greater chance of triggering conflict over chemistry. Yes, you heard it right. If you literally apply, "Do unto others as you would have them do unto you," you'll make problems for yourself with up to 75% of the types of people you meet. Following the Golden Rule verbatim means treating others from your point of view. That means you naturally tend to speak in the way you are most comfortable listening; or sell to others the way you like to be sold; or manage the way you want others to direct you.

When you treat people as you seek to be treated, it can cause tension. Why? Because the other person may not like your way. Perhaps you fill your own needs instead of his or hers. Or speak in a way that's easy for you to follow, but hard for the other person. That brings us to the second reason the Golden Rule can actually damage relationships. It implies all people want to be treated the same when, in fact, our preferences are not all alike. So application of this principle varies from one individual to the next based on their personality differences.

Margaret treats you as she wants to be treated

The Golden Rule would work only in a perfect world where all of us were identical. But we're not. For instance, Tony's mother devoutly practices it, but it backfires. She treats everybody alike. The world population is part of her extended Italian family. To understand her, try picturing the women in the Italian family from the hit movie *Moonstruck*. You'll have a sense of what she's like . . . only more so.

Tony's mother is an exceptionally people-oriented, outgoing person. She's so gregarious, she makes Bruce Willis look like an introvert. Anyway, when she goes to a restaurant, she greets the hostess and other patrons as though they're in her kitchen. Anyone who makes eye contact with her is fair game.

As she approaches a table of complete strangers, she typically says, "Hello? My name is Margaret. What's yours? Are you an Italian girl? No? Too bad . . ." And on and on. She joins in other people's conversations. She doesn't mind being asked personal questions. Readily and willingly misapplying the Golden Rule, she asks other people personal questions—whether they want to answer or not. "What is the special occasion?" Or, "What do you do for a living?"

"I'm an actuary."

"An actuary. Is that a religious society or something? And what do you do as an actuary?"

"I calculate rates for insurance companies."

"Do you make good money? Yes? How much?" (She also likes to prospect for her daughter Linda.)

If we take a poll at that restaurant, half the people will probably think that Margaret Alessandra is wonderful. "Boy, I wish my mother acted like that," or, "The woman is a national treasure." The rest of them are likely to react or think differently. "I enjoy my privacy when I go out to eat," or even, "Who let her loose?" As well-meaning and people-oriented as she is, she often unintentionally steps on people's toes. She doesn't want to, but . . .

What has happened? Margaret puts the Golden Rule into action and, by doing so, impresses some people and depresses others. Well, maybe she doesn't exactly depress them, but heightens their tensions. By acting the way she likes to be treated, there are mixed reviews. When behaving from only her own perspective, she doesn't take others' preferences into account. Why not? Simply because it's okay if strangers approach her and ask about her intimate, private thoughts; so she naturally figures it's okay for her to do the same thing. It's true for the rest of us. If we don't think first of the other person, we run the risk of unintentionally imposing a tension-filled win/lose or lose/lose relationship on them.

The Platinum Rule

We believe in refining The Golden Rule to take into consideration the feelings of the other person. Notice we don't say break the rule. We redefine it into the Platinum Rule—"Do unto others as they want to be done unto." Treat others the way they want to be treated. By platinum, we don't mean to imply *better*. We simply want to capture the true spirit or actual intention of the Golden Rule so we consider and respond appropriately to the other person's needs. We can learn to treat different people differently, according to their needs, not ours. That leads to greater understanding and acceptance.

Doing what comes naturally

Imagine Bruce Willis of MOONLIGHTING trying to motivate Mr. Spock of STAR TREK—with both of them practicing the Golden Rule. The problem that inevitably surfaces is Bruce will try to inspire Spock as he himself would like to be inspired. "Hey, this new plan is incredible!" Spock's typical reaction would probably be, "This does not compute." He wants concise, factual, accurate information. "Where's the proof? Can you document that?" while Bruce prefers to deal with the bigger, more generalized picture.

When we treat another person from our perspective, the result is often tension, whether it's expressed or not. In Neil Simon's THE ODD COUPLE, Felix and Oscar represent opposites. Oscar perceives himself as a *real* man—rough and tumble; Felix sees him as what he sometimes refers to as a slob. Felix thinks he's a *model of perfection*; Oscar figures Felix is an uptight worrywart. Whenever Felix approaches Oscar with his own expectations based on his needs—tidiness, punctuality, and moderation—Oscar explodes. Even though the two characters exaggerate many behaviors that we're likely to encounter, they represent clear examples of how we can turn people off when we *act naturally* en route to meeting only our own needs. While watching them clash may be entertaining for us, it's not so much fun in the daily lives of the real, although less dramatic, Felixes and Oscars around the world.

A steady dose of conflicting needs can end a promising relationship unless we treat the other person appropriately! If

Felix and Oscar made the effort to understand each other's needs, they could begin to gain greater appreciation of, and learn more about, their differences. Then they could find practical, optional ways of solving their own naturally occurring conflicts. The two of them collide when they expect each other to act like clones of themselves.

Archie Bunker says:

"Edith, do you know why we can't communicate? Because I'm talking in English and you're listening in dingbat!" Well, maybe Archie could benefit from learning how to communicate in *dingbat*! Then, he could mentally change places with Edith to understand her expectations instead of just his own.

Every day we face the potential for conflict or success with different types of people. Conflicts are inevitable, but the outcome from how you handle dissension is much more controllable. At the very least, you can manage your end of it. You can choose to treat somebody from his perspective—the way he wants to be treated—by modifying your own behavior; or you can choose to meet only your own needs—facing consequences such as dissatisfaction, frustration, confusion, and distress. It's up to you.

Modify your spots

"Modify my behavior? Hey, I don't want to change! And I hate phonies!"

We're not talking about changing a leopard into an elephant. We mean acting in a sensible, successful way. When someone wants to move at a faster pace, move at that pace. If others want more facts and details, provide them.

But wait? Isn't it phony to act in a way that isn't natural for you? We think acting in a way that is responsive to Japanese behavior patterns in a Japanese environment is more likely to be appreciated and accepted there. The result is greater success! It helps dispel the "Ugly American" stereotype that has been associated with some tourists who *act themselves* and expect others to do likewise. Of course, anything that's new feels strange at first, until you get more comfortable with it through repeated practice.

People learn to become more adaptable through education, experience, and maturity. We simply have to allow the opportunity for appropriate behaviors to surface. As we've mentioned, if you're able to put yourself in the other person's position, you become more open-minded in dealing with him or her. When you understand the way the other person feels comfortable communicating, you can modify your approach to get on the same wavelength. You haven't changed your own natural personality. You've merely added to it still other consciously learned, behavioral insights and strengths for dealing with different types of people and situations. The best part is that people will teach you how to communicate with them if you're willing to learn their signals by *reading* and then appropriately responding to them.

A suggestion for Felix and Oscar

Felix Unger and Oscar Madison, television's ODD COUPLE, have known each other for years. But they don't always choose to apply what they know. When each considers only himself, he unconsciously tends to plunge ahead towards meeting only his own needs. When they do this, they ignore the signals of how to allow each other to meet their own needs.

Imagine this more productive exchange:

"Oscar, your room is a mess. Here, I'll help you straighten it up by throwing away these old newspapers."

"Okay, but don't touch anything else in my room without my approval, Felix. You'll ruin my personal filing system."

Oscar's housekeeping is intentionally looser than Felix's. If Felix can tolerate a more "lived in" look and Oscar can learn to pick up after himself, they'll become more successful at meeting each other's needs. Regarding the housekeeping issue, Felix needs orderliness while Oscar needs freedom. With this realization in mind, they can communicate more effectively by letting each other know they've received these two signals. Then they can explore ways for satisfying both types of needs.

One option is trading off. Oscar can keep his room as sloppy as he wants as long as the door is closed and their common living area is neat. Or they can collaborate by cleaning Oscar's room together.

"Oscar, I know you like your freedom to do what you want, but your room is so filled with personal expressions you seem to be a prisoner in it. (How does he find his bed?) I'd like to help you organize your room so that it's more comfortable for you and for me."

(Ha! Felix would probably throw everything out if it was his room.) "I like it the way it is, but I'll go along with your idea if you don't throw anything away without asking me first."

There! Felix and Oscar have reached a naturally acceptable solution based on understanding and accepting each other's needs. Good for them!

Background of behavioral types

People have been both frustrated and fascinated with each other's differences for thousands of years. The earliest recorded efforts to explain our differences were made by astrologers who recorded the positions of the heavens. The twelve signs in four basic groupings—Earth, Air, Fire, and Water—are still used today.

In ancient Greece, Hippocrates' concept of four temperaments followed—Sanguine, Phlegmatic, Melancholy, and Choleric. He viewed personality as shaped by blood, phlegm, black bile, and yellow bile. As unpalatable as this might sound to us, people accepted these physical or bodily causes for varying *humors* for centuries. Respected figures from medical/physical sciences, metaphysics, mathematics, and philosophy observed these four temperaments—including Aristotle, Empedocles, Theophrastus, and, in Roman times, Galen. References to Hippocrates' Big Four can be found in Shakespeare's plays. We still use these terms, especially in the SAT college admissions test and in reference to babies and young children. "Jason looks so serious and melancholy for a one-year-old," or "Jennifer has a sanguine, ruddy-faced disposition."

In 1923, Dr. Carl Jung wrote his famous *Psychological Types*, at that time the most sophisticated scientific work on personality. In it, he again described four behavioral styles—the Intuitor, Thinker, Feeler, and Sensor.

This basic, four-type model spans all cultures. East and west, north and south. For instance, contemporary Japan still studies behavior and physical composition. Advice on *How to Form a Good Combination of Blood Types*, a best-seller by Toshitaka Nomi, claimed 100,000 documented cases of cross-referencing personalities with blood types. Nomi indicated that 40 percent of Japan's population has Type A blood. He associated this with the conscientious, hard-working behavior expected of engineers and technicians. He hypothesized that this explained Japan's emphasis on high-technology excellence.

Four styles with a difference

Today's Information Age features more than a dozen varied models of our behavioral differences. But they all have one common thread—the grouping of behavior into four categories.

Most of these explanations of behavioral styles have focused on internal characteristics leading to external behaviors. *People Smart* focuses on patterns of observable, external behaviors which each style shows to the rest of the world. It also demystifies those lesser known, but scientifically proven, internal forces which are the motivating clues behind our behaviors. In other words, this book will help you understand why you do what you do. Because we can see and hear these external behaviors, that makes it much easier for us to *read* people. Therefore, our model is simple, practical, easy to remember and use, and extremely accurate.

Our model divides people into four natural, core behavioral types:

— The Dominant Director
— The Interacting Socializer
— The Steady Relater
— The Cautious Thinker

So . . . which are you?

Chapter 2

I Know Who You Are, But What Am I?

So how do you identify your behavioral type? Here's how! You begin by choosing those traits that most and least describe you from a list of one-word possibilities. At first, you might think, "All these sound like me," or "None of them do," but select your personal traits from these commonly found choices with a clear focus in mind. Your reward will be in arriving at one behavioral type that is more descriptive of you than any of the others.

Any of us occasionally may behave like each of the four types, but we behave in predominantly one style more of the time. The most familiar place where you operate most comfortably is called your core behavioral type—your own unique personality style. This is most evident when you just act yourself. This natural tendency appears when you don't think about how to act. It's where you're found when your mind is on automatic pilot. This type of core behavior is your home base. To discover your behavioral type, read the instructions carefully and answer accordingly.

PERSONAL ASSETS INVENTORY *

INSTRUCTIONS FOR RESPONDING & SCORING

1. In the space provided below, identify those behaviors which have typically been MOST-TO-LEAST characteristic of you. Working left to right, assign "4" points to the MOST characteristic, "3" to the next most characteristic, then "2" and finally "1" to your least characteristic behavior.

EXAMPLE

_3_ DIRECTING   _4_ INFLUENCING   _1_ STEADY   _2_ CAUTIOUS

2. **Total** the numbers in each of the **four** columns. Place the **total** number for **each** column in the **blank** at the bottom of the column.

3. **Check** the accuracy by **adding** all the columns together. When **all four** columns are **added** together, they will equal 50.

COLUMN 1	COLUMN 2	COLUMN 3	COLUMN 4
_____ Directing	_____ Influencing	_____ Steady	_____ Cautious
_____ Decisive	_____ Optimistic	_____ Patient	_____ Restrained
_____ Daring	_____ Enthusiastic	_____ Stabilizing	_____ Analytical
_____ Competitive	_____ Talkative	_____ Accommodating	_____ Precise
_____ Forceful	_____ Charming	_____ Easygoing	_____ Curious
_____ **TOTAL**	_____ **TOTAL**	_____ **TOTAL**	_____ **TOTAL**

HOW TO DETERMINE YOUR "CORE" STYLE

If your highest column TOTAL is under **column 1,** you are a **Dominant Director.**

If your highest column TOTAL is under **column 2,** you are an **Interacting Socializer.**

If your highest column TOTAL is under **column 3,** you are a **Steady Relater.**

If your highest column TOTAL is under **column 4,** you are a **Cautious Thinker.**

IT'S YOUR PICK . . . AFTER ALL, IT'S REALLY YOU!

This personal inventory is a realistic measure of your actual behaviors. Think of your personal traits across the variety of environments and periods of your life. In other words, complete this inventory as you see yourself. To do this, start asking yourself, *"Is this or isn't this really me?"*

Look at the overall results to determine which of the four *behavioral patterns* you see as the single MOST and LEAST characteristic of you. Also notice the *specific behaviors* within the inventory which you may have identified as MOST or LEAST characteristic of you. Later, you may want to use the same instrument to help you reevaluate your own and others' pattern(s) in four major settings--work, social, family, and romance.

* Reproduced with permission of Life Associates, Inc. (Adapted from the "Personal Style Survey")
©copyright 1982 Life Associates, Inc.

The Personal Assets Inventory

This inventory is designed to help you take stock of those personal assets related to the goals and results which are important to you in different settings. It is a valuable personal resource for identifying: 1) your already developed personal characteristics and 2) other potential strengths you can further develop. These potential strengths can be especially helpful. You can learn to adapt your style to handle different types of situations, even those more *difficult* ones we don't prefer, but must manage in the real world laboratory of life.

It's your pick . . . after all it's really you!

This personal inventory is a realistic measure of your actual behaviors. Think of your personal traits across the variety of environments and periods in your life. In other words, complete the inventory as you see yourself. "Is this or isn't this really me?"

An Overview of the Four Types

The Dominant Director:
Look at My Accomplishments!

Goals and Fears

Dominant Directors, driven by the inner need to lead and be in personal control, take charge of people and situations so they can reach their goals. Since their key need is achieving, they seek no-nonsense, bottom line results. Their motto is: "Lead, follow, or get out of the way." They want to win, so they may challenge people or rules. Similarly, Dominant Directors also accept challenges, take authority, and go head first into solving problems. Closely related to Dominant Directors' goals are their fears: falling into a routine, being taken advantage of, and looking *soft*. So they may go to extremes to prevent those fears from materializing. They may act impatient, but they make things happen.

"Do as I say"

Since Dominant Directors need to have control, they like to take the lead in both business and social settings. The song *Don't Fence Me In* may have been written for this type, because they behave almost claustrophobically if they perceive someone is trying to stymie them. As natural renegades, Dominant Directors want to satisfy their need for autonomy. They want things done their way or no way at all.

Strengths and weaknesses

They often prefer strong directive management and operational tendencies and work quickly and impressively by themselves. Dominant Directors try to shape their environments to overcome obstacles en route to their accomplishments. They demand maximum freedom to manage themselves and others, using their leadership skills to become winners. Additionally, Dominant Directors often have good administration and delegation skills. This matches their motivating need. In fact, if they could delegate their exercise regimens or visits to the dentist's office, they probably would.

These assertive types tend to appear cool, independent, and competitive. They opt for measurable results, including their own personal worth, as determined by individual track records. Of all the types, they like and initiate changes the most. We symbolize this personality type with a lion—a leader, an authority. At least, they may have the inner desires to be #1, the star, or the chief.

Less positive Dominant Director components include stubbornness, impatience, and toughness. Naturally preferring to take control of others, they may have a low tolerance for the feelings, attitudes, and *inadequacies* of co-workers, subordinates, friends, families, and romantic interests.

From general to specific

Dominant Directors process data conceptually by using deductive reasoning—from general to specific information. They are more comfortable using the left brain than the right. When combined with their need for control, this helps us better understand the emphasis on getting down to the bottom line results.

Masters of "mind control"

They may use various *mind control* techniques to help them focus on one task priority at a time. For instance, some are adept at blocking out distractions when they immerse themselves in projects. They don't hear voices, sirens, or doorbells. They seem to channel all their energies into specific jobs. Similarly, in a summer biology class, the instructor, Dr. Rains, seemed oblivious to the smell (and the grumbling) when his students dissected decomposed fish. While the class choked and hurried from their desks to the windows to gulp for air, Dr. Rains instructed them as if the odor were an everyday occurrence. No big deal. Not to him, anyway.

Venting relieves their tension

Under pressure, Dominant Directors are likely to rid themselves of anger by ranting, raving, or challenging others. They naturally react to tense situations with a fight response. This tendency reflects the Dominant Directors' natural blind spots concerning other people's views and feelings. Although this venting allows the relief of their own inner tensions and hostilities, other personality types may feel intimidated by this natural, (for them!) stress reducing practice. But the Dominant Directors' barks usually exceed their bites, and they may soon forget what specifically upset them in the first place.

"Watch this performance"

Dominant Director musicians and performers typically seek to simultaneously command the stage and awe their audience. They envision themselves rising above their admirers and peers and moving into the position of number one, the best ever. Frank Sinatra, Evel Knievel, Reggie Jackson, Mike Tyson, and Jane Fonda all fit into this competitive category that tends to welcome any and all challenges.

Vince Lombardi, the former coach of the Green Bay Packers, coined this typical Dominant Director statement: "Winning isn't everything; it's the only thing." And who can forget that confrontational baseball coach, Billy Martin! Other famous Dominant Directors include Barbara Walters, Margaret Thatcher, Mike Wallace, General George Patton, Telly Savalas as KOJAK, Ed Asner as LOU GRANT, and Bea Arthur as MAUDE or as Dorothy in the show GOLDEN GIRLS.

Dominant Director territory

Two cultures which have produced many Dominant Directors are northern, industrialized Germany and South Africa. These examples are not meant to over-generalize or stereotype individual behavior; instead, they help us understand how cultures tend to socialize or group people into patterns of behavior which are more consistent with past customs and expectations. In this regard, it's easier for us to understand the more natural Dominant Director behaviors. These have emerged as the expected norms or preferred behavioral patterns over the long, colorful histories of both Germany and South Africa. How often have you described people you know of German or South African background by the following behavioral descriptions of the Dominant Director temperament mentioned throughout this chapter?

- take charge—naturally seek direct control and want to run things their way
- controlling—fear losing personal power or status
- competitive—want to win
- motivated to be #1—seek being first or *on top* whether other people approve or not
- task-focused—strive to get the job done, often less aware or oblivious to others' feelings—which may make them appear insensitive
- *no nonsense*—view life in terms of overcoming the obstacles to their achievement of desired results
- strong-willed—once they make up their minds, preferring to stick to their ideas; even becoming headstrong, especially under stress
- impatient—expect other people to help them get results, ASAP!!!
- fast-paced—often somewhat involved with many projects simultaneously; may even exhibit *workaholism* tendencies

Action Plan . . .

DOMINANT DIRECTOR CHARACTERISTICS

SO YOU . . .

DOMINANT DIRECTOR CHARACTERISTICS	SO YOU . . .
Concerned with being #1	— Show them how to win, new opportunities
Think logically	— Display reasoning
Want facts and highlights	— Provide concise data
Strive for results	— Agree on goal and boundaries, then support or get out of their way
Like Personal Choices	— Allow them to "do their thing," within limits
Like changes	— Vary routine
Prefer to delegate	— Look for opportunities to modify their work-load focus
Want others to notice accomplishments	— Compliment them on what they've done
Need to be in charge	— Let them take the lead, when appropriate, but give them parameters
Tendency towards conflict	— If necessary, argue with conviction on points of disagreement, backed up with facts; don't argue on "personality" basis

The Interacting Socializer:
Hey, Look at Me!

Outgoing, Supporting, Interacting Socializers

He-e-e-ere's the Interacting Socializer!—the person who likes to go where the action is. Typically, he is outwardly energetic or fast-paced, and relationships tend to naturally take priority over tasks. The Interacting Socializer tries to influence others in an optimistic, friendly way focused on positive outcomes, whether in the social or work environment. In other words, if he shows others he likes them, he figures others will be more likely to reciprocate by responding favorably towards him. Since recognition and approval motivate him, he often moves in and around the limelight and hub of activity.

Goals and Fears

He wants your admiration and thrives on acknowledgment, compliments, and applause. "It's not just whether you win or lose . . . it's how you look when you play the game." People's admiration and acceptance typically mean more to this type than to any other. If you don't talk about him, he may spend considerable time talking about his favorite subject—himself— to gain the acceptance he wants. His biggest fear is public humiliation—whether appearing uninvolved, unattractive, unsuccessful, or unacceptable to others. These frightening forms of social rejection threaten the Interacting Socializer's core need for approval. Consequently, he may go to extremes to avoid public humiliation, lack of inclusion, or loss of social recognition.

Strengths and weaknesses

Interacting Socializers' primary strengths are their enthusiasm, persuasiveness, and friendliness. They are idea people who have the ability to get others caught up in their dreams. With great persuasion, they influence others and shape their environments by building alliances to accomplish results. Then they seek nods and comments of approval and recognition for those results. If compliments don't come, Interacting Socializers may invent their own. "Well, Harry, I just feel like patting myself on the back today for a job well done!" They are stimulating, talkative, and communicative. This type can be represented by a porpoise—playful, sociable, and talkative.

Their natural weaknesses are too much involvement, impatience, aversion to being alone, and short attention spans. This causes them to become easily bored. When a little data comes in, Interacting Socializers tend to make sweeping generalizations. They may not check everything out, assuming someone else will do it, or may procrastinate because redoing something just isn't exciting enough. When Interacting Socializers feel they don't have enough stimulation and involvement, they get bored and look for something new again . . . and again . . . and again. When taken to an extreme, their behaviors can be seen as superficial, haphazard, erratic, and overly emotional.

Talk, talk, talk . . .

Picture Willard Scott, the smiling weatherman on the TODAY show. He strikes up conversations with everyone from Iowa pig farmers to visiting dignitaries. He smiles and laughs with most people he meets, somehow managing to sandwich in a few comments about the day's weather forecast. We believe Willard when he wishes a *beautiful 100-year-old darling* a happy birthday or endorses a pecan pie as "the best I've ever had."

Irrepressible Willard alternately dazzles us with his footwork and baffles us with his homespun corn. But we can't help liking him. He seems so genuinely moved by his fans' gifts—moose hats with antlers, lopsided cakes, and one-of-a-kind T-shirts—that both we and his co-workers catch ourselves smiling as we think, "What a warm person he is!" This man would probably talk as naturally to the President as he does to anyone else. Willard Scott epitomizes the down-to-earth, person-to-person, Interacting Socializer tendency which minimizes role and status differences among people.

"Let me entertain you!"

If they pursue the entertainment field for careers, Interacting Socializers typically allow their natural, animated emotions to show and flow. They become stimulated by the movement and reactions of the audience, trying to get the audience to figuratively fall in love with them by acting charming and friendly. They want viewers to feel, "He (or she) is fabulous!" Interacting Socializer performers who mesmerize and win over their fans include Dolly Parton, Mickey Rooney, Tracy Ullman, Muhammad Ali, Bill Cosby, Tony Danza, Dom DeLuise, Eddie Murphy, Carol Burnett, Sammy Davis Jr., David Brenner, *Magic* Johnson, and Liza Minnelli.

Two countries brimming with Interacting Socializers

Every country, culture, and subculture socialize their society's members into typical daily patterns of behavior. In this respect, both Ireland and Italy are often mentioned as settings where this Interacting Socializer type seems quite commonplace. Globally, people refer to them as highly emotional people who tend to "wear their hearts on their sleeves." The Irish are known for their animated, interactive storytelling and neighborhood socializing. In fact, many areas of the Northeastern United States have become settled as Irish-Italian communities by these immigrants with similar lifestyles.

Italians' Interacting Socializer attributes have made them world famous in the performing arts, restaurant and hospitality fields, and other person-to-person areas such as fashion and sales. How often have you described a native Irishman or Italian you have met by the following general description of the Interacting Socializer tendencies?

- optimistic—prefer to view life's positives; often block out negative situations, facts, concerns
- fast-paced—talk, move, and do most activities rather quickly
- emotional—readily show their own feelings and respond to others' feelings
- approval-seeking—look to others for acceptance and re-energizing; want people to approve of and like each other, too

Action Plan . . .

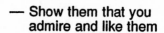

INTERACTING SOCIALIZER CHARACTERISTICS

SO YOU . . .

INTERACTING SOCIALIZER CHARACTERISTICS	SO YOU . . .
Concerned with approval and appearances	— Show them that you admire and like them
Seek enthusiastic people and situations	— Behave optimistically and provide upbeat setting
Think emotionally	Support their feelings when possible
Want to know the general expectations	— Avoid involved details, focus on the "big picture"
Need involvement and people contact	— Interact and participate with them
Like changes and innovations	— Vary the routine; avoid requiring long-term repetition by them
Want others to notice THEM	— Compliment them personally and often
Often need help getting organized	— Do it together
Dislike conflict	— Act non-aggressively and avoid arguing directly on a personal basis
Look for action and stimulation	— Keep up a fast, lively, pace
Surround themselves with optimism	— Support their ideas and don't poke holes in their dreams; show them your positive side
Want feedback that they "look good"	— Mention their accomplishments, progress and your other genuine appreciation

- fun-loving—seek an upbeat, positive, casual atmosphere and love a good party, especially with friends
- excitable—show emotions and become enthusiastic, at best; rattled, at worst—when pressured or tired
- spontaneous—behave impulsively; dislike planning or dealing with follow-through details
- expressive—at times, they may forget and divulge secret information; they may say too much to the wrong people

The Steady Relater: Notice How Well-Liked I Am

Goals and fears

This type, as sung by Aretha Franklin in her hit record, may privately want a little *R-E-S-P-E-C-T*, as demonstrated by your sincere personal attention and acceptance of them. Steadiness and follow-through actions characterize these people. They prefer a slower and easier pace: "It's not whether you win or lose . . . it's the friendship that counts." They focus on building trust and getting acquainted because they aim for long-standing personal relationships. Pushy, aggressive behavior secretly irritates them.

Steady Relaters strive for security. Their goal is to maintain the stability they prefer in a more constant environment. To Steady Relaters, while the unknown may be an intriguing concept, they prefer to stick with what they already know and have experienced. *Risk* is an ugly word to Steady Relaters. They favor more measured actions, like keeping things as they have been and are, even if the present situation happens to be unpleasant. Related to their goal of keeping things very similar is their accompanying fear of change and disorganization. Consequently, any disruption in their routine patterns can cause distress in Steady Relaters. Fearing sudden changes, they are naturally concerned with what may happen. A general worry is that the unknown may be even more unpleasant than the present. They need to think and plan for changes. Finding the elements of sameness within those changes can help minimize their stress by identifying the specific assurances required to cope with such demands.

Strengths and weaknesses

America's favorite *Uncle*, Walter Cronkite, is a classic example of a low-keyed, sincere-acting, Steady Relater. He visited millions of homes each week night via TV for decades. People still reminisce about his soothing voice and comforting delivery. Whether the news was good, bad, or indifferent, his manner had a unique way of adding a sense of stability, calmness, and reassurance to the evenings at the end of our busy workdays.

Like *Uncle Walter*, other Steady Relaters also naturally *wear well* and are an easy type to get along with. They prefer stable relationships which don't jeopardize anyone, especially themselves. Steady. Relaters can be represented by the koala with its accompanying slower, steady pace, its relaxed disposition, and its appearance of approachability and warmth. Steady Relaters have a tendency to plan and follow through. This helps them to routinely plug along. But they have their own type of unique difficulties with speaking up, seeming to go along with others or conditions, while inwardly, they may or may not agree. More assertive types might take advantage of this Steady Relater tendency to give in and avoid confrontation. Additionally, Steady Relaters' reluctance to express themselves can result in hurt feelings. But if Steady Relaters don't explain their feelings, others may never know. Their lack of assertiveness can take a toll on this type's health and well-being.

Take it slow

Steady Relaters yearn for more tranquillity and security in their lives than the other three types. They often act pleasant and cooperative, but seldom incorporate emotional extremes such as rage and euphoria in their behavioral repertoire. Unlike Interacting Socializers, Steady Relaters usually experience less dramatic or frequently-occurring peaks and valleys to their more moderate emotional state. This reflects their natural need for composure, stability, and balance.

"Just plain folks"

Picture Edith Bunker of the classic sitcom ALL IN THE FAMILY. She lends a tone of continuity, coziness, and *motherliness* to virtually every scene in which she appears. Edith mothers everyone around her. With her easygoing manner, she projects a genuine liking and acceptance of her family, friends, and acquaintances. She's a comfortable person to watch and listen to who emanates that "I'm just a regular person" modesty. She puts on no airs and projects contentment with present conditions—just as they are and always have been.

"May I entertain you?"

In the same respect, Steady Relater celebrities tend to give predictable deliveries. Both the audience and performer may seem to merge because the Steady Relater feels so in tempo with his or her viewers. Typical audience responses may include: "He's truly one of us!" Or, "It's like being with a member of the family or my closest friend!" Steady Relaters welcome group participation, and their performances reflect their natural give and take. Steady Relaters that we know and are fond of are: Perry Como, Kenny Rogers, Mr. Rogers, Mary Richards (THE MARY TYLER MOORE SHOW), Elise Keaton (FAMILY TIES), MARCUS WELBY, M. D. (in vintage reruns with Robert Young in the title role), Mother Theresa, Pope John Paul II, Gary Collins, David Hartman, John Denver, Hugh Downs, Ed Sullivan, and Martina Navratilova.

Two countries with many Steady Relaters

Two Steady Relater countries that seem to have emphasized this lifestyle as a cultural norm, resulting in a disproportionate number of such individual styles, are Poland and Spain. Both cultures have historically found ways to get along with foreign elements while methodically plodding forward in the direction expected, even though that direction has often been dictated by others in the short run. The Polish people are world famous for their friendly, hard-working perseverance despite the obstacles which may confront them. And the Spanish people make others feel at home while practicing such distinctive customs as their renowned midday siestas. Taking siestas actually allows them to go home to their families during the work day. This is consistent with the preferred slower lifestyle of this temperament, without disrupting the differing customs of guests in their homeland.

Citizens of both countries are known in their native lands and in the United States for their neighborhood restaurants and extensive group social activities. Compare the following distinguishing characteristics of this Steady Relater type which describe people you know who've been influenced directly by their own ethnic, social group, or cultural roots:

- easygoing—calm, measured, low-key behavior and outlook
- slower paced—wait until they know the steps or guidelines before acting, then move forward in a pre-set manner
- patient—tend to define themselves by their desire for stable relationships with others; often view problems or concerns as workable
- predictable—favor routine and stable conditions and practices
- persevering—likely to stick to a project for longer periods of time or at least until the concrete results have been produced
- modest—less likely to blow their own horns, but are often appreciative when others sincerely acknowledge their contributions
- accommodating—like to get along with others through predictable role relationships
- neighborly—prefer friendly, pleasant, helpful working relationships

Action Plan ...

STEADY RELATER CHARACTERISTICS

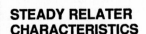

SO YOU...

STEADY RELATER CHARACTERISTICS	SO YOU...
Concerned with stability	— Show how your idea minimizes risk
Think logically	— Show reasoning
Want documentation and facts	— Provide data/proof
Like personal involvement	— Demonstrate your interest in them
Need to know step-by-step sequence	— Provide outline and/or one-two-three instructions as you personally "walk them through"
Want others to notice their patient perseverance	— Compliment for their steady follow-through
Avoid risks/changes	— Give them personal assurances
Dislike conflict	— Act non-aggressively, focus on common interest or needed support
Accommodate others	— Allow them to provide service or support for others
Look for calmness and peace	— Provide relaxing, friendly atmosphere
Enjoy teamwork	— Provide them with a cooperative group
Want sincere feedback that they're appreciated	— Acknowledge their easy-going manner and helpful efforts, when appropriate

The Cautious Thinker:
Have You Noticed My Efficiency?

Goals and fears

Cautious Thinkers concern themselves more with content than with congratulations. They prefer involvement with the performance of products and services under specific, and preferably controlled, conditions so the process and the results can be correct. Since their primary concern is accuracy, human emotions may take a back seat with this type. After all, emotions are subjective and tend to distort objectivity. Cautious Thinkers' biggest fears of uncontrolled emotions and irrational acts relate to their goals. More precisely, Cautious Thinkers fear that these illogical acts may prevent goal achievement. Similarly, they fear emotionality and irrationality in others. This type strives to avoid embarrassment, so they attempt to control both themselves and their emotions.

Strengths and weaknesses

Cautious Thinker strengths include accuracy, dependability, independence, clarification and testing skills, follow-through, and organization. They often focus on expectations (e.g., policies, practices, and procedures) and outcomes. They want to know how things work so they can evaluate how correctly they function. We picture a fox as an appropriate symbol for Cautious Thinkers—cagey, resourceful, and careful. Because they need to be right, they prefer checking processes themselves. This tendency toward perfectionism, taken to an extreme, can result in "paralysis by overanalysis." These overly cautious traits may result in worry that the process isn't progressing right, which further promotes their tendency to behave in a more critical, detached way.

Complex and serious

They prefer tasks over people, clearly defined priorities, and a known pace which is agreeable to them, especially where task timelines and deadlines are involved. Other types typically live life through a single, predominant time orientation—past, present, or future. But Cautious Thinkers are apt to be concerned about all three, as one aspect of their complex mental makeup. They tend to see the serious, more complicated sides of situations as well as the lighter—or even bizarre side—which accounts for their natural mental wit.

As the most cerebrally oriented of the four types, Cautious Thinkers concentrate on making decisions in both logical and cautious ways to ensure that they take the best available action. (This cerebral quality refers to the way they process information and experiences, and does not relate to I.Q.) "It's not whether you win or lose . . . it's how you play the game" —the more technically perfect, the better.

Think deeply

Visualize Woody Allen, the quiet, unassuming director, actor, and clarinet player who covets his privacy. In most of his movies, either he or his characters agonize over what to do next, what and how their feelings operate, and how to ultimately do the right thing. He typically puts his emotions under a microscope where he analyzes and reanalyzes them. In HANNAH AND HER SISTERS, for instance, Woody Allen's character thinks repeatedly about his *wrong feelings* for his sister-in-law, while viewing his wife Hannah as a saint. He mentally vacillates between the two women for the duration of the film. Like Woody Allen's Cautious Thinker characters, this type can even become overwhelmed by indecision when pressure builds.

Due to compliance to their own personal standards, they demand a lot from themselves and others and may succumb to overly critical tendencies. But Cautious Thinkers often keep their criticisms to themselves, hesitating to tell people what they think is deficient. They typically share information, both positive and negative, only on a need-to-know basis when they are assured that there will be no negative consequences for themselves.

When Cautious Thinkers quietly hold their ground, they do so as a direct result of their proven knowledge of facts and details or their evaluation that others will tend to react less assertively. So they can be assertive when they perceive they're in control of a relationship or their environment. Having determined the specific risks, margins of error, and other variables which significantly influence the desired results, they will take action.

The "mystery" First Lady

Visualize Jacqueline Kennedy Onassis, the private, yet national figure who is consistently on *The Ten Most Admired Women in America* list. She is and was impeccably groomed and has subsequently made dozens of lists of *Best Dressed Women.* Her mystique and personal style have captivated Americans since the days of *Camelot* when John F. Kennedy was President. She even received an Emmy award for the perfection of her televised tour of the White House. Many people remember her obvious grief, but refusal to cry, at her husband's funeral.

Cautious Thinkers entertain uniquely

Cautious Thinker entertainers want to move beyond the audience, since they are motivated to deliver a one-of-a-kind, captivating, near-perfect performance. They want spectators to think, "What a unique performance" or "Nothing else is quite like it!" When they take their varied stages, Mikhail Baryshnikov, Neil Diamond, Barbra Streisand, Katharine Hepburn, Larry Bird, and Wayne Gretsky have meticulously prepared themselves to provide a memorable experience with each intense performance—a key reason why they seem more emotionally drained from their own efforts. Other well-known Thinkers include: Meryl Streep, Dr. Joyce Brothers, Dick Cavett, Albert Einstein, Henry Kissinger, Dustin Hoffman, STAR TREK's Mr. Spock, and Sherlock Holmes. And, of course, Jack Webb from the vintage DRAGNET series, the now classic *patron saint* of Cautious Thinkers—"The facts, Ma'am . . . just the facts."

Cautious Thinker countries

Under adverse political and geographic conditions, two Cautious Thinker countries have historically figured out creative, intuitive ways to survive. Both Sweden and Switzerland have harsh winter climates, but they've mastered the art of survival. Switzerland, especially, boasts a substantial corner on the market of world finance. For a small country, it controls a disproportionate amount of the world's money. And Sweden, long known as a land which appreciates beauty, continues to have a worldwide impact in exporting its aesthetic talents, products, and services resulting from cultivated efforts.

Whether watching a professional tennis match or beauty contest, we frequently see a representative from sparsely populated Sweden in the running for top honors. And, whether shopping for distinctive items—such as Scandinavian sweaters, needlework, furniture, crafts or other unique objects—or tasty and eye-catching bakery goods, the artistic flair of the Swedish heritage has universal appeal.

Which of the following Cautious Thinker characteristics listed below match individuals you know with cultural roots similar to those discussed above?

- careful—methodical and cautious; don't jump into things initially
- precise—need to be accurate, so they check and recheck in their effort to find the right or best available answer
- proper—more formal, discreet, and inclined to allow others to be in their own space, expecting the same for themselves
- private—keep thoughts to themselves; do not willingly disclose their own or others' thoughts and feelings
- reserved—somewhat formal and cool; take time to get to know them—they have few close relationships
- logical—process-oriented seekers of reason
- inventive—like to see things in new or unique ways; often have a unique perspective that includes or addresses both themselves and others
- contemplative—introverted and reflective, they ponder both the why and how elements in situations

Four types, just acting themselves

With the natural differences among the four behavioral types in mind, pretend that you want to give four people 15-20 minutes to make three simple decisions:

Action Plan . . .

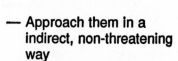

CAUTIOUS THINKER CHARACTERISTICS	SO YOU . . .
Concerned with aggressive approaches	— Approach them in a indirect, non-threatening way
Think logically	— Show your reasoning
Seek data	— Give it to them in writing
Need to know the process	— Provide explanations and rationale
Utilize caution	— Allow them to think, inquire and check before they make decisions
Prefer to do things themselves	— When delegating, let them check on others' progress and performance
Want others to notice their accuracy	— Compliment them on their thoroughness and correctness when appropriate
Gravitate toward quality control	— Let them assess and be involved in the process when possible
Avoid conflict	— Tactfully ask for clarification and assistance you may need
Need to be right	— Allow them time to find the best or "correct" answer, within available limits
Like to contemplate	— Tell them "why" and "how"

1. Where the next meeting will take place
2. When it will happen
3. The theme of the meeting

Quite by accident, your group consists of one Steady Relater, one Cautious Thinker, one Dominant Director, and one Interacting Socializer who all believe in practicing The Golden Rule. Do you think they'll get the job done? Perhaps, or perhaps not, depending on how each responds to one another in handling the simple task. Let's see why this may not work out. As they walk into the room, the Dominant Director typically speaks first. "Here's my plan . . . "

The Interacting Socializer says, "Hey! Who died and left you boss?"

The Cautious Thinker says, "You know there seems to be more here than meets the eye. We might want to consider some other relevant issues and break into sub-committees to explore them."

The Steady Relater smiles and says, "We may not get this done if we don't work as a team like we have before."

If you think that we're stacking the deck, consider putting all four of one behavioral type into the room to make those decisions. They'd get the job done, wouldn't they? Not if they follow the Golden Rule verbatim!

What do you call it when you send four Dominant Directors into the same room? War!

Or four Cautious Thinkers? A laundry list full of questions!

And four Steady Relaters? Nothing! They sit around smiling at each other: "You go first."

"No, why don't you go first. By the way, how's the family?"

When four Interacting Socializers walk out, try asking them if they've gotten the job done. "Get what done?" They've had a party and instead come out with 10 new jokes and stories.

We admit that we may be exaggerating to make a point, but in some cases, not by much. Dominant Directors tend to have the assertiveness and leadership initiative to get tasks started. They may then delegate to others for follow-through, enabling the Dominant Directors to start still other new projects which interest them more.

Cautious Thinkers typically are motivated by their planning and organizational tendencies. If you want a task done precisely, find a Cautious Thinker. Of the four types, they're the most motivated to be correct—the quality control experts.

Steady Relaters have persistence, people-to-people strengths —patience, follow-through, and responsiveness. When we have a problem, we may choose to go to a sympathetic-appearing Steady Relater because he or she listens, empathizes, and reacts to our feelings.

Interacting Socializers are natural entertainers who thrive on involvement with people. They also love to start things, but often do not finish them. In fact, they may pick up three balls, throw them in the air, and yell, "Catch!" Emotional, enthusiastic, optimistic, and friendly, Interacting Socializers usually pep up an otherwise dull environment.

A behavioral knight-time story

Here is a story to reinforce the differences among the four basic behavioral types:

Four of King Arthur's knights, each representing a different behavioral type, were convicted of a crime and sentenced to death by decapitation. On execution day, they mounted the stairs together to position their heads in a custom-made, four-person guillotine. (For you skeptical types who may be wondering why King Arthur uses a French product, maybe it's a gift from King Louis.) The Lord High Executioner swings his royal ax, the rope snaps, and the blade comes down—stopping inches from their necks. King Arthur interprets this as a sign of innocence, so he pardons all four men. They all rejoice—some noisily, some silently—with everyone reverting to his own type of instinctive response.

Almost immediately, the Dominant Director knight turns to the others and yells, "You see! I told you I'm innocent!"

The Interacting Socializer knight screams, "Let's eat, drink, be merry . . . and party, party, party!"

The Steady Relater knight walks up to the executioner and says, "I want you to know that I don't hold this against you. You were just doing your job and I know you're a good person at heart. Would you like to join me for dinner sometime?"

The Cautious Thinker knight pauses, looks up at the mechanism, scratches his head, and says, "Hmmm, I think I see the problem."

Pick a type . . . any type

After our general introduction to the basic four, core behavioral types, you may already know which one is most like you. Did you also recognize other people you know? Besides deciding which type is most like you, you may have thought of people who sounded quite similar to one or more of the personality types in this chapter—those you harmonize with and those who tend to rub you the wrong way. Now that you know which type *you* are, you can better determine *other people's* types. Integrating what you know about yourself with what you can observe and learn about others reveals valuable information to help you relate more effectively with them. The next chapter explains how to determine other personality types by focusing on specific verbal, vocal, and visual signals they provide. So get ready to become a people reader in Chapter 3.

Remember . . .

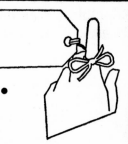

TASK ORIENTED

Cautious Thinker
Dominant Director

PEOPLE ORIENTED

Steady Relaters
Interacting Socializers

FASTER PACED

Dominant Directors
Interacting Socializers

SLOWER PACED

Steady Relaters
Cautious Thinkers

WHO SEEKS WHAT?

Dominant Directors . . . . Power & Control
Cautious Thinkers . . . . Accuracy & Precision
Interacting Socializers . . . . Popularity & Prestige
Steady Relaters . . . . Sincerity and
Appreciation

KIND OF DECISION MAKER

Dominant Director . . . . Decisive
Cautious Thinker . . . . Deliberate
Steady Relater . . . . Conferring
Interacting Socializer . . . . Spontaneous

Chapter 3
How Will You Know One When You Meet One?

Now that you're familiar with your core behavioral type, how can you recognize other types when you meet them? Since relationships depend on your appropriate interactions with each behavioral type, the immediate question is, "How can I identify someone's behavioral type and how can I do it quickly?"

Two important dimensions for recognizing another person's behavioral type are Directness/Indirectness and Supportingness/Controllingness. We all exhibit a range of these characteristics in our expressed, observable behaviors. But we need to focus on how people act in order to determine their core type.

"Excuse me, Mr. Smith, but would you mind giving me some information about how Indirect or Direct and how Supporting or Controlling you are so I can figure out your behavioral type?" definitely won't do. Neither will guesswork, but that approach is seldom necessary because people give so many clues, if you just know what to look for. To identify someone's type, observe what he does by tuning in to both his verbal, vocal, and visual behaviors.

Verbal, vocal, and visual clues

The verbal channel of communication includes the words people use to express themselves—the content. The other two areas convey the intent of the message—how people want to say it. The vocal channel includes all the subtle aspects of voice intonation—volume, speed, resonance, pitch, inflection, and rhythm. The visual channel includes all the aspects of body language—the range of movements and positions—from the subtle raising of an eyebrow to the precise movements of the trained actor.

We have assembled a range of verbal, vocal, and visual characteristics into a list of observable behaviors for each type. But beware! These descriptions refer to actions you can see, not value judgments you may be tempted to make about them. If you see a woman hopping up and down, is it because she is throwing a temper tantrum, has stepped on a nail, has a foot that has fallen asleep, or is very excited? All you can say is she is hopping up and down. Finding out why requires more observable verbal, vocal, and visual clues.

Is the person more Direct?

Directness, the first of two dimensions in our expressed behavior, is the amount of involvement a person uses to meet his needs by seeking to influence people and situations. Directness means the tendency to move forward or act outwardly by expressing thoughts, feelings, or expectations. Direct people come on strong, take the social initiative, and create a powerful first impression. They tend to be assertive, fast-paced people who make swift decisions and take risks. They can easily become impatient with others who cannot keep up with their pace. As active people who talk a lot, they appear confident and sometimes dominant. Direct people tend to express opinions readily and make emphatic statements. Such individuals try to shape their environment and relationships— "Tell McCullough that I want to talk to him ASAP." Indirect people typically act in a more measured way—"I'll get back to you about McCullough, Jack."

Direct people are faster paced, more assertive, and more competitive. At worst, these tendencies can transform into hastiness, combativeness, or lower awareness of others' needs. More outspoken, talkative, and dominant, Direct people are extroverts who focus their attention on interests in their environment. In other words—action! They tend to work and play faster. When at a social gathering, they're the ones who introduce themselves as a natural way of seeking to influence others in their surroundings.

They prefer to make rapid decisions, becoming impatient when things don't move fast enough or don't go their way. Checking for errors is something other people can do. It's too time-consuming and self-involving for Direct people. Instead of checking, they busily rush into new areas where the more Indirect may fear to tread. In fact, they rush into so many new areas that their time seems to evaporate into thin air. That's one reason why they have difficulty consistently being prompt—because something comes up at the office or somewhere else. Meanwhile, their more punctual, Indirect friends learn to busy themselves with time killers, such as projects or magazines, while waiting for their more easily side-tracked companions.

Direct people may enjoy risks and want results now, or yesterday. Risks are a way of life with them. Not only are they less worried about rocking the boat, they'll often tip it over and splash around in the hot water they find themselves in. They crave excitement, so they do as much as possible to get it.

This type feels that if they throw enough against the wall, something has to stick. Who cares if the output isn't perfect! Quantity beats quality (within limits known only to them) most days of the week. So they're likely to tolerate a higher error rate than their Indirect counterparts to gain a higher number of trial opportunities, even if their success ratio is lower. They generally figure that the number of successes is more important than the percentage of successes.

Anyone involved in telemarketing or outside sales realizes that the road to success is littered with setbacks. Direct people excel in these arenas because they're able to take no's; they simply go out and find more prospects. Aware the yes's are out there somewhere, they're determined to unearth them. "The odds are definitely in my favor now. I'm due for a big hit!" Indirect people tend to take those no's as personal rejections, responding by examining other alternatives which don't force them to go out again. "Maybe if I send out a direct mail letter first, then follow up by phone, I'll increase my chances of getting a *yes*."

Direct people point, finger jab, or otherwise more observably express themselves in methods ranging from open arms to forearms—literally, a hug or a shove. They are verbally intense. "Tough toenails! This is the way it is, so get used to it." They emphasize their points of view with confident-sounding vocal intonations and assertive body language.

They speak with conviction. "This bozo got an advanced degree from a diploma mill!" Fast-talking, Direct people like to tell, not ask, about situations. If you want to know the answer, just ask them. They can even become brutally blunt— "That's supposed to be a custom suit? It looks more like a horse blanket."

Impatient and quick-paced, they jump into things, so they get into more "iffy" situations than their indirect counterparts. Just as the songs of the sirens lured sailors to their doom, the *windows of opportunity* beckon to Direct people. Entrance sometimes nets them huge results and sometimes slaps them with dramatic disasters. Wherever inclination takes them, their natural tendency is to do their own thing.

When the windows of opportunity crack open, the Direct types can't wait to tell somebody. So they seek willing listeners—usually of the Indirect variety—and they say, "I've found a gray area."

What sort of feedback do you suppose the Indirect types probably provide? "It sounds interesting, but it also raises a lot of questions. Have you asked anyone else for their opinion? Your boss, for instance?"

"Ask my boss? Forget it! He might say no! Then what would I do? My hands would be tied."

This more Direct person's motto in these cases is, "It's easier to beg forgiveness than seek permission." When in doubt, do it anyway. You can always apologize later.

Or Indirect?

On the opposite side of the Directness spectrum, Indirect people are more quiet and reserved. They are seen as more easygoing, or at least more self-contained. Indirect people ask questions and listen more than they talk. They typically reserve their opinions. When asked to take a stand, they may make tentative statements. They often appear more objective, quiet, and indecisive. When taken to an extreme, these positive traits can be viewed as negative ones—wishy-washy, tight-lipped, unassertive behaviors. Indirect people are also less confronting, less demanding, less assertive, and less socially competitive than their Direct counterparts. They're team players who allow others to take the social initiative. For instance, when they want to go to the movies or a restaurant, they might think to themselves, "Gee, I'd really like to see that new Kevin Kline movie." Then they wait for someone to invite them to go instead of outwardly expressing interest to others.

They tend to be more security-conscious—moving slowly, meditating on their decisions, and avoiding bigger risks. As a result, they often avoid taking bold chances or spontaneous actions. After all, what's the best way to keep from failing? One way is to do nothing until you're satisfied it will be an improvement. In other words, do only sure things. Those sure things result in a higher success ratio, so they are more natural for Indirect people. Number of successes divided by number of tries equals success. In a given month, they may try 10 things. Nine may be successfully completed, one not—for a success ratio of 90%.

When Indirect people flop, they tend to take the setback personally. They are likely to internalize or privately think about it, often wondering if there's something wrong with them. "How could I have been so stupid?" Just give them a hint that something is going wrong, and reserved folks may engage in negative self-talk for days.

Indirect people tend to move at a slower or more measured pace. For them, sooner or later is good enough. They speak and respond more slowly since they are more cautious or stability-focused when considering change. If the behavior becomes too measured, detractors (usually Direct people) can view this as dragging their feet, or even lacking interest.

Predictability is more important to such Indirect people, so they tend to consider the pros and cons, attend to details, and fact-find. Caught in a gray area with no clear-cut guidelines, they usually ask for clarification or permission before they take action. They seek to meet their needs by accommodating the requirements of their environment. Generally they operate according to established formats and rules, so when you make an appointment with an Indirect person, you can expect him to show up on time, or possibly wait for you!

Indirect people tend to communicate by asking instead of stating. Their questions clarify, support, or seek more information—"By that, do you mean . . . ?" They prefer qualified statements—"According to my sources, the candidate received an advanced degree from a non-accredited university." They speak more tentatively and take a roundabout or step-by-step approach—"It seems to me that this is so." If they don't like something, they respond subtly—"Well, I think your other suit looks better." They reserve the right to express their opinions or keep them to themselves. But, they can also act like impregnable rocks when they don't want to crack.

Some are more, some less

It is important to realize that people vary in their location on this scale of Direct to Indirect behavior. Bob Newhart and Mary Tyler Moore both portray Indirect individuals on their long-running sitcoms, but Mary Richards exhibits comparatively more Direct behavior than Bob. Similarly, although they're both Direct, Ronald Reagan is much more Indirect when compared to Archie Bunker of ALL IN THE FAMILY.

Think of someone you know who irritates you. Now that you know about Direct and Indirect characteristics, have you figured out which trait best describes him or her? One important consideration is to determine the person's preferred pace. Pace refers to natural rate of speed—whether he does things quickly or slowly. Bearing in mind pace and other trait descriptors for Direct and Indirect people, let's determine whether that person is more Direct or Indirect. Nobody fits exactly in the middle.

You may be wondering which are better—Direct traits or Indirect ones. We can answer with an unqualified, "It depends." Sometimes it's better to act more Direct and sometimes it's better to act more Indirect. Comparing the two is like evaluating San Diego and New York City. Each is very different, yet we could build a strong argument in either one's favor.

Appropriateness depends on the requirements of a situation. The real question isn't which is better, but how to best use the positive aspects of each trait while recognizing accompanying less developed attributes. Since each of our lives involves a variety of situations requiring differing responses, remember there is no one best personality type. The idea is to maximize people's natural traits while understanding and trying to minimize their accompanying drawbacks.

Survey of Directness Versus Indirectness

This is an informal survey designed to provide you with a general description of how you see others in daily situations. Answer as objectively as possible. This is a non-judgmental assessment—there are no right or wrong answers. Choose one person you know (socially, personally, or at work) and answer these nine questions in terms of how you see that person most of the time, in most situations. This will help you determine if this person is more Direct or Indirect. For each number, choose the one statement that best applies to the person you are evaluating.

Is the Person More Direct or Indirect?

1. (I) A less frequent contributor to group conversations OR
   (D) A more frequent contributor to group conversations
2. (I) Tends to keep personal thoughts or feelings private, sharing only when asked and necessary, OR

(D)   Tends to express personal thoughts or feelings about things, whether asked to or not

3. (D)   Frequently uses gestures, facial expressions, and voice intonation to emphasize points, OR

    (I)   Less likely to use gestures, facial expressions, and voice   intonation to emphasize points

4. (D)   More likely to make statements: "That's the way it is!" or, "I feel . . .", OR

    (I)   More likely to ask questions or speak less assertively: "How does this fit?" or, "As I understand it . . ."

5. (I)   More likely to wait for others to introduce him (or her) at social gatherings, OR

    (D)   More likely to introduce self at social gatherings

6. (I)   Tends to remain involved with known situations, conditions, and relationships, OR

    (D)   Tends to seek new experiences, situations, and opportunities

7. (D)   Likely to express own views more readily, OR

    (I)   Likely to reserve the expression of own views

8. (I)   Tends to react more slowly and deliberately, OR

    (D)   Tends to react more quickly and spontaneously

9. (I)   Likely to respond to risk and change in a more cautious or predictable manner, OR

    (D)   Likely to respond to risk and change in a more dynamic or unpredictable manner

Total number circled: D's_____   I's_____
                  (Directness) (Indirectness)

Supporting or Controlling

Besides Direct to Indirect behaviors, we've also found that people tend to be either Supporting or Controlling—the other major dimension which describes our daily actions. Basically, Directness and Indirectness describe people's observable behavior—how others see and hear us behaving. The second behavioral scale explains the motivating goal behind these daily actions. Why we do the things we do in the way we do them. When combined, these two scales explain both the tendency to reveal our thoughts and feelings plus the degree to which we tend to support other people's expressions of their thoughts and feelings.

Is the person more Supporting?

If he talks with his body, uses more vocal inflection, makes continual eye contact, and speaks in terms of feelings, then he's projecting more Supporting than Controlling behaviors. Other Supporting cues that show greater responsiveness include animated facial expressions, much hand and body movement, a flexible time perspective, and immediate non-verbal feedback. Supporting people also like to tell stories and anecdotes and make personal contact.

Supporting people are more open to responding to digressions than Controlling personalities are. They need to make conversation more enjoyable, so they look favorably upon straying from the subject to discuss personal experiences. As long as it's in the ball park, they figure it's probably relevant. "That reminds me of the time Uncle Jed got stuck on the Garden State Freeway for five hours . . . " And exaggeration of details just adds interest by fully depicting their experiences.

Supporting types are also more negotiable about time. Their time perspective is organized around the needs of people first and tasks second, so they're more flexible about how others use their time than the Controlling types. "I'm sorry I'm late for work today, but my son was crying this morning because Jason broke his science project. So I had to write a note to the teacher and cheer him up before I dropped him off at school."

Of course, like any behavior that's overused, these same Supporting characteristics can also drive people up the wall if they get out of hand. For example, self-disclosure can be seen as neediness, digression as inattention, animation as melodrama, acquiescence as weakness, and friendliness as patronization. As with Direct to Indirect tendencies, too much of anything can become a liability.

Or Controlling?

If Supporting types seem more like open books, then Controlling ones tend to be more *poker faced*. Controlling individuals prefer to play their real cards closer to the vest—

increasing the probability of getting the upper hand and decreasing the probability of appearing foolish. They usually like to keep their distance, both physically and mentally. They don't touch you and you don't touch them. People often say this about a Controlling person they know: "Once you get to know him, he's a really great guy." But you must become acquainted by breaking through that exterior shell that he erects. Consequently, Controlling people tend to stand further away from you, even when shaking hands. They have a strong sense of personal space and territory, so make sure you don't take anything from their desks. At home they might set traps with a rug or a sofa cushion to see if someone used them when they weren't supposed to. You know—the tiny fold in the rug or the perfectly aligned pillow on the couch. "You sat on that couch today, didn't you? I asked you not to go in my room when I'm not there. I have proof that someone walked on that rug and sat on that couch."

Controlling people show little facial expression, use controlled or limited hand and body movement, and adhere to a more time-disciplined agenda. They push for facts and details, focus on the issues and tasks at hand, and keep their personal feelings private. They don't touch, and they tend to respond coolly if anyone touches them. Unlike their Supporting counterparts, they give little non-verbal feedback.

By contrast, Controlling types place higher priority on getting things done. They prefer working with things or through people—rather than with or for them. "I can't talk now, Frank. I have a two o'clock deadline to meet," or "I'll let you know when I have time to do that," are characteristic comments of this pattern.

Controllers like structure, since they expect results within that structured environment. When negatively motivated, these types of individuals can be viewed as coercive, restrictive, or overbearing. They prefer to stick with the agenda, at least their own. As more naturally independent workers, they need to control the conditions around their tasks—either in terms of input and output (Directness) or the process itself (Indirectness). These more self-contained people make use of either key talent or key procedures to meet their goals. Thus, they view the planning and supervision processes as ways of reaching goals. The Direct individuals need to control people while the Indirect types need to control their environment.

Because time equals money to Controllers, they're more disciplined about how other people use their time. In part, this explains their tendency not to show, discuss, or willingly listen to thoughts and feelings like Supportives. Controllers are more matter-of-fact, with more fixed expectations of people and situations. Just as facts place second for Supportives, feelings take a back seat for Controllers. You might say that Supportives experience life by tuning in to the concerns or feeling states (of themselves and others) and then reacting to them. Controllers focus on the points or ideas in question.

Controllers like to know where a conversation is going. Idle, non-directed chitchat is not for them. If Supporting types stray from the subject, Controllers find a way to bring them back on track. They usually need clarity before they move on to the next topic. If you get off the subject, they're likely to ask, "Can you sum that up for me?" or, "What is the key point you're trying to make?"

Because of their different priorities, Controlling types can perceive more Supporting ones as time-wasting or wishy-washy. And Supportives may view these Controllers as cold, unsympathetic, or self-involved. As a result, misunderstandings can quickly grow out of proportion when we don't discern and respond to these types of differences. You may still wonder which is better—Supporting or Controlling behavior. And again, the answer is, "It depends." As with Directness and Indirectness, circumstances determine the appropriateness of any type of behavior. Our awareness of potential pitfalls for each personality pattern can save multitudes of problems for ourselves and others as well as for our workplace, social groups, and organizations.

Whereas Supporting people may feel any attention is better than no attention at all, Controllers tend to be more selective about whom they associate with. They feel more comfortable retaining firm control over their emotions.

Ranges of behavior

Whether a person is more Supporting or Controlling, remember there are degrees of these characteristics that vary from individual to individual. These range from the more Direct Captain Kirk character on STAR TREK to the more Indirect, less talkative, and more reserved Mr. Spock. Bruce Willis (of MOONLIGHTING) and Bill Cosby are both Supportive, but Willis gives his openness more free rein. And then, of course, there's Vanna White, the best-known card turner in the country. Everyone from toddlers to octogenarians seems to relate to her warmth as she roots for all the contestants on WHEEL OF FORTUNE.

Controllers, too, cover a wide range of less-than-open behaviors. When we compare Charles Bronson's characters to MAGNUM P. I.'s Higgins, Higgins is more open. Again, both are Controlling, but Bronson is usually more so. Other Controlling TV personalities include MURPHY BROWN and Julia Sugarbaker on DESIGNING WOMEN.

When the chips are down, Supportives tend to spare others' feelings at the expense of completing a task. Controllers want to get things done, even though feelings may get hurt as part of the emotional cost of accomplishment. This doesn't necessarily mean that Supportives don't believe in responsibly doing their work; it just means that people are a higher concern. Similarly, it doesn't mean Controllers don't value other people. They simply think the best way to deal with people is by a more controlled style of behavior.

Survey of Supporting Versus Controlling Behaviors

Follow the same guidelines for this set of nine questions as you did for the Direct and Indirect ones earlier in this chapter. Focus on the same person that you did previously.

Is the Person More Supporting or Controlling?

1. (S) More open to getting to know people better and establishing new relationships, OR

(C) Exerts more control over who he/she gets involved with, including how well you get to know them

2. (C) Focuses conversations on tasks, issues, business, or subject at hand, OR

   (S) Allows conversations to take the direction of interest of the parties involved, even though this may stray from the business or subject at hand

3. (C) Tends to make decisions based on objectives, facts, or evidence, OR

   (S) Tends to make decisions based on feelings, experiences, or relationships

4. (C) More likely to expect and respond to conflicts, OR

   (S) Less likely to expect conflict and more motivated to personally deal with conflicts when they arise

5. (S) More likely to accept others' points of view (ideas, feelings, and concerns), OR

   (C) Less likely to accept other people's points of view (ideas, feelings, and concerns)

6. (C) Tends to focus mostly on the idea, concept, or outcome, OR

   (S) Tends to focus primarily on the interest level, persons involved, and process

7. (S) More open about own time involvement with others, OR

   (C) Less open about own time involvement with others

8. (C) Likely to stick with own agendas and concerns while tuning in to the power motives of others, OR

   (S) Likely to tune in to others' agendas and concerns while   minimizing any conflict or disagreement

9. (C) Prefers to work independently or dictate the conditions as it involves others, OR

   (S) Prefers to work with and through others, providing support when possible

Total number circled: C's_____   S's_____

                             (Controlling)   (Supporting)

To identify a person's behavioral style

Simply use the process of elimination. If the person is more Direct than Indirect, then you can eliminate the Steady Relater and Cautious Thinker types (the two Indirect styles). If the person is also more Supporting than Controlling, then eliminate the Dominant Director (the more Controlling type). Now you arrive at the remaining style, in this case, an Interacting Socializer.

Which type is this?

You have an appointment with a client whose secretary sets the time for exactly 10:10 a.m., not 10:00 or 10:30. After acknowledging you in the reception area with a fixed, polite smile, she gives several detailed instructions to her secretary. Gathering behavioral clues, you notice that she dresses impeccably. She again smiles politely at you and asks you to follow her into the office. She tells you where to sit, checks her watch, and actually says, "You have exactly 15 minutes. Go."

During your presentation, the client remains as expressionless as a statue in a museum. No emotion shows. She asks for highly specific facts, assesses your responses, and then extends the discussion in areas of interest to her. She invites you to stay longer and literally closes the sale herself after getting specific answers to her time, schedule, and cost questions.

There are many clues to help you determine the behavioral style of this client. First, look at her Direct versus Indirect behaviors. You can be fairly sure of placing her as Direct: She directs the conversation, confronts the issues head-on, controls both you and the situation (when to begin, where to sit, what to discuss), and closes the sale herself. That's Directness!

Next, look at her Supporting or Controlling tendencies. By nature of her time discipline, fact and task orientation, formality, and expressionless face, she is fairly easily to classify as Controlling.

When you put together the two aspects which determine behavioral style, you have a combined rating of high Directness/low Supportingness. These two classifications tell you that the client is a Dominant Director.

One more time

You conduct a seminar which begins at 8:30 a.m., following an 8:00 coffee and doughnut session. When you arrive at 7:45, the first participant is already seated in the room, pad and pencils neatly lying in front of her. She says nothing until you approach. Then she politely shakes hands. She is totally noncommittal. You ask a few questions and receive polite, short answers.

Around 8:15, with several other people in the room, a person stops hesitantly at the door and softly asks, "Excuse me. Is this the training seminar for salespeople?" When he hears, "yes," he breathes a sigh, walks in, takes a cup of coffee, and mentions how interesting he hopes the seminar will be, saying it really could be helpful in business and at home. He asks a few questions, listening intently to other's remarks. He expresses some concern for role-playing in front of a group.

At this moment, another participant strides in, loudly asking, "Hey, is this the sales seminar?" Upon hearing, "yes," this person dramatizes relief and asks where the coffee is, explaining that he *can't function without that black poison*. He has overheard the role-playing comments and leaps in on the conversation to say how he likes doing those things. He follows this with a tale of how he embarrassed himself in the last role-play session he attended.

Which style is the first person? The second? The last?

The first person's apparent disinterest in conversation and restrained gestures identify her as Indirect. This narrows the possible choices to either a Steady Relater or Cautious Thinker. She is also clearly in control of her emotions and the setting—Controlling, as opposed to Supporting. Another name for an Indirect/Controlling person is a Cautious Thinker.

The second participant speaks with a soft voice, requests clarification, and hesitates before starting the seminar. All these clues add up to an Indirect behavior pattern (Cautious Thinker or Steady Relater). He volunteers information about personal feelings and gives rapid feedback with his sigh and comments. These are Supporting characteristics. This person shows a Steady Relater style.

Participant number three demonstrates Directness through his speed of response, fast movements, and high quantity of conversation (Dominant Director or Interacting Socializer). He also shows Supporting behaviors by telling stories and responding quickly. These are traits of the Interacting Socializer.

How Will You Know a Dominant Director When You See One?

At the office

When entering Dominant Directors' offices, look around. The overall tone suggests authority and control. Their desks may be covered with projects and papers, stacked in neat piles. Both their in- and out-baskets typically bulge with busywork. They tend to surround themselves with trophies, awards, and other evidence of personal achievement. Virtually everything about the place suggests hustle, bustle, formality, and power. This type is the one that often favors a large chair behind a massive authority structure known as a *power desk*. Besides nonverbally announcing, "I'm important," the desk separates them from visitors, literally keeping them at a distance.

Notice the walls

The walls may include diplomas, commendations, and other evidence of success. One wall may have a large planning sheet or calendar on it . . . the better to juggle with, my dear. If Dominant Directors have family photos, they may hang behind them or someplace where they don't readily see them. To this type, their offices are places of business and the fewer distractions they have, the better.

Hustle, bustle, and busywork

Dominant Directors like constant activity, so you'll seldom catch them idle. Between existing tasks, they pick up new ones. They perk up when competing and appear to thrive with a pressure cooker schedule. They often squeeze you onto their calendars and let you know that their time is limited, either by telling you outright or by showing you. Looking at a watch or clock, they frequently shift their gaze elsewhere, or make and take phone calls while you sit in their office.

They walk fast in pursuit of a tangible goal, so Dominant Directors may not notice people around them or may just hurriedly grunt something to acknowledge them. They often act both brisk and brusque without realizing it. When under stress, impatience emerges and they may push others aside to reach their goal—completing a report, getting served first, or running out the door to make an appointment. When pressure intensifies, Dominant Directors often rise to the occasion. Under time constraints, they may concede to impatience and rely on educated guesses, even their own hunches.

Power symbols

Dominant Directors tend to dress comfortably and typically pay less attention to their appearance than the other types. They may program themselves primarily for work results, so wardrobe tends to play a secondary role in most fields of work. They may be candidates for a time-saving personal shopper or tailor who can choose or measure outfits for them in the privacy of their own offices. Dominant Directors gravitate toward authority symbols, so they may wear navy blue or charcoal gray *power* suits.

Dominant Directors may like to let people know they've *made it* without having to tell anyone about it, so they often prefer possessions that emit success and authority messages—like a black or steel gray Mercedes or BMW. Someone once suggested they'd buy a Sherman tank, if they could.

Observable Characteristics of Dominant Directors

Verbal	Vocal	Visual
States more than asks	More vocal variety	Firm handshake
Talks more than listens	More forceful tone	Steady eye contact
Primarily verbal, not written, communication	Communicates readily	Gestures to emphasize points

| Makes strong statements | High volume, fast speech | Displays impatience |
| Blunt and to the point | Challenging voice intonation | Fast moving body language |

How Will You Know a Dominant Director by Phone?

When speaking on the phone to a Dominant Director, treat her the same way as in a person-to-person contact. Think of the ABC's: Keep it abridged, brief, and concise. Then we prepare our delivery with the bottom line in mind: "The trend in your industry is toward computer-generated graphics. The research we've conducted with other typesetters in your area indicates increased profits of 20 to 30% over two years. I'd like to meet with you for 10 minutes to show you the numbers and see if this concept interests you."

They waste no time

It's not unusual for a Dominant Director to call someone and, without saying hello, launch right into the conversation. "You've got to be kidding; the shipment from Hong Kong will kill us . . . by the way, this is Jack." When other people can't keep up with their speed, they may view them as incompetent.

On the telephone, determine whether the person sends power signals. Dominant Directors want to pick the time and place to meet. They often speak in a sort of shorthand—concisely and pointedly—and sound cool, confident, and demanding. When Dominant Director Dennis phones, he actually says: "Janice? Dennis. Tony there?" Talking to him is like speaking to a human telegram. He reduces the concept of *brief and to the point* to another dimension. As commanding speakers who tend not to listen to others, they naturally want to direct the conversation toward their goals. Under stress, they can become defensive and aggressive, attacking others personally to show who's in control. They dislike using *touchy-feely*, emotional terms and prefer sensible *thinking* terminology. "I think we'll implement this plan tomorrow," or, "I think this discussion is over."

Their letters are brief and to the point

A letter from a Dominant Director tends to be brief, forceful, and to the point. They may mention highlights of conversations or materials, but they don't belabor them. They may give specifics for your follow-through or raise questions they want answers to now. "The Mulvany account needs to be reworked. I hear he's got a new partner and a different address. Track him down and get the data we need so we can let him know that we've studied his account and we know our stuff."

Even notes and cards take on abbreviated forms and may show little or no indication of feelings. "Todd, hope you're doing well. I'm working hard . . . " We know more than one Dominant Director who signs personal birthday and Christmas cards with no closing, not even *Sincerely*, but with just their names. Steady Relaters and Interacting Socializers gravitate more toward *Warmly*, *Fondly*, or *Cordially*. But Dominant Directors, perhaps in their efforts to get as many things accomplished as possible, tend to opt for brevity.

Pick a Dominant Director co-worker

Think of a co-worker who is a strong Dominant Director in the workplace. What characteristics does he or she exhibit that reveal those Dominant Director traits? How do you get along with this person? Why?

How Will You Know an Interacting Socializer When You See One?

At the office

When you enter the working area of an Interacting Socializer, look around his office. What does it look like? Even if you've never been to this type's office before, you may recognize it from across the room. Remember Oscar Madison? He and other high Interacting Socializers may strew paperwork across their desks, sometimes trailing it along the floor, too. They react to visual stimuli, so they like to have everything where they can see it. Consequently, their desks often look cluttered and disorganized. If anyone comments, "How do you find anything?" they like to say that they're *organized in their disorganization.*

And the walls?

Interacting Socializer walls may sport prestigious awards. They may be broad, liberal arts degrees, motivational or upbeat slogans, generalized personal comments, or stimulating posters. You may see notes posted and taped all over the place with little apparent forethought, rhyme, or reason. Overall decor reflects an open, airy, lively atmosphere that often reveals the personality of its occupant. Likewise, the furniture arrangement tends to indicate warmth, openness, and contact. An Interacting Socializer seldom sits behind a desk when he talks. He often opts for comfortable, accessible seating, enabling him to meet his goal of getting to know people better. He prefers to sit next to us at a table or on a couch so he can see and hear us better and get a feel for how we respond to him. He talks a lot and shows emotion with both his body language and speech.

Feelings take priority

Interacting Socializers have a natural preference for talking and listening in *feeling* terms. Unconsciously, they may become uncomfortable when talking to a person who, instead, uses *thinking* words. (The opposite also is true). Statements like, "I feel that we should have been consulted about moving our office," or, "I feel good about what we've accomplished today," tend to put this people-oriented type more at ease.

They like glitz and pizzazz!

The way Interacting Socializers dress often relates to their need for recognition. Since they like others to notice them, they may dress in the latest style. *Look at me* Socializers like bright colors and unusual clothes that prompt others to compliment them. Many Interacting Socializers even prefer negative comments to none at all. "Are you dressed for Halloween today, Rhonda?" At least she's getting the attention she craves.

In an informal poll taken by Tony at his many seminars, red ranks number one with Interacting Socializers as their color choice for clothes or for a sports car or convertible. They like glamour, flash, and excitement . . . and their purchases often express their preferences. Musical choices even include energizing songs like *Celebration* or *Fame.*

Observable Characteristics of Interacting Socializers

Verbal	Vocal	Visual
Tells stories, anecdotes	Lots of inflection	Animated facial expressions
Shares personal feelings	More pitch variation	Much hand/body movement
Informal speech	More variety in vocal quality	Contact oriented
Expresses opinions readily	Dramatic	Spontaneous actions
Flexible time perspective	High volume	
Digresses from conversation	Fast speech	

How Will You Know an Interacting Socializer by Phone?

"What's up?" or "What's happening?" are usual Interacting Socializer opening lines. They are sometimes so animated that their gestures can be transmitted via the phone lines. How? By their varied, emotional vocal inflections/intonations and their colorful choice of words that may tend toward exaggeration. "Really? That's fantastic!" or, "You have to be kidding me!" The telephone can be a favorite toy that enables them to both prolong conversations and recharge themselves, especially when no one else is physically around. "I just called because I'm bored." You may also detect background noise when you speak to individuals of this type. They sometimes put on the TV or radio just for the sound, visual stimulation, and activity.

On the phone, Interacting Socializers speak rapidly and emotively. "I feel that if we go through with this plan, the community will resent us as anti-environmentalists," or, "I feel that I've contributed enough to this organization over the years to allow me to talk about this." Other styles may more naturally use *thinking* words, instead.

Say it with feeling

Typically, you'll notice a wide range of vocal inflection and intonation and a tendency to want to know your reaction. "Do you feel that way, too?" They liven up conversations with personal anecdotes and may keep you on the phone longer than you had anticipated. If you need to extricate yourself from an extended monologue, try something like, "Well, Don, it's been great talking with you. I'm really looking forward to our appointment on Monday!" If you say it with feeling, the Interacting Socializer may already eagerly anticipate your meeting.

By Letter?

Letters, too, can reveal the Interacting Socializer behind the correspondence. Often, this type overuses exclamation points, underlining, and bold highlighting. You can almost hear her emphasizing those picturesque adjectives and adverbs. Just as the Interacting Socializer tends to speak in a stimulating, energetic way, so does she write. She may also throw in an image-provoking personal anecdote or reference to some mutually satisfying experience. "I'll never forget our adventure on the freeway en route to Los Angeles—in rush hour, of course!" When she's finished a letter or note, she may add a postscript (P.S.), a P.P.S., or even a P.P.P.S.

Caution: Again, these tendencies may not as readily reveal themselves if the Interacting Socializer has learned to tone down her natural flair while conducting business. And there's always a possibility that the secretary *cleans up* her copy before typing it out, especially if she is a more exacting, less animated behavioral type.

How Will You Know a Steady Relater When You See One?

Office memorabilia

When you enter a Steady Relater's office, be alert for conservatively framed personal slogans, group photos, serene landscapes and posters, and other personal items. Since they seek close relationships, also look around for telltale family pictures and mementos, usually turned so they can view them from their desk chair. They often favor nostalgic memories of stabilizing experiences and relationships in our increasingly high tech world. These remembrances of a pleasant, uncomplicated past allow them to transform their offices into an environment of friendly, warm ambience. They prefer to arrange seating in a side-by-side, more congenial, cooperative manner. No big power desks for them! If they do have one, though, they'll typically come out from behind it to *reach out* by opting for a more personal touch.

Service certificates

Their educational background often includes more specialized areas of attention and interest within their professions. You may also see certificates recognizing volunteer hours for various hands-on activities in their community. While other behavioral types may contribute in other ways—such as gifts of money—Steady Relaters typically enjoy giving their time for causes they feel strongly about. Besides the possibility of meeting more potential friends, this also helps satisfy their need to see for themselves: (1) what's really going on, (2) where they fit into the group effort, and (3) how they can get meaningful, concrete results.

Steady Relaters are natural listeners

You can recognize Steady Relaters by their natural listening patterns and slower, lower-key delivery. Their questions often focus on concrete topics and experiences. "What did you say the terms for payment were again?" They walk casually, acknowledging others and sometimes getting sidetracked by chance encounters.

Nothing too loud for them

Steady Relaters dislike calling attention to themselves, so they tend to wear subdued colors and conservatively cut clothing, favoring conventional styles that don't stand out too much. Their cars also reveal these preferences. They often like beige or light blue station wagons or vans, factory recommended tires, and in the best of all worlds—no horn. To Steady Relaters, using a horn is like yelling at somebody. Steady Relaters often tell us they like most songs by Lionel Ritchie or Barry Manilow. Both have more predictable, Steady Relater styles of performing mellow, soothing, easy listening music.

Observable Characteristics of Steady Relaters

Verbal	Vocal	Visual
Ask more than state	Steady, even-tempered delivery	Intermittent eye contact
Listen more than talk	Less forceful tone of expression	Gentle handshake
Reserve opinions	Lower, quieter volume	Exhibit patience
Less verbal communication	Slower rate of speech	Slower moving body language

How Will You Know a Steady Relater by Phone?

"How are you?" or "I'm glad to hear from you again," are typical Steady Relater greetings. Like those telephone company TV commercials, their warmth can seem to transcend the limitations of the phone lines. Although they prefer more personal interactions with people, they will also settle for indirect contact—especially if the person is pleasant and non-threatening. They project this people orientation by phone and like to build a personal, first-name relationship with callers. Even if they don't know you, they may say, "You don't have to be formal. Just call me Alice." They may project a desire to know you personally or provide you with good service.

They communicate with steady, even vocal intonations to convey friendliness, comfort, and a sense of relaxation. Steady Relaters tend to be naturals at listening to others' ideas and feelings, whether on the phone or in person. They tend to be interested in the blow-by-blow, point-by-point description of what you did yesterday or the sequential pattern of how to complete a certain task. You're probably talking to a Steady Relater if you notice slower than average speech patterns, more moments of listening than of speaking, and references to actual, real-life experiences regarding either products or mutual acquaintances.

"I'll look it up for you"

Steady Relaters tend to express themselves in a rather tentative manner in both their face-to-face and telephone conversations. "I'll need to consult Mrs. Adams before I can make that decision," or, "I'm not sure we can do that, but I'll get back to you as soon as I find out." As in other aspects of their lives, they often defer to the more human, proven way things have always been done. They typically feel more comfortable making decisions based on conferring with others rather than by themselves. "What do you think?" and "How do you feel?" and "What do you recommend?" are all common questions this type may ask.

When They Think About Someone, They May Drop a Line

In their written correspondence, Steady Relaters may send letters just to keep in touch or to let you know they're thinking of you. Of the four personality types, this one is likely to send thank you notes for almost anything—inviting them to a party, driving them to the dry cleaners, or saving coupons for them. They may even send a thank you note to acknowledge your thank you note. Again, they are likely to organize their letters, writing as they do their other *to do* task lists—probably in sequential *in-out* order. Since they tend to write in a slower, more methodically paced manner, their work tends to follow a systematic outline pattern.

Visualize a Steady Relater friend

Picture a friend of yours who best typifies the Steady Relater. What does he or she do that fits the type? How do you tend to interact with him or her?

How Will You Know a Cautious Thinker When You See One?

At the office

Cautious Thinkers often carry their organizational tendencies into their work environments. Environmental clues include neat, highly organized desks with cleared tops so they can work unimpeded by clutter—clean, shipshape, and professional with everything in the appropriate place. Charts, graphs, exhibits, models, credentials, and job-related pictures are often placed neatly on their office walls or shelves. Cautious Thinkers favor a functional decor that will enable them to work more efficiently. They tend to keep most objects within reach, readily available when needed. Where appropriate, you may notice state-of-the-art technology to further enhance efficiency.

Cautious Thinkers ask pertinent questions

People of few words, Cautious Thinkers tend to ask pertinent questions instead of making statements. They typically speak more carefully and with less expression than the other types. Reluctant to reveal personal feelings, they often use *thinking* words (like the Dominant Director), as opposed to *feeling* words. "From what I've read, I think Product X may be better for our situation than Product Y because of its superior filtration system," or, "I think that Jones is overreacting in this matter."

Formality is more comfortable

Cautious Thinkers are non-contact people who prefer the formality of distance. This preference is reflected in the functional, but uninviting arrangement of their desks and chairs, usually with the desks physically separating you and them. They generally are not fond of huggers and touchers, and prefer a cool handshake or a brief phone call. When Cautious Thinkers walk, they usually move slowly and methodically toward a known destination.

Noticeably understated

Picture Felix Unger, the neat, perfectionistic one on television's THE ODD COUPLE. Like Felix, Cautious Thinkers tend to wear more conservative clothes, but with unique, often perfectly matched accessories. While the Interacting Socializer may draw attention to himself with glitz and glitter, Cautious Thinkers usually prefer a more understated, faultlessly groomed look with nary a hair out of place. But their taste may differ from the people around them.

They like expressions of individuality and creativity, but within guidelines. For some reason, male Cautious Thinkers with beards seem to prefer short, well-manicured ones. If they smoke, they often prefer pipes—perhaps, someone noted, this is because taking a puff from a pipe gives them more time to think before they answer. Since they may prefer exploring life's complexities, they may enjoy the intricacies of a specific kind of music or individual musical piece, whether jazz, classical, rock, etc. You may spot them driving well-built, practical cars that perform well, often in more conservative, understated, but less common colors.

Observable Characteristics of Cautious Thinkers

Verbal	Vocal	Visual
Fact and task-oriented	Little inflection	Few facial expressions
Limited sharing of feelings	Few pitch variations	Non-contact oriented
More formal and proper	Less variety in vocal quality	Few gestures

| Focused conversation | Steady, mono-tone delivery | Slower moving |
| Less verbal, more written communication | Lower volume, slower speech | |

How Will You Know a Cautious Thinker by Phone?

"Good afternoon, Mr. Lomis. This is Jonathan Williams. You asked me to call back Monday morning." Formal greetings are one tipoff that you may be dealing with a Cautious Thinker. Time-conscious individuals of this type often get to a task just when they say. they will. Monday morning it is! In this example, the Cautious Thinker also calls himself Jonathan, not Jon. We've noticed that many people in this category call themselves by their given names, not by nicknames. It's Elizabeth, Rebecca, Donald, and Peter, not Beth, Becka, Don, or Pete. Of course, there are exceptions. Actually, Jon may prove to be an effective and logical alternative for some Cautious Thinkers, but this type seems less likely to tolerate what they perceive as cute nicknames for themselves, such as Johnny, Ricky, Cindy, or Becky.

"May I speak with Mr. Holmes or Dr. Brothers?"

They prefer brief, to-the-point telephone calls. Although they may not tell you, call them Mister or Ms. or Doctor or whatever their titles happen to be. Cautious Thinkers sometimes view jumping into a first-name basis as invasion of privacy, so they deal with others on a more formal basis. If you think you're talking to Sherlock Holmes or Dr. Joyce Brothers, chances are you've contacted a Cautious Thinker. They typically retain their ground in stressful situations when they can maintain their position with concrete facts or reverse-control questions. They do this quietly and independently, by first avoiding others. Then they take on the problem in an orderly way which is aligned with their own plan.

"Need to know" basis

They're inclined to talk in rather structured, careful speech patterns, almost weighing their words as they say them. They tend to ask pertinent questions and talk in a quiet, observant, cautious way. Additionally, they may not volunteer much about their personal selves beyond the equivalent of name, rank, and serial number. "Yes, I'm married with two children. We live in New York." They prefer to keep the relationship formal, yet pleasant and businesslike. Less can be more to a Cautious Thinker—less conversation, self-disclosure, and verbal communication equals more comfort zone. So we must learn to hear between the lines: Longer than average silences, especially when we ask them more private questions, may signal annoyance or reluctance. When this occurs, ask, "Am I getting too personal?" or "If I'm asking uncomfortable questions, how could you let me know so I don't make a problem for either of us?" They may relax more if they think they have an out.

Careful and correct

Like Steady Relaters, Cautious Thinkers tend to express themselves in a rather tentative manner. "I'll check on that and let you know tomorrow." Or they may want to provide you with information so you can form your own conclusions. "I have a copy of the Governor's report in my files. If I send it to you, perhaps you can find what you're looking for." Both these approaches satisfy Cautious Thinkers' need for caution and correctness. They simply may not want to get misquoted or, possibly, involved in the first place.

How Will You Know
a Cautious Thinker by Letter?

Cautious Thinkers typically send letters to clarify or explain positions. Consequently, these letters may become rather long and filled with data. "I was struck by the similarities between the Noonan and Kilgary lawsuits." But they may also be somewhat reserved or vague. "I'm researching a company's file now that I literally can't talk about." Or the letter may be on the short side with enclosures, citings, or references to specific information. Whether they prefer the long or short form, they usually concentrate on processing data. They like to cover their bases so they are neither misinterpreted, incomplete, nor incorrect.

Like Dominant Directors, in the interest of time, they may sign personal cards with just their names or with individual mottos, like "In the spirit of growth, Jonathan Williams." Even if you know them well, this type may include their surnames so there's no mistaking who sent this card.

If the shoe fits

The dimensions that determine type—Direct/Indirect and Controlling/Supporting—have their own innate strengths and weaknesses. In fact, the strengths are closely allied to the weaknesses—the strengths taken to an extreme. The Direct-Controlling type can become overbearing when he pushes persistence too hard. Similarly, the Direct-Supporting type may turn manipulative; the Indirect-Supporting type, wishy-washy; or the Indirect-Controlling type, unreachable. These and other positive or negative characteristics shade the actions of all four types. Individuals representing all four may have the same assignment, but use different approaches. If a monthly report is due, one type may keep a day-by-day journal (Indirect-Controlling), another may delegate the work (Direct-Controlling), another may prefer completing it with a co-worker (Indirect-Supporting), and yet another may prefer to pull an *all nighter* to complete it at the last minute (Direct-Supporting). Take a look at two charts which further summarize many of the Distinguishing Characteristics and Daily Examples of these four basic types of individuals.

By now, you know how to recognize the four core types by observing environmental clues and external behaviors. The four combinations we've just discussed—Direct/Controlling, or Dominant Director; Direct/Supporting, or Interacting Socializer; Indirect/Supporting, or Steady Relater; and Indirect/Controlling, or Cautious Thinker—all behave differently from each other in various situations. Whether at home, work, a social activity, or in a romantic encounter, they all naturally act true to their own type. It's their attempts to fill their type's needs and expectations. By acting themselves, they show their true core behavioral colors.

In the next chapter, *Adaptability*, you'll read about getting along with all the behavioral types in their natural, and less natural, life environments. You'll learn how to have more productive relationships with people of all types. Thereafter, you'll read about applying People Smart concepts in the workplace (Chapter 5), leading and being led by each type (Chapter 6), and selling to and being sold by them (Chapter 7). Then you'll discover personal applications in Chapters 8 through 10 when you learn about the different types in social, family, and romance settings. So read on to discover more about your People Smart potential in different life environments.

DISTINGUISHING CHARACTERISTICS OF THE FOUR STYLES

	STEADY RELATER	CAUTIOUS THINKER	DOMINANT DIRECTOR	INTERACTING SOCIALIZER
1) BEHAVIOR PATTERN	Indirect/Supporting	Indirect/Controlling	Direct/Controlling	Direct/Supporting
2) PACE	Slower/Relaxed	Slower/Systematic	Faster/Decisive	Faster/Spontaneous
3) PRIORITY	The Relationship/ Communication	The Task/ Process	The Task/ Results	The Relationship/ Interaction
4) FEARS	Sudden changes, Instability	Personal criticism of their work efforts	Being taken advantage of	Loss of Social recognition
5) GAINS SECURITY THROUGH	Friendship, Cooperation	Preparation, Thoroughness	Control, Leadership	Playfulness, Others' approval
6) MEASURES PERSONAL WORTH BY	Compatibility with others, Depth of contribution	Precision, Accuracy, Quality of results	Quality or impact or results, Track record & process	Acknowledgments, Applause, Compliments
7) INTERNAL MOTIVATOR	The "Participation"	The "Process"	The "Win"	The "Show"
8) APPEARANCE	Casual, Conforming	Formal, Conservative	Businesslike, Functional	Fashionable, Stylish
9) WORKPLACE	Friendly Functional Personal	Formal Functional Structured	Efficient Busy Structured	Interacting Busy Personal

DAILY EXAMPLES
OF THE FOUR STYLES

	STEADY RELATER	CAUTIOUS THINKER	DOMINANT DIRECTOR	INTERACTING SOCIALIZER
1) SEEKS	Acceptance	Accuracy	Control	Recognition
2) STRENGTHS	Listening Teamwork Follow-through	Planning Systematizing Orchestration	Administration Leadership Pioneering	Persuading Enthusiastic Entertaining
3) WEAKNESSES (GROWTH AREAS)	Oversensitive Slow to begin action Lacks global perspective	Perfectionists Critical Unresponsive	Impatient Insensitive to others Poor listener	Inattentive to detail Short attention span Low follow-through
4) IRRITATIONS	Insensitivity Impatience	Disorganization Impropriety	Inefficiency Indecision	Routines Complexity
5) UNDER STRESS	Submissive Indecisive	Withdrawn Headstrong	Dictatorial Critical	Sarcastic Superficial
6) DECISION MAKING PATTERN	Conferring	Deliberate	Decisive	Spontaneous
7) OCCUPATIONS	Family doctor Social services Teacher	Engineer Researcher Artist	Executive Military leader Newspaper editor	Sales Public relations Actor
8) CELEBRITIES	Kenny Rogers Edith Bunker Martina Navratalova	Mr. Spock Sgt. Joe Friday Katherine Hepburn	Mike Wallace McGarrett (Five O) Rambo	Carol Burnett Tony Danza Dom Deluise
9) SONG	"You've Got a Friend"	"Don't Rain On My Parade"	"My Way"	"Celebration"
10) VEHICLE	Station Wagon	"Best Rated Buy"	Full-Size Luxury Car	Sports Car
11) ANIMAL	Koala	Fox	Lion	Porpoise

People Smart Principle #4—The Adaptability Principle:
"Your willingness and ability to adapt your behavior
is a prerequisite for your personal effectiveness."

Chapter 4
Creating Personal Power Through Behavioral Adaptability

What is it?

Behavioral adaptability is the key to success with the different types. With adaptability, we can treat the other person the way he wants to be treated. We define it as the willingness and ability to engage in a range of behaviors not necessarily characteristic of your style in response to effectively dealing with the requirements of a situation or relationship. Behavioral adaptability is something applied more to yourself (to your patterns, attitudes, and habits) than to others. It involves making strategic adjustments to your methods of communicating and behaving, based on the particular needs of the relationship at a particular time. Adaptable people try to meet the expectations of others by practicing tact. They make the choice to go beyond their own comfort zone so others feel more comfortable—especially with the derived results.

What adaptability isn't

Adaptability does not mean imitation of the other person's behavioral style. It does mean adjusting your Supportiveness, Controllingness, Directness, and Indirectness in line with the other person's preference. At the same time, it means maintaining your own identity and good sense. You modify your spots.

So does that mean that Cautious Thinkers prefer the company of Cautious Thinkers and that the other types prefer people who share their type? Yes and no. Two clichés apply. *Birds of a feather flock together*, and *Opposites attract.* Dominant Directors may personally admire other Dominant Directors like themselves for their accomplishments and success rates, but prefer to be more guarded with them at work in order to maintain their own power and authority.

Cautious Thinkers may appreciate Interacting Socializers for their joy of life, but steer clear of them at work because of their imprecision. Interacting Socializers may enjoy Cautious Thinkers for their command of matters of interest to them, but may stay aloof at work because of the Cautious Thinkers' desired perfectionism. Steady Relaters and Dominant Directors may also admire each others' qualities or feel alienated by them. So what's a person to do?

Remember, the willingness to try behaviors not necessarily characteristic of your type is called *behavioral adaptability*. It is not the same as your behavioral type. No members of any type corner the market on adaptability. No style is *naturally* more adaptable than another. In other words, Steady Relaters as a group are no more adaptable than Interacting Socializers, Dominant Directors, or Cautious Thinkers (and vice versa).

Your adaptability level affects the way other people perceive you. Raise your adaptability and you'll discover trust and credibility go up; lower it, and they go down. Behavioral adaptability means adjusting your behavior to allow others to be more at ease, encouraged, and successful in your relationship.

Which style is most adaptable?

No one style is naturally more adaptable than another. For a given situation, the strategic adjustments each behavioral style makes will vary. The decision to employ specific techniques of behavioral adaptability is made on a case-by-case basis. You can choose to be adaptable with one person and not with another. You can also choose to be quite adaptable with one person today and less with that same person tomorrow. Behavioral adaptability concerns the way you manage your own communication and behaviors. It also involves how you manage the requirements that exist for a task or situation—whether other people are involved or not.

For example, when an Interacting Socializer works with a Cautious Thinker on a common task, one of the ways she can practice behavioral adaptability is by talking less, listening more, and focusing on the critical facts. Behavioral adaptability means adjusting your own behavior to make other people feel more at ease with you and the situation. You practice adaptability every time you slow down for a Cautious Thinker or Steady Relater—or when you move a bit faster for an Interacting Socializer or a Dominant Director. Adaptability occurs when the Dominant Director or the Cautious Thinker takes the time to listen to a human interest or family story told by an Interacting Socializer or a Steady Relater.

The Adaptability Recipe

Adaptability is a phenomenon which has many characteristics. In fact, formal research studies in which we have been involved have identified at least 10 such attributes of people who are highly adaptable and 10 characteristics of those who have lower adaptability—a total of 20 traits in all. Of course, no person is likely to be either totally adaptable or nonadaptable. Instead, each of us possesses:

- different general, overall levels of adaptability ranging from higher (more characteristic) to lower (less characteristic)
- personal differences in various situations regarding our level of the two basic ingredients of adaptability—flexibility and versatility
- specific key strengths and possible growth areas in the 20 behaviors which make up your overall level of development in adaptability potential

The 10 behaviors which define the person with high adaptability potential are different from behavioral type, so anybody can choose to enter the higher range characteristics of a more enlightened, functionally mature human being. Unfortunately, the 10 at the lower end represent the darker side more characteristic of lower order animals and species. But you (and every other individual) have the personal power to increase your level of adaptability if you are willing to learn the abilities to get there.

The high and low adaptors

The research conducted on flexibility has shown you view yourself as both more flexible and versatile than you actually are. In part, this is because you aspire toward who and what you want to be. As a result, your view of yourself includes both how you intend to act and how you actually do act. However, the reality of how you act is based only on the second element.

Another factor that explains this gap in our idealized versus actual level of adaptability is that it's not easy. If you're like most people, you may not be aware of all 10 behaviors which allow you to achieve your potential, let alone have already developed them as personal strengths. Similarly, you may not have thought about the 10 others which undermine your potential strengths. Here are all 20, broken down into 10 flexibility strengths and weaknesses and 10 versatility plus and minus points.

Higher flexibility is characterized by these personal attitudes:
- confidence—the attitude of belief in one's self, trusting your own judgment and resourcefulness
- tolerance—open-minded state of acceptance; willingness to defer judgment on the basis of limited time or information
- empathy—sensitivity to another's point of view; caring approach towards others (without being overwhelmed or manipulated by people)
- positiveness—maintaining a state of positive expectations about people and situations, including a positive state of energy in your thoughts and emotional patterns

- respect for others—desire to understand, accept, and consider mutual and separate interests, choices, and commitments

Lower flexibility is characterized by these personal attitudes:
- rigidity
- competition with others
- discontent
- being unapproachable
- difficulty in dealing with ambiguity

Just think of the more successful individuals you have admired, both personally and from afar, and you'll probably notice your list is full of people with high flexibility strengths. Those with lower flexibility characteristics seldom seem to make the cut.

Now, for the other half of this adaptability formula—versatility. Our research indicates people have a more clear-cut understanding, and generally a higher developed level, of flexibility than versatility. Versatility, instead, involves a set of personal aptitudes which are distinctly different from merely being willing to adapt. Many people are willing to modify their behaviors, but simply lack the required set of abilities. Versatility is a complex set of mental and emotional abilities which we acquire over time through a variety of sources. These include formal education, daily life experiences, and observations of others who demonstrate these same behaviors.

The good news is that versatility can be learned. People aren't born either high or low in versatility. But more versatile people tend to approach every situation in each day of their lives as new opportunities for learning and growing. And, of course, others make a personal decision to opt for the lower road—getting the consequences that go along with the easier way of doing things in life.

Higher versatility is characterized by these personal aptitudes:
- resilience—learning how to cope in spite of setbacks, barriers, or limited resources
- vision—foresight, creativity, and imagination

- attentiveness—being mindful and aware of stimuli in the environment; reality-focused
- competence—capability of managing required tasks and being knowledgeable about required subjects and people; including uses and updates of appropriate abilities
- self-correction—able to initiate and evaluate by oneself, seeking feedback as appropriate, characterized by a problem-solving mind set/approach to matters

Lower versatility is characterized by these personal aptitudes:
- subjectiveness
- bluntness
- resistance
- single-mindedness
- unreasonable risk-taking

Flexibility

The flexibility dimension of adaptability is the half that involves your personal attitudes toward yourself, others, and the situations you face. It indicates your degree of willingness to change your perspective and/or position, when appropriate. Examples follow of a lower and higher level of adaptability in a person, and the way each one is likely to respond.

Here's a brief summary of some of these key differences between such people:

Higher flexibility attitudes indicate . . .
- a higher level of security and sense of personal worth or well-being
- an open-minded, searching attitude in dealing with people and situations
- positive expectations about your own goals and desired results, and those of others

Lower flexibility attitudes indicate . . .
- a tendency to be reactive to people, conditions, or events—often responding out of fear or anxiety
- predetermined views, conclusions, or patterns of behavior which are non-negotiable

- a tendency to be negative about what may occur, especially if points of view or opinions change

As you review the following statements, you can see the differences in higher versus lower flexibility.

Lower personal flexibility

"What do you expect of me? That's just the way I am. It's me . . . my type of person or style I'm stuck with . . . so I can't do anything about it."

Higher personal flexibility

"Well, one thing I've learned is that each of us can be our own worst enemy in our own unique way. That's the real benefit I've gained from this *type* kind of behavioral style idea. Now, I realize my more natural strengths, preferences and short suits. As a result, I've made conscious efforts to monitor these to make sure they stay in the positive range while also learning how I can become better by modifying myself, at times."

Lower personal flexibility

"Look, each of us has our own cross to bear in terms of other people. I can't be expected to get along with everyone. There are such things as personality conflicts and that's all there is to it. So I try to seek those people I get along with and stay away from all those other types that pose problems for me—and themselves, too."

Higher personal flexibility

"Obviously, since no two people are identical and there are few Prince Charming/Cinderella matches in the real world, each of us has to work at our relationships if we want them to be mutually satisfying. This means I have to be willing to accept every person as worthwhile, regardless of their style or values. The key is being willing to understand as well as accept them as people I want to get along with. When I do, I've found that things usually work out quite well; and when I don't, then it usually doesn't. The choice and the consequences belong to me."

Lower personal flexibility

"Look, I'm just your average, hard-working kind of person. I mean, I'm good at handling some types of situations, and not so successful with others. But I've learned to accept this fact. After all, nobody's perfect. So I just don't deal with those situations that pose problems for me. Instead, I either avoid them or try to get someone else to handle them. After all, why should I get all bent out of shape about these?"

Higher personal flexibility

"A few years ago I attended a public seminar on Situational Leadership. I found it really fascinating and since then have read some books and listened to tapes on the subject. Now, I consider myself a lot more effective as a person—both at work and in my personal life—because I've learned how to adjust my own preferred style of doing things when it gets in the way of the kinds of results I want to achieve. This has been a real breakthrough for me and has given me a much greater sense of confidence in my ability to deal with situations that arise. And it wasn't that I didn't have the ability to deal with them. It's just that this model helped me better process my own attitudes when I got stuck over how to handle different situations."

Versatility

By comparison with flexible individuals, highly versatile people demonstrate a set of distinctive abilities in realistically and productively managing a variety of situations. This includes the stresses that accompany this higher activity level. In addition, their actions are clearly goal oriented, serving a meaningful purpose in their own personal aspirations, their relationships with others, and the desirable outcomes of situations. They also exhibit appropriate problem-solving actions which match the requirements that exist in dealing with a broad range of different situations.

Lower versatility is characterized by a tendency to be responsive only to one's personal preferences or expectations, discounting the reality of other factors that require consideration. As a result, these people tend to be more one-dimensional in their behavior. If they are Supporting and Direct, for instance, they have difficulty demonstrating other behaviors, even when different actions are more appropriate in a specific situation. Additionally, while they tend to be very adept at finding problems and passing them off to other people, they lack the same skillfulness when it comes to contributing to the solution of such problems.

Higher versatility individuals

Employee: "One of the things I really like about my job is that every day is different. I'm always learning something new and have the opportunity to respond to many types of situations where I can use my talents as well as develop other ones. In fact, our company gives us the chance to take a variety of training programs—both in-house and through continuing education programs—and they reimburse us for part of the cost. I'm always on the lookout for ones that fill in the gaps for my job and areas where I'd like to get better."

Homemaker: "I used to work before I had children, but now I really enjoy being at home. There are a wide variety of tasks and challenges I face in the job my husband calls chief executive officer of our home. We have three children, and as you might guess, each of them is quite different. My husband is, too. That significantly impacts the way I organize schedules, and respond to the many little stresses each one faces, from their own point of view. I also keep an eye on the bigger picture involving where we were, are, and want to go individually and as a family. That's sure a full-time job, requiring a lot of different skills to understand and manage the range of situations which arise."

Lower versatility individuals

Teenager: "I hate school. It's always the same old thing, day after day and year after year. About the only really good thing about it is I get a chance to meet a lot of people and get invited to a lot of great parties and things. In that way it's a lot better than just sitting around. But I don't really see how a lot of the stuff they try to teach us is really going to apply to what I do. After all, I have a part-time job at a local store and I don't really need hardly anything they teach me to get the things done that they expect of me. So, what's the point?"

Manager: "You know, one of the problems with people nowadays is that they expect a lot more than people did in the good old days. Back then, people just came to work and did what they were told. Even customers were satisfied with what they got as long as it worked and the price was fair. But now the whole world seems to have turned upside down. As a manager, I've got to also deal with a lot of other things that I didn't before. One of the most difficult is knowing how to deal with all of these different expectations which have dramatically changed the nature of the business we're in and how I have to do my job—handling all these people and their concerns. I just do the best I can at this point and try not to make too many waves, but it's confusing. I can't say I'm real clear as to what's expected of me nowadays, let alone how to do these things."

These comparisons indicate that you do not have to be a prisoner of your own behavioral tendencies and patterns. Instead, by increasing your personal flexibility and versatility, you can gain personal success and effectiveness by managing yourself, your relationships, and the situations you encounter. You are in charge of whether you choose to be a person with higher or lower flexibility and versatility.

Everyone can become more adaptable

So the good news is you can, in fact, become more adaptable. The accompanying bad news is that it doesn't happen overnight, by wishing for it, or without occasional regressions back to the old behaviors you felt more comfortable with. Since adaptability involves learning techniques of mind over matter, you can speed up the process and increase your probability for success by focusing once again on the matter of who you are. Coming full circle, this means dealing with who you are. It also means personally committing to work toward overcoming these easier, more natural behaviors you will occasionally slip back into. After all, you've done them thousands of times more than these newer, competing behaviors.

The Road Map to Personal Adaptability

	How to Increase FLEXIBILITY	How to Increase VERSATILITY
IF you are a . . .	Lower your over-emphasis on . . .	Develop and demon strate more . . .
DOMINANT DIRECTOR	control of other people and conditions	supportive skills and actions Examples: listening, open-ended questions, positive reinforcement of others
INTERACTING SOCIALIZER	approval from other people or groups as the primary determinant of appropriate choices for you	directive skills and actions Examples: self-assertion, conflict resolution, negotiations
STEADY RELATER	resistance to try or seek out new or different opportunities; limiting your options by undue demand for, dependence on, stability or risk-free choices	directive skills and actions Examples: negotiation, divergent thinking
CAUTIOUS THINKER	unnecessary perfectionism and the tendency to focus on weak nesses (rather than strengths) and on faults of self and others	supportive skills and actions Examples: empathic listening, positive reinforcement of others, involvement with others with complementary strengths

Just as you consult a map when you swerve off course, you can remind yourself to stay on the road to adaptability when you fall back into your old habits. The *Road Map to Personal Adaptability* will help you increase your own flexibility and versatility. You can also use it to coach and assist your friends, family, co-workers, and others through the same learning process. Again, this process begins with who you are. From there, you can work on either those appropriate attitude changes or aptitude changes to develop the potentials related to your own unique behavioral tendencies.

Here's how to use your own road map. First identify your strongest behavioral tendency ("D", "I", "S", or "C"). Select just one goal—either flexibility or versatility—not both at once. Then look across the appropriate row and under the corresponding column to find what you can do to further develop yourself.

Since we don't behave in a vacuum, these general self-adaptations can obviously be further refined for greater success when used more selectively with some types of individuals, and less so with others. Here, then, is a brief *to do* list for ready reference use in deciding what specific types of adaptations are more appropriate when you are interacting with each of the four types of different individuals.

These four basic development action strategies for increasing flexibility and versatility are a good starting point for increasing your own effectiveness. But based on the natural human condition, they tend to be ongoing challenges. Therefore, a second approach which complements this lifelong *road map* focuses on one of the many adaptability strengths noted above.

To see how this might work, picture some well-known characters who are generally agreed to be lower in either flexibility or versatility. The classic TV character Archie Bunker is a great example of low flexibility. As we review the prior list of higher flexibility strengths, notice how Archie could improve his relationships and his management of situations if he chose to work at developing four of the five strengths mentioned: tolerance, respect for others, empathy, and being more positive.

Action Plan . . .

Steady Relaters

Cultivate a casual, easy going, personable, one-on-one relationship. Treat them with warmth, feeling, and sensitivity.

Cautious Thinkers

Use an orderly, logical, accurate approach which zeroes in on the process and procedures. Give them well thought-out, accurate documentation.

Dominant Directors

Get right to the point quickly and decisively without getting bogged down in minute details. Operate with conviction, know what you're doing, and don't try to bluff.

Interacting Socializers

Show your energy and liveliness while focusing on the give-and-take interaction. Make your encounter fun, upbeat and enjoyable!

Another vintage TV character who is quite flexible—at times, too much so—but quite low in his versatility is Gilligan, the feature character of GILLIGAN'S ISLAND. He could be a more successful person if he develops the following key strengths of a versatile person: vision (the foresight to think ahead before letting himself get drawn into unfavorable situations); attentiveness (tuning in to what is going on around him); being realistic (about the motives and methods of other people); and competence (being both more self-initiating/evaluating and using a problem-solving approach). The benefit to Gilligan of his increased versatility would be reduced dependence on others to define both the problems he must deal with and the solutions he must put into action—without his consideration of whether their ideas will be in his best interests.

Creating Personal Power Through Increased Adaptability

A wise person once commented, "A little knowledge can be a dangerous thing." In the field of formal education, this quote is sometimes called the sophomoric syndrome. That is, as people begin to learn about a new topic, they tend to jump to oversimplified and incomplete conclusions. When that happens, they are often less successful than is possible. But with continuing effort, thought, and increased study, they eventually graduate to a higher level of excellence. In terms of adaptability, this means it is essential for us to understand the following principles:

1. Adaptability is not a goal in and of itself, but a means to the end of increased personal effectiveness and success.

2. A key to effectiveness is to realize what level and type of adaptability component(s) are the critical factors in achieving a targeted goal.

   Examples:
   "The key to getting this sale is to be a lot more flexible than I am naturally with this type of strong-willed person."

"If I don't lower my already high tendency to be overly flexible and accommodating, I'm likely to continue giving away the store. Conditions have changed and I can't afford to do that any longer because it conflicts with the results I'm looking for."

3. Being adaptable also means assessing the other available resources which can allow you to get your desired outcomes by acting smarter.

Example:
While you have developed the competencies required to successfully complete a known task, you work with three other people who also possess these same talents. But they don't have the same pressing, competing priorities facing them as you. So in this case, adaptability also includes having the vision and self-corrective aptitudes to seek one or more available resources to help you appropriately manage your adaptabilities. Isn't that better than trying to be superhuman and doing it all yourself?

Adaptability, then, is important because it directly relates to your degree of achieved success in a wide variety of life's opportunities. These range from relationships with other people, to coping with changing conditions around you, to managing different types of situations.

Extreme behavior can raise others' tensions

At times people may perceive extreme adaptability as acting wishy-washy, sashaying back and forth across the fence line, or acting two-faced. Former California Governor Jerry Brown had that problem when he ran for President. His flexibility disintegrated into vacillation on the issues to the degree that some reporters dubbed him the human windshield wiper.

Additionally, a person who maintains high adaptability in all situations may not be able to avoid personal stress and ultimate inefficiency. This was suggested previously by the superperson myth of doing it all yourself. There is also the danger of developing tension from the stress of behaving in a *foreign* manner with others. This is usually temporary and may in fact be worth it if you gain rapport with the other person.

The other extreme of the continuum is no behavioral adaptability. This causes people to view someone as rigid and uncompromising. He insists on behaving at his own pace and priority. An example is Stephanie Vander Kellan, the fish-out-of-water maid on THE BOB NEWHART SHOW.

Adaptability is important to successful relationships of all kinds. People often adopt at least a partially different role in their professional lives than they do in their social and personal lives. This is to successfully manage the professional requirements of their jobs. Interestingly, many people tend to be more adaptable at work with people they know less and less adaptable at home with people they know better. Why? People generally want to create a good impression at work, but at home may *relax and act themselves* to the point of unintentionally stepping on other family members' toes. Not an attractive family portrait, but often an accurate one.

We can gain a better understanding of how adaptability impacts the effective management of situations by looking at its application to a variety of professions and their related role or job requirements. This process is essentially the same one which is used by major selection, recruiting, and career development consulting firms around the world. To better acquaint you with this process, we'll examine a public service profession familiar to you—the Presidency of the United States. What does that job require from the perspective of the general voting public who have the power to select and replace this job holder?

To better understand this concept, compare the competing choices or finalists for this job in two of the elections. Incidentally, both elections included candidates with distinctly different types of behavioral styles. Picture Ronald Reagan (a Dominant Director with strong Interacting Socializer tendencies) versus Jimmy Carter (a Steady Relater); and George Bush (a Steady Relater) versus Michael Dukakis (a Cautious Thinker).

Ronald Reagan was a classic case of high flexibility who, as an actor in the White House, dazzled people with his different moves, about-faces, and social adeptness. Most critics, however, gave him low marks for his performance abilities or versatility: increased budget deficits, mass dismissal of staff for improper public performance, and lack of knowledge of specifics related to various critical tasks.

In contrast, Jimmy Carter was viewed as a highly qualified individual in terms of versatility, but he projected only a moderate level of flexibility regarding his willingness to play ball with other officials. Similarly, Michael Dukakis was perceived as having moderate-to-high versatility (the well-informed man who brought Massachusetts back from its legislature's well-documented mismanagement through its political *football games*), but he became known as "poker-faced Mike" in the Presidential campaign. In other words, he was seen as a highly inflexible individual who was not open to others' points or concerns.

Compare him with George Bush, a moderately flexible man. To capsulize the observations of many commentators, "There's not much choice between the two as the public views it—it seems to be which is the least undesirable of the two candidates." Whether or not these perceptions are true is questionable, but they reflect the reality of the desired characteristics of a Presidential jobholder requiring higher flexibility and a moderate to higher level of versatility.

You can profile any role or job in the same way. That's not to say a person's behavioral style isn't also important. After all, there have been more people who exhibit aspects of Dominant Director and Interacting Socializer types who have been elected to that highest public office than individuals with the other two styles (more about mixed styles in Chapter 11). However, once in office, their levels of flexibility and versatility distinguish the higher performers from the lower performers. Again, with the sophomoric syndrome in mind, let's take a deeper look at this concept as it relates to some other types of position requirements. A sales job which involves a single, simple product line is most likely to require high flexibility, but may not require much versatility. Another sales job involving multiple products that are complex and changing usually requires both high flexibility and high versatility.

Contrast this with the position of nuclear researcher which requires very high versatility, but much lower flexibility. This lower flexibility actually protects this person and others from being open to trying possibilities that may literally blow up in their faces. Finally, picture the job requirements of a single working parent of two teenagers. Here again, versatility is the key ingredient in managing the myriad of competing expectations and demands. Of course, a moderate level of flexibility allows the lid to stay on so peace and order prevail and the children don't end up parenting the adult!

Adaptability works

Effectively adaptable people meet the key expectations of others in specific situations—whether it's in personal or business relationships. Through attention and practice, you can achieve a balance of strategically managing your adaptability by recognizing when a modest compromise is appropriate. You'll also understand when it's necessary to adapt to the other person's behavioral style.

Practice managing relationships in a way that allows everyone to win. Be tactful, reasonable, understanding, non-judgmental, and comfortable to talk to. This results in a moderate position between the two extremes. You're able to better meet the needs of the other person as well as your own. Adapt your pace and priority. Work at relationships so everybody wins at work, with friends, on dates, and with family.

So self-knowledge of how Direct/Indirect and Supporting/ Controlling you are provides help in better dealing with yourself and others. Just as you discovered your own unique behavioral type and the characteristics that go along with it, you'll learn to identify others' key strengths and weaknesses. Recognizing *sterling traits* and potential pitfalls of diverse people means you can better understand their behaviors and relate more effectively with them.

When you try to accommodate the other person's expectations and tendencies, you automatically decrease tension and increase trust. Adaptability enables you to interact more productively with difficult people, helps you in strained situations, and assists you in establishing rapport and credibility. It can make the difference between a productive or an ineffective interpersonal relationship. And your adaptability level also influences how others judge their relationships with you. Raise your adaptability level—trust and credibility soar; lower your adaptability level—trust and credibility plummet.

Another way of looking at this whole matter is from the perspective of maturity. Mature persons know who they are. They understand their basic behavioral type and freely express their core patterns. However, when problems or opportunities arise, they readily and deliberately make whatever adjustments are necessary in their core patterns to meet the need. Immature persons, on the other hand, lose effectiveness in dealing with the real world when they lock into their own style. By disregarding the needs of others, they end up causing conflict and tension which lead to less satisfaction and fulfillment in their life environments.

There are four key payoffs which make our efforts at becoming more mature and adaptable worth the effort. These benefits define the characteristics of people who are the higher performers in life. By reading, reflecting, and then taking the guided actions suggested in this book, you too can achieve this same level of excellence in your own life. The only questions are whether you wish to become more:

- successful
- effective
- satisfied
- fulfilled

If so, then today is your first opportunity to get started based on what you've already learned in these first four chapters. Now you can read the remaining chapters for even more powerful insights about how you can become all that you can truly be.

Part Two

Workplace Applications

**People Smart Principle #5—The Principle of Comple-
mentarity: "People have the potential to complement
other types of individuals at work tasks."**

Chapter 5
On the Job

Problem solving in the workplace

As you read this chapter, think of specific individuals you
know at work who represent each of the four behavioral
styles—Dominant Director, Interacting Socializer, Steady
Relater, and Cautious Thinker. How can you apply what you
learn about them to improve your working relationships with
each one? What are some characteristics that work to the
advantage of these people in their job performance? Which
characteristics work against them?

It can be most helpful for your increased understanding of
the connection between your behavioral type and your daily
work performance to realize these four tendencies define the
way you go about your work. In other words, they describe
your *work style* or *how you actually perform your work duties.*

All jobs essentially involve different types of problem-
solving tasks which have to be achieved to ensure satisfactory
job performance. And, since such job requirements differ, so
too does the degree of natural match or fit with your own
preferred behavior pattern. As jobs become more complex, they
call for increased adaptability to fulfill these job expectations
which may be quite different from your own sources of natural
inner motivation. Let's look further at how adaptability is
critical in influencing these four behavior patterns. The graphic
entitled "Our Problem-Solving Work Styles" provides you with

a summary illustration of the four distinctly different types of problem-solving approaches to your daily work efforts.

Dominant Director Behavior in a Work Setting

Preferred jobs

Higher power positions and career areas where they can take charge
• President or CEO; i.e., the formally recognized leader
• Politician
• Policeman/woman
• Military officer
• Executive or manager
• Entrepreneur
• Owner of his or her own company
• General contractor

"I'll solve that problem"

A typical Dominant Director point of view consists of seeing himself as a problem-oriented manager who enjoys a challenge just because it's there. He likes the opportunity to complete tasks in a creative manner—which aligns with his way, of course! He's independent, strong-willed, restless, and goal-oriented. Other people tend to view him as having a high level of confidence, although this may not be the case. However, when he reads something he doesn't understand, he may instinctively react as if it must be a misprint. His self-image is high, and so is his output.

Because of their drive for specific and concrete results, Dominant Directors often put in extra hours at the office. At the extreme, their high results orientation can manifest in an overextended work pattern. When this happens, they pay a high price for their success—their personal and social lives may fall apart from neglect while their work-related attainments accumulate.

PROBLEM-SOLVING WORK STYLES

The Dominant Director (D) Style	The Interacting Socializer (I) Style
– Pragmatic – Reactive – Decisive – Competitive – Harsh	– Supporting – Trusting – Instinctive – Exploring – Appeasing
The Cautious Thinker (C) Style	**The Steady Relater (S) Style**
– Analyzing – Evaluating – Planning – Investigating – Critical	– Observing – Reflecting – Implementing – Applying – Avoiding

D's can juggle faster than the eye can see

When the Dominant Director perceives others' output as less than exemplary, he may react with a message to stimulate others to action: "Don't just stand there. Do something!" Dominant Directors typically show administrative and leadership qualities that reflect their ability to initiate and accomplish tasks, then juggle them.

They have the ability to pick up three balls (tasks) and keep them all in the air at the same time. They're multi-phasic behavior specialists—able to simultaneously do many things well. After adapting to juggling three balls, they pick up another and another. They end up juggling all of them faster than the eye can see where one begins and the other ends. However, the pressure mounts as they try to maximize the quantity of tasks or the quality of results.

Logically, it makes sense to drop one ball to relieve some of the pressure. Not so with the Dominant Director. Admission that they can't do it all tarnishes their macho image. They like impressing other styles with their workloads until they get bored or tired of not-enough-hours-in-the-day balancing acts. Then they drop everything to take up a new direction or focus for their activities until they tire of the same pattern again. Dominant Directors typically refer to this as *reordering priorities*.

Efficiency is the name of the game

Adult Dominant Directors often like to accumulate items—especially ones they think will save time or money. Efficiency is the name of the game. One Dominant Director told us he's so impatient that he never buys green tomatoes. Another one is exhilarated by the fast-forward feature which lets her eliminate the time taken up by TV commercials as she plays her VCR. A third enjoys using her car phone so she doesn't have to waste time while driving, let alone stopping for pay phones; she can't wait to get others to implement her ideas. Yet another tells his secretary to *fax* his mail to him when he's away from the office.

Despite their *strongman* images, D's, too, have their own unique limitations. They're selective listeners who tend to tune out small talk. To increase their adaptability, their listening skills and awareness of others' needs require improvement. Instead of telling others what to do, hearing their thoughts and opinions can help them get things done more smoothly—for the good of everyone involved. Otherwise, people may interpret the Dominant Director's behavior as, "When I want your opinion, I'll give it to you."

Consequently, Dominant Directors tend to work more favorably with complementary types who contribute stability, predictability, and support towards their common objectives. Each of these other types can help the Dominant Director put tasks into perspective, recharge his or her batteries, or bolster a temporarily bruised ego. Other people's feedback can also help D's stay on track in terms of objectivity, accuracy, and responsiveness to others' needs.

D leaders

The Dominant Director is an outspoken, no-nonsense, take-control type of individual. *Give 'Em Hell* Harry Truman summed up the Director's work-style attitude with his now famous statement: "If you can't stand the heat, get out of the kitchen." In fact, many Presidents of the United States have shared this same Dominant behavioral tendency with Harry. They include John F. Kennedy, Franklin D. Roosevelt, and Ronald Reagan. Each of them exhibited a personal need to decisively lead—including their willingness to use force to do it, if required. And each of them preferred the roads to the most direct action for fast results. When under stress, they lashed out and forcefully took charge in differing ways. All can be described as either strong, hard to budge, or both.

Generals George Patton and Napoleon Bonaparte, two Dominant Director military leaders, depict this "Go for the gusto!" "No guts, no glory!" perspective of their type. In battle, Dominant Director mottos translate to *Charge!* or *Follow me!* but not necessarily in that order. When taken to the extreme, Dominant Directors may, at times, seem to live by the watchwords, "Ready! Fire! Aim!" because they tend to naturally plunge in without a lot of risk-assessing forethought.

They may not be too busy for that, after all

Sometimes others may interpret the Dominant Director's hustle and impatience as, "Don't interrupt me. I'm busy." Ironically, when this happens, the Dominant Director may sabotage the very control which he desires. If co-workers and employees perceive him as swamped with too much work, they may hesitate to disturb or delay him. So the Dominant Director may know less about what's happening than he would if he had made himself more accessible.

Risk-taking excites D's.

Consider car manufacturer John DeLorean—a maverick who broke some written and unwritten rules in pursuit of his goals. Dominant Directors don't feel as bound by conventional practices as the other types. "That's for other people, not me." The higher authority they prefer to answer to is themselves; they sense a need to be their own boss so they can have control over the results they want. Opportunities for change are sought or created just to satisfy their need for results. They gravitate toward high-risk situations because the excitement of challenges fuels their actions.

They may combine pleasure with business

Dominant Director Dan decided to give his employees a special surprise for Christmas—a combined business/pleasure trip to Honolulu. From bus excursions to daily seminars and discussion groups, Dan arranged everyone's itinerary. He thought his staff would eagerly embrace his plans, but was extremely disappointed to overhear a few of them complaining about his fixed agenda:

"Who does he think he is? Giving us a supposed vacation and bouncing us around in workshops and seminars, not to mention spending every breathing minute with him!"

"Yes, I know what you mean. Just once, I wish he'd ask us what we want instead of doing what he wants."

"Here, here!"

Dan's first impulse was to rush in and tell those ingrates a thing or three, but he held himself back and decided to call his wife Jean to tell her what happened:

"I can understand their point, Dan. It sounds as though they just want to be part of the decision-making process instead of your telling them what to do," Jean observed.

"Hmmm. I guess the way I did it could seem a bit autocratic."

"I'm glad you see it that way, Dan," said Jean.

"Maybe I'll call an informal meeting so they can let me know just what they want," Dan decided.

So he did. The employees thanked him, but also told him they'd like a few days just to be with their families without having to check in with anyone but themselves.

"Is that all?" Dan asked. The group agreed. "This was a lot easier than I thought it would be," Dan observed.

Fortunately, Dan put himself in his employees' shoes and became willing to see their point of view—they wanted to help decide. For Dan, it seemed much easier to make the decisions and then tell everybody else to follow through. But what he wanted and what they wanted didn't necessarily match.

We know an elementary school principal who chose to manage her school in typical Dominant Director fashion—her way. She decided to arbitrarily rescind the privilege for parents to request teachers for their children because reading all those forms *wasted her secretary's time.* The parents had different ideas and became angry they hadn't been consulted. The resulting furor could have been prevented if she had only stopped to ask, "What do you think?" Actually, she didn't even have to do what the parents wanted, so long as she got their input. They resented her *dictatorial approach.*

The principal, following her Dominant Director instincts, focused on the result, not the steps leading to it. To accomplish that end, she tried to shape the environment by overcoming the opposition. Unfortunately for her, she discovered the parents didn't necessarily want their environment shaped, especially without their feedback. Even benevolent dictators collide with their subjects when they try to rule by themselves.

People, products, and profits

Lee Iacocca, another person with a Director work style, talks about how he learned to merge his temperament with other styles as he finally arrived at the following management philosophy, as described in his biography, *Iacocca*: "In the end, all business operations can be reduced to three words: people, products, profits. People come first. Unless you have a good team, you can't do much with the other two." Iacocca, a living Dominant Director legend, illustrates the fact that collaborative team playing pays off for Dominant people and others!

Hail to the chief!

Since he views himself as a chief, not just one of the tribe, the Dominant Director may resist deeper involvement in work teams. Stress, especially, brings out his natural apprehensiveness about people. When under duress, he may even seize control and make himself the leader—his natural *me first* tendency. Do you remember this happening when former General Alexander Haig tried to take charge when President Reagan was shot? Additional well-known Dominant Directors include ALL IN THE FAMILY's Archie Bunker, Margaret Thatcher, Dan Rather, FAMILY TIES' Alex P. Keaton, and Barbara Walters.

Consequently, the Dominant Director needs a co-worker who draws him into the group. Dominant Directors often take themselves too seriously and can benefit from gentle reminders to take life less seriously and laugh at themselves.

Competition motivates D's

Because he's so competitive, he may view himself as participating in perpetual contests with others. Other styles may see themselves as merely giving reports—period. Not so for the Dominant Director. His report jockeys for position against yours. He needs to have control, so one-upmanship can become one of his favorite games. In this extreme Dominant Director game, he fills the role of the all-seeing, all-knowing expert. Everyone else, by contrast, becomes a babbling idiot. Not a particularly appetizing thought for the rest of us.

D's can learn how to occasionally walk away

He can also help himself by learning when to walk away from a project and let others assume control. Otherwise, his tendency to hold on can frustrate the other types. People also tend to respond more favorably to the Dominant Director when he verbalizes the reasons for his conclusions and paces himself to project a more relaxed state. He can also soften his propensity for reprimanding others by tempering criticism with healthy doses of genuinely appreciative praise. Otherwise, about the only time you'll hear a Dominant Director say, "Well done!" is when he orders a steak.

Remember, people have feelings

As natural doers, they may need some help channeling their energies. Why? Because they may have trouble distinguishing the realistic from the awe-inspiring. Of all the types, this one is the most likely to try even harder if told, "That's impossible."

When Dominant Directors learn to become aware of other people's feelings, they become more successful in developing satisfying relationships with them. Since this type has a natural inclination toward authoritarianism, he can work on recognizing when it's appropriate to consciously back off, slow down his fast pace, and listen more to other people's opinions, ideas, and concerns. Besides bolstering his people skills, he can also attend to analyzing tasks more thoroughly. He instinctively wants to hurry on to the next challenge, but he can ward off many problems that result from his typical hastiness by learning more details about projects than he would otherwise seek out.

Other behavioral types may not share the Dominant Director's preferences for quick results and blunt straightforwardness. By becoming less rigid in his direct approach with others, he can better learn to manage the differences between people and modify his own.

Remember . . .

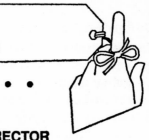

DOMINANT DIRECTOR
BUSINESS CHARACTERISTICS

- Prefer time frames
- Seek personal control
- Get to the point
- Strive to feel important and be noteworthy in their jobs
- Demonstrate persistence and single-mindedness to reach a goal
- Express high ego strength
- Prefer to downplay feelings and relationships
- Focus on task actions that lead to achieving tangible outcomes
- Implement changes in the workplace
- Tend to freely delegate duties, enabling them to take on more projects

DOMINANT DIRECTOR:
PREFERRED BUSINESS SITUATIONS

- Like to call the shots and tell others what to do
- Like challenging workloads which fuel their energy levels
- Tend to personally oversee, or at least know about, their employees' or co-workers' business activities
- Like to say what's on their minds without being concerned about hurting anybody's feelings
- Enjoy taking risks and being involved in changes
- Prefer to interpret the *rules* and answer to themselves alone
- Interested in the answers to *what* questions, not *how* ones
- Like to see a logical road toward increasing and on-going advancement, since *bigger is better* to them

At Work with the Interacting Socializer

Preferred job positions

Careers that maximize influence with people where they can socialize, mingle, and gain positive feedback
- Public relations
- Entertainment—acting, singing, reporting, public speaking —being on stage or in the public eye
- Professional host or hostess (talk show, party, restaurant, airline, etc.)
- Recreation director
- Politician
- Personnel interviewer
- Salesperson

People are their business

The Interacting Socializer likes to be treated with warmth, friendliness, and approval. Because he favors interacting with people on more than just a business level, he wants to be your friend before he does business with you. If a client suggests meeting for lunch, a social drink, or dinner and asks things like, "What exciting things are happening with you?" you're probably dealing with an Interacting Socializer.

Like the Dominant Director, the Interacting Socializer shares a quick pace. While the Dominant Director busies himself with tasks, the Interacting Socializer tends to move about the office in a flurry of activity. He even walks in a way that reflects his optimism and quick pace . . . lively and energetically. He observes and "sight-sees" as he goes, avoiding obstacles and potential problems.

I's like to bounce ideas off others

Interacting Socializers think out loud. Desks confine them, so they typically stroll around the office talking to nearly everyone, from the custodian to the boss along the way, calling them by their first names. All the while they seek others' reactions to almost anything and everything, but they visibly warm up to comments about themselves.

Non-Interacting styles may view Interacting Irv's behavior as goofing off. "That Irv spends more time gabbing at the soda machine than he does working. What does he get paid for, anyway?" But appearances may fool us. While Irv weaves his way toward a drink, he bounces ideas off the people along the way. "John, if you got a coupon in the mail for free dessert at Cafe Eduardo's with any dinner for two, would you go? I'm working on new advertising possibilities for them. What would motivate you to try a new restaurant?"

Irv often doesn't merely talk—he actually brainstorms out loud with virtually anyone he encounters. It's important for him to find out how other people feel about his ideas. He likes the feedback and the occasional pats on the back which his conversations provide. He enjoys a casual, relaxed environment where he can allow his impulses free rein. Desk-hopping also satisfies his need for companionship. Like other Interacting Socializers, he seeks out people to first share the present, with one eye on future additional experiences with them. Talking with co-workers happily mixes business with pleasure for this type. They like to play and mingle as they learn, earn, and do practically everything else.

I's seek "people power" positions

Since the Interacting Socializer is naturally talkative and people-oriented, these positions of people power meet his needs for inclusion by others, popularity, social recognition, and (probably) freedom from a lot of detail. They utilize his natural strengths. As with the other types, jobs do not equal behavioral type; but many Interacting Socializers tend to gravitate toward people-oriented, high visibility professions to fill their innate needs.

Take Disneyland employees, for example. Disneyland seems to hire vast numbers of Interacting Socializers who act as peppy and people-oriented at 10 p.m. as they did at 10 a.m. Tour guides usually still smile and carry on verbal repartees with guests at the end of their shifts. This characteristic cannot be taught; employees either become energized by mingling with people, or they don't. Interacting Socializers do. Disneyland even provides people-free *decompression* areas for their employees during breaks so they can maintain their positive energy levels with guests.

They're smooth-talking dreamers

At heart, the Interacting Socializer is a dreamer who is good at getting others caught up in his ideas. His persuasive powers may simultaneously amaze his admirers and frustrate his detractors. The Interacting Socializer shows smooth-talking tendencies which, at the extreme, can be interpreted as either silver-tongued oration or evasive double-talk. He can appear to be a verbal Pied Piper with a seemingly unending gift of gab or a wheeling and dealing chatterbox.

Chin up!

As a leader, the Interacting Socializer likes spontaneous, expressive actions for noticeable results. "Chin up! Think positively," he may say, to encourage his employees, peers, or superiors to function smoothly. Statements like "Follow that dream," and "Climb every mountain," sum up Interacting Socializer feelings. Though typically somewhat less motivated by change than Dominant Directors, Interacting Socializers become more susceptible to risk-taking when pressured by others to take the chance. If they haven't fully considered the ramifications, they may regret their impulsiveness after it's too late.

A classic Interacting Socializer who sought the U.S. Presidency was Hubert Horatio Humphrey, the charismatic Minnesota Senator. When he died, he received a stately funeral with more attention and sympathy than many who had won the Presidency. Without such triumph, he moved the hearts of the entire nation.

What do I's want at work?

Interacting Socializers want companionship and social recognition, so their contributions to group morale often satisfy these needs. At work, they like to know everybody's first name and something about everyone. They can benefit from feedback from their co-workers, especially those who represent other behavioral types. Just as Steady Relaters contribute stability,

Cautious Thinkers seek accuracy, and Dominant Directors add decisiveness, Interacting Socializers give their enthusiasm and energy. Tactfully reminding and assisting them so they will prioritize and organize can help the entire office function more smoothly. Since Interacting Socializers tend to be *open books,* the other types can detect when they are having an off day and give them a boost with a compliment or two.

As true extroverts, Interacting Socializers typically look outside themselves to renew their energies. They enjoy motivating books, tapes, and speeches—pick-me-ups that recharge their batteries to help them overcome obstacles. These are viewed as practical growth opportunities. They even prefer the terms *opportunity* or *challenge* instead of *problem.* A problem is too mired in negativism to comfortably fit with an Interacting Socializer's optimistic nature.

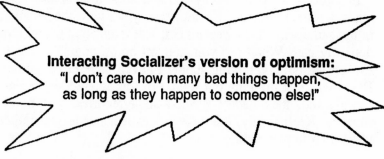

Interacting Socializer's version of optimism:
"I don't care how many bad things happen, as long as they happen to someone else!"

They prefer the "big picture"

As inductive thinkers, Interacting Socializers naturally think first about the big picture, then of supporting details. After seeing the broad overview, they prefer not to personally dwell on specifics. "Collins can work out the details." Interacting Socializers are intuitive and may naturally come up with assorted ideas—some practical, some not—but if they *feel right* to them, they *talk up* those ideas to others to elicit their feedback and enthusiasm. This can also serve the purpose of pulling Interacting Socializers back to reality if they venture too far out into *La-La Land* (one Dominant Director's description of this behavior at its most extreme). "Earth to Fred, earth to Fred!" may get an Interacting Socializer who's become too carried away back on course by using one of his own techniques—humor.

I's think out loud

Since Interacting Socializers like to talk more than average —to others and to themselves—they're likely to say inappropriate things more often than most of the other types. When talkativeness and emotionality mix, then hoof-in-mouth problems may set in with this behavioral type. Learning when to stop talking and start listening can help Interacting Socializers grow. Sometimes their naturally impulsive behaviors energize us; at other times their spontaneity requires more restraint.

They're idea people who throw ideas out. "Hal, we could do this (and this, or this, etc.)." This impulsive habit can get them in trouble. Why?

Because other people may think a commitment has been made, but the Interacting Socializer may not view the situation in the same way. Two weeks later, Hal may say, "Okay, I've done my part. When can you start action on yours?" "What part are you talking about? I never agreed to anything, Hal. I was just thinking out loud." In this Interacting Socializer's mind, they hadn't formed an agreement, just brainstormed. Realistically, this type is much better at generating ideas than implementing them.

Fire! Fire! Fire!

Interacting Socializers can pump up their flexibility by better controlling their time and emotions and by developing a more objective mind set. They can benefit by spending more time checking, verifying, specifying, and organizing, or getting someone else to do it for them. Otherwise, Interacting Socializers may succumb to their excitable *Fire! Fire! Fire!* tendencies. If they concentrate on the task and take a more logical approach, then they can improve their follow-through.

For instance, Interacting Socializers may have so many things going that they may forget to finish tasks by a deadline; or they procrastinate until the last minute because of their multiple priorities. Writing things down and prioritizing can help the Interacting Socializer remember when to do what

Remember . . .

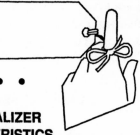

INTERACTING SOCIALIZER BUSINESS CHARACTERISTICS

- Like to brainstorm and interact with colleagues and others
- Want freedom from control, details, or complexity
- Like to have the chance to influence or motivate others
- Like the feeling of being a key part of an exciting team
- Want to be included by others in important projects, activities, or events
- Get easily bored by routine and repetition
- May trust others without reservation—take others at their word and don't check for themselves
- Typically have short attention spans, so they do well with many short breaks

INTERACTING SOCIALIZER: PREFERRED BUSINESS SITUATIONS

- Like to work participatively with others
- Need immediate feedback to get, or stay, on course
- Like to mingle with all levels of associates and call them by their first names
- Enjoy compliments about themselves and their accomplishments
- Seek stimulating environments that are friendly and favorable
- Motivated to work toward known, specific, quickly attainable incentives or external motivators (dislike pursuits which drag out over long time periods)
- Open to verbal or demonstrated guidance for transferring ideas into action
- Like to start projects and let others finish them

with whom. They can benefit from handy pocket calendars that go everywhere with them. If you fit the M.O. of this type, you can forget about using some little corner of an envelope to write on. You're probably too impatient to rifle through piles of paperwork to find it later.

Steady Relater Behavior at Work

Preferred job situations

Secure positions and careers where they can specialize in some areas and be part of a team
- Financial services
- Social worker
- Family doctor/nurse
- Residential or community services
- Teacher
- Personal assistant/secretary
- Insurance agent
- Librarian
- Customer service representative

Stability motivates them

In business and in their personal lives, Steady Relaters take one day at a time and may consciously avoid gambles and uncertainties. They tend to respect traditions and often demonstrate loyalty to everyone else while they trek along. Because stability in the workplace motivates them, Steady Relaters are apt to have the most compatible of all working relationships with each of the four types. Steady Relaters have patience, staying power, and stick-to-it-ivity, so they commit themselves to making relationships work.

They are extremely uncomfortable with conflict. In the workplace, this type may notice how others complete their tasks, but typically say nothing negative about their observations (with the possible exception of a close friend or family member). Why? They don't want to make waves and they don't want to appear to be know-it-alls. Silently, Steady Relaters may think they're shouldering the lion's share of duties, but they generally won't tell the boss or fellow employees. They'll just continue performing their own work and make the best of it.

"Be prepared"

If they need to make a presentation, Steady Relaters will probably thoroughly prepare and organize their material in advance. Since they feel comfortable with proven methods, they like to carefully acquaint themselves with each step of a procedure so they can duplicate it later. When taken to an extreme, this adherence to following instructions and maintaining the status quo can limit their actions.

Since Steady Relaters wear well and favor step-by-step procedures, they're natural choices for assisting/tutoring others, maintaining existing performance levels, and organizing systems. They often enjoy helping set up or implement guidelines that allow others to be more organized. Remember, Steady Relaters are the ones who assemble all their equipment first, set up their tools, and begin to work only when everything is in place.

For instance, when she's ready to collate, Steady Relater Paula places all the pages in descending order on a table. Next, she places *Tacky Finger* on one side of the desk, then a stapler on the other, extra staples close to that, and finally a large enough opening near page one for the completed stacks. When everything is ready, she begins to work on the completion of this task. Many a Dominant Director and Interacting Socializer who initially rolled their eyeballs at what they viewed as a laborious preparation stage have later found themselves marvelling at such assembly line efficiency. At this point, a sincere compliment on her work procedure might be both appropriate and welcome. "Paula, your collating technique is more efficient than I could have imagined, let alone be likely to do myself."

The typical Dominant Director may want to delegate and oversee such a procedure: "Paula, you can start without assembling all that paraphernalia, can't you?" But for Steady Relaters, that's not a comfortable approach because they're advocates of the *Be Prepared* and *Plan Ahead* schools of thought. An Interacting Socializer may tend to haphazardly set up such a collating area, possibly on the floor, and omit key items like extra staples or adequate copies of page 13. "Darn, I need to go to the closet again," or, "Oh, no! I'll have to run to the store for more paper." Both of these individuals can waste more time than they thought they'd save because they didn't prepare as well as the Steady Relater.

Both the personalized people factor and going along with established practices rate high with this type. So when problems bombard Steady Relaters, they try to solve them by helping or working with others, following tried and true procedures, or a combination of the two. If these tactics fail, they may quietly do nothing. Doing nothing may include higher absenteeism; when conflict and stress increase, Steady Relater tolerance may decrease.

"Are we ready yet?"

As with any trait, the Steady Relater's propensity for studying procedures and doing repetitious tasks can sometimes be taken to an extreme. For instance, the following anecdote about the Steady Relater type illustrates this point. After Michelangelo (a Cautious Thinker, our next type) completed the frescoes on the ceilings of the Sistine Chapel, the Pope asked him to draw up architectural plans for St. Peter's Cathedral. Since Michelangelo had passed his 80th birthday, he drew up the massive and complex plans in less than two years and then turned them over to his most promising apprentice—a Steady Relater. This slower moving cohort's approach to implementing these plans was to study them step by step, day after day, year after year, time and again. Finally—after 23 years—he was ready to direct his efforts to the actual building of this world famous cathedral.

Service is their business

Steady Relaters tend to gravitate toward relationships which provide them with security, stability, and large doses of routine; these positions satisfy some of their rather maternal or paternal needs. While we know that not all elementary school teachers are Steady Relaters, this personality type is inclined to pursue careers that fit their natural desire for repeated group and one-to-one people contact, preference for sameness, and the opportunity to help or support others. Personally, we've observed many Steady Relater preschool, elementary, and middle school teachers—especially among those employees reporting higher levels of job satisfaction.

Service is Tony Gwynn's business

If the job doesn't necessarily fit a Steady Relater's requirements, then, like the other styles, he too may shape it accordingly to fit with his personal performance style. For instance, even when Tony Gwynn, the three-time champion National League batter, seemingly single-handedly wins a baseball game, he has been quoted as saying things like, "I couldn't have done it without a lot of help from my teammates. Today's game was a real group effort." On the other hand, a typical Dominant Director may respond: "Well, it's because I've been practicing so hard that I had this outstanding performance that resulted in our winning today's game." He may toss in a salute to his teammates as an afterthought, but the primary focus of his remarks is clear—he did it. Similarly, an Interacting Socializer may bask in the adoration of his fans. "Moments like this make it all worthwhile." He may include his team in the spotlight, too, but not as easily, as often, or as naturally as the Steady Relater does.

In a community service role, Steady Tony Gwynn volunteered to emcee at an award ceremony for an elementary school Jog-a-thon, casually dressed in a sweat suit and an old baseball cap. Shortly after he congratulated all the runners for their hard work, he commented, "Kids, I'm so nervous standing up here in front of you that my knees are knocking together. Playing baseball is one thing, but talking to all of you is another." Although Tony Gwynn was apparently not as at home in the speaking arena, he still couldn't refuse doing a good deed by servicing the kids of his community.

Actions speak louder than words

Inherently modest and accommodating, Steady Relaters usually think their actions speak for themselves. While Dominant Directors and Interacting Socializers pat themselves on the backs, Steady Relaters tend to simply nod and listen. Inwardly, they may want to divulge a personal triumph, but they won't volunteer it. If someone asks them about it, fine. Or, better yet, an ally may pipe up about the Steady Relater's coup. Steady Relaters tend to adopt a *Me last, if there's time,* attitude. At work, this type may think he should get a promotion, but is likely to just wait for the boss to notice what a good job he's doing, rather than bring it to his supervisor's attention.

S leaders

Politically, Steady Relaters act approachable and down-to-earth. Consider President Dwight D. Eisenhower, who also served as NATO's Supreme Allied Commander during World War II. His Presidential campaign button said simply, "I like Ike!" a Relater-like understatement if there ever was one. The man was probably one of our most popular Presidents ever. Voters warmed to his down-to-earth, *Aw, shucks* mannerisms and easygoing smile. But despite their likability, Steady Relaters naturally have difficulty taking tough stands. Both President Gerald Ford and Vice President "Fritz" Mondale have shared this problem, as did U.S. Vietnam military leader General George Abrams.

Steady Relater military leaders go by the book—a manifestation of their deductive, convergent, left brain orientations. They are driven by a basic need to use predictable, steady actions to yield known, proven results. At the most extreme, their battle cry is *Ready! Ready! Ready!* In fact, they might still be getting ready when the enemy fires. Then they may react by saying to others in their group, "Hold the fort!" Or "Toe the line!" Or "What's the SOP (standard operating procedure) for us to follow in this kind of situation?"

S's want to be part of the group

Since Steady Relaters seek security and inclusion with the group, they can contribute to the workplace with their natural planning skills, consistent pace, and their desire to fit in. Like Interacting Socializers, they favor work relationships on a casual, first-name basis; but Steady Relaters generally prefer developing special, more in-depth friendships with selected co-workers than do their social butterfly, Interacting Socializer, counterparts. So while Interacting Socializers may talk to anyone who will listen, Steady Relaters prefer involvement with a closer group of confidants.

Steady Relaters also want stability, steadiness, and a calm atmosphere in the workplace. They contribute to harmony in the office, so they usually fit comfortably into the work environment, but they also often become overly dependent on using the same old methods over and over again. Sometimes these procedures include steps needed when they learned the procedure, but which can now be discarded. They may improve their work productivity by using shortcuts that eliminate extra labor. Dominant Directors and Interacting Socializers can often help them with this. And, when asked, Cautious Thinkers can generally demonstrate new ways to get things done through other processes.

Why change?

The Steady Relater is the optimistic realist among the four types. A pragmatist, he likes to do routine things with familiar people to maintain the same situation. He performs regularly and deliberately toward this end of holding onto or striving for continuity, peace, and orderliness. Changes and surprises make him uncomfortable because they alter the current formula. Instead, he prefers to refine existing practices.

"Modesty is the best policy"

Just as they may think their own job performance needs no self-promotion, they may think (not say) the same about others' work. "I wish John would stop boasting about what a wonderful job he does. He seems to spend half the day promoting himself, rather than doing the work that's already on his desk." They often figure that if the boss (or anyone else) doesn't see what's going on, they don't want to have to be the ones to confront others about this unpleasant reality.

Remember . . .

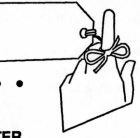

STEADY RELATER
BUSINESS CHARACTERISTICS

- Need to know the order of procedures
- Operate well as members of a work group
- Motivated by usual, known, and proven practices
- Oriented toward more concrete, repeatable actions
- Want order and ability in the workplace
- Focus on how and when to do things
- Work in a steady and predictable manner
- Like a long-term relationship with their business place and their fellow employees

STEADY RELATER:
PREFERRED BUSINESS SITUATIONS

- Like to perform the same kinds of duties day after day (no matter what the importance of the type of work involved)
- Prefer to work cooperatively with others to achieve common results
- Dislike taking risks
- Enjoy working in a stable, steady, low-key environment which has a minimum of changes
- Like to know each step toward completing their duties
- Prefer to make decisions by group consensus or other accepted practices rather than by themselves
- Enjoy feeling like valued members of the work group

How do they know, unless they see it themselves?

Steady Relaters operate predominantly from a deductive perspective. Instead of naturally sensing (Dominant Director), or feeling (Interacting Socializer), Steady Relaters think about things: "I think that something is really troubling John. His eyes are bloodshot, he's short-tempered and edgy, and he's been getting to work about an hour late for two days in a row." Even their feelings about others seem to be based on their thoughts about them. This ties in with the Steady Relater's more concrete or literal orientation. He often needs to see something with his own eyes before he's sure about it.

S's take the indirect route

As naturally interested listeners, Steady Relaters appreciate this same behavior from others. They like others who genuinely share a common interest in exchanging thoughts, feelings, and experiences. This sometimes takes some extra effort, however, because Steady Relaters tend to speak indirectly. They seldom come right out and say what's on their minds, especially if they think something may be amiss. For example, a Steady Relater may know that everyone thinks a certain employee isn't pulling his own weight or has brown-nosed his way to the executive suite. Yet when pressed on this situation, he's likely to respond, "I don't want to say anything. I'd rather you observe things for awhile and come to your own conclusions."

At Work with the Cautious Thinker

Preferred jobs

Careers in which they can strive for perfection, creativity, and completeness
- Forecasters (political, weather, etc.)
- Critics (film, history, literary, etc.)
- Engineers
- Research scientists
- Data analysts
- Accountants/auditors

- Artists/sculptors/architects
- Inventors

Process and perfection

They see themselves as problem solvers who like structure, concentrate on key details, and ask specific questions about identified factors. They're masters at following important, established directions and standards, while still meeting the need to control the process by their own actions. Process-oriented, Cautious Thinkers want to know why something works, since such insight allows them to determine for themselves the most logical way to achieve the expected results—from themselves and others.

In business, Cautious Thinkers are practical and realistic. They seek neither utopias nor quick fixes. Because of their low risk-taking tendencies, they may overplan when change becomes inevitable. They like working in those existing circumstances which promote quality in products or services. When possible, they prepare ahead of time for their projects and then work diligently to perfect them to the nth degree. Their thorough preparation is designed to minimize the probability of errors. They prefer finishing tasks before or on schedule without mistakes caused by last minute rushing and inadequate checking or review.

Cautious Thinkers rank second only to Steady Relaters in their pursuit of logic. They rely on reasoning to avoid mistakes, so they tend to check, recheck, and check again. But they may become mired down with data collection. Amassing facts and specifics, they are uncomfortable with giving opinions or partial information until they've exhausted all their resources. This can frustrate people who want to know what's going on now, the types with faster paces. Additionally, all that checking can result in a disruption of the work flow.

They can benefit from checking only the critical things rather than everything. This procedure allows them to sort out and control the important details, and still get things done well. They can hold onto their high standards without becoming bogged down in relatively trivial business details. Cautious

Thinkers need to learn to accept that perfection is an impossible quest, worth the effort in some instances, but not in others.

C's prefer the "right" way

When airline pilots prepare to fly a commercial plane, they have a checklist of safety points before take-off. Cautious Thinker pilots have been found to focus far more on the most critical factors, using the remaining time to review the less crucial ones. In their typical Cautious Thinker style, they complete the checklist the *right* way, by checking known factors against unknown variables. By contrast, Dominant Director pilots have been known to delegate this duty to someone else. With this, they then see to it that the task gets done their way. Interacting Socializer pilots have been observed getting *off task* by talking to co-workers they see during this process. Then they may wait till the last minute, due to their difficulty in assessing the amount of time needed to complete such detailed tasks. Steady Relaters go through each point, in the listed order, completing it in a step-by-step way, but without the same rigorous attention paid to those most critical items that the Cautious Thinker pilot scrutinizes. Although all four types finish the checklist, they have completed this task quite differently—according to their different work styles—and with the possibility of different outcomes as a result of their different approaches to the same task.

Old questions, new answers

Whether or not this type opts for a scientific or artistic career, they often follow a scientific method or intuitive, logical progression to achieve their objectives. Because of their natural inclination to validate and improve upon accepted processes, Cautious Thinkers tend to generate the most native creativity of the four types. Consequently, they often find new ways of viewing old questions, concerns, and opportunities.

Many artists and inventors fall into the Cautious Thinker category, many leaning toward experimentation and the possibility of coming up with new answers. Just as Michelangelo's creative mind envisioned completed sculptures entrapped in a solid piece of marble, Leonardo da Vinci perfected the

Mona Lisa's expression in such a manner that its meaning still evades contemporary experts. Similarly, Galileo's creativity formulated precisely detailed plans of "impossible" futuristic inventions. These three Renaissance men left lasting memorials as evidence of the quality-consciousness often associated with Cautious Thinker tendencies.

C leaders

Political Thinkers range from Thomas Jefferson to Henry Cabot Lodge and Adlai Stevenson. Each was a private person who exhibited calm, cool, objective behaviors which detractors at times viewed as aloofness and insensitivity. President Woodrow Wilson, often dubbed by scholars as the most intellectual 20th century president, also predictably fits this Cautious temperament. A former university professor, Wilson established far-reaching policies and practices, some of which still exist today. An intense, though private and contemplative individual, he was known as a man who was far ahead of his time in his Think(er)ing. The press had a heyday with *Silent Cal*(vin) Coolidge and his typical one or two word comments which often amounted to a clipped yes or no.

Cautious Thinker military leaders may use planned, careful actions to achieve their desired results. They may instruct their troops, "Don't ever let your guard down," or, "CYA (Cover your anatomy)!" If under extreme pressure, Cautious Thinker leaders may tend toward the *Aim! Aim! Aim!* mind set. They just keep aiming until they think they'll make a perfect shot.

People may complicate things

Like Steady Relaters, Cautious Thinkers are basically more introverted individuals who seek solace and answers by turning inward. Cautious Thinkers' natural orientation is toward objects and away from people. From their perspective, people are unpredictable and complicate things. The more people added to the formula, the more chance of getting unpredictable results.

Cautious Thinkers often choose to work with colleagues who promote calmness and thoroughness in the office—often either other Cautious Thinkers or Steady Relaters. Since Cautious

Thinkers seek perfection, the other two types may help them modify that quest into a more time-efficient procedure. Dominant Directors can contribute by helping to explain realistic deadlines and parameters, so Cautious Thinkers can build those time frames into his procedures. Interacting Socializers, too, can help them *lighten up* more at work and teach them that there is more to the workplace than working alone eight hours a day.

When encouraged to do so, Cautious Thinkers can share their rich supplies of information with small groups of co-workers who can benefit from their wealth of experience and knowledge. This can enhance the Cautious Thinker's status with colleagues and become a bridge toward building teamwork and mutual understanding. Sharing with others can also serve to lessen Cautious Thinkers' reservations and suspicions about associates or even encourage C's to stand up for themselves against those very people they may prefer to avoid.

They can also participate in more coffee machine conversation that may just give them a better understanding of co-workers, and possibly, some work problems. Carrying on a dialogue with associates may even provide them with insights into themselves. For instance, someone may observe, "Harold, you're furrowing your brow again."

Cautious Thinker Harold replies, "I am? I wasn't aware that I was."

"Yes, you do that a lot. That's why I've never said more than 'hello' to you. I thought you were either deep in thought or worried about something."

"Thank you for bringing that to my attention," Harold says. "I'll monitor that from now on."

Since Cautious Thinkers want clarity and order, they can contribute a natural sense of thoroughness to their company. They usually don't care about knowing everyone's name in their department, but they may make it a point to find out who they think exhibits the same thoroughness and precision they themselves have: "What's the name of the artist who drew up the graphics for the Robinson account?"

When the going gets loud

Cautious Thinkers (prefer to) get going. When discussions and tempers become hot and heavy, "I want to get out of this place," may represent the Cautious Thinker viewpoint. Because they want peace and tranquillity, they avoid and reject hostility and outward expressions of aggression. At the extreme, they can numb themselves to conflict to such an extent that they may have difficulty tapping into their feelings . . . not only anger and hatred, but caring and love.

By learning to accept others' expressions of emotions, Cautious Thinkers can also learn to accept their own feelings. Ideally, if the Cautious Thinker can consciously raise his tolerance for aggression, he can then begin to increase his ability to successfully deal with it in a more open manner through mutual exchanges.

C's take themselves seriously

Since Cautious Thinkers often detect many of life's complexities which escape the other types, they can become perfectionistic and worrisome, with both themselves and others. While this quality control aspect can be very positive, when taken to an extreme, associates may dismiss the Cautious Thinker's caution as *crying wolf*. When C's are willing to bend their standards on small matters, co-workers are more likely to listen to them for the bigger issues.

In the NASA space shuttle disaster, for instance, engineers repeatedly emphasized the need for more research. But after a few delays, the public pressure became so great that the Challenger was launched prematurely. That time, pushing the researchers harder and faster resulted in tragedy. The message: Listen to Cautious Thinkers about the big things. At the least, both positive and negative sides will come to light; at the extreme, the bleakest results will be projected. In either case, unknown factors become more clearly defined. At the same time, the obstacles and resources required for success are identified. The C's exploratory process results in moving closer to the more desired goal or state shared by all parties.

Remember . . .

CAUTIOUS THINKER
BUSINESS CHARACTERISTICS

- Concerned with process; want to know *how* something works
- Intuitive and original; once they know the expected structure, they may invent their own structure, method, or model
- More interested in quality than quantity; prefer lower output to inferior results
- Want to be right, so they employ logical thinking process to avoid mistakes
- Over-attend to details, sometimes impeding progress with regular checking and rechecking
- Dislike changes and surprises
- Reject aggression

CAUTIOUS THINKER:
PREFERRED BUSINESS SITUATIONS

- Colleagues and superiors do not criticize their work or ideas
- Can set the quality control standards and check to see if they're properly implemented
- Work with complete data systems, or can formulate some themselves
- Superiors value correctness and let them know they are key workers in the organization
- Workplaces are organized and process-oriented, with a minimum of socializing

People Smart Principle # 6—The Principle of Personal Leadership: "To know and accept who you are—including strengths, weaknesses, and growth potentials—is essential for effective leadership behavior."

Chapter 6
Leadership Styles

Making this chapter meaningful to you

Picture a Dominant Director, Interacting Socializer, Steady Relater, and Cautious Thinker who manage you or whom you manage. As you read, bear in mind each of these particular people and specify what you can do to improve your relationships with them. Focus on each one's more productive traits as well as each one's less productive characteristics.

To begin answering these questions, we have found a common *universal leadership language* which exists around the world in management circles. Whether you are a corporate president, chairman of the board, head of a small company, a board member, director of a non-profit organization, an independent consultant, or senior pastor of a church, you can greatly increase your effectiveness as a leader by learning to speak this language. It involves the most widely known leadership concept in continued practice today—the managerial grid—which reveals a person's leadership influencing approach.

The essence of this concept is that all people have their own natural, and thus preferred way, of doing things, including exerting influence over people and/or managing tasks or organizations. In this respect, Dominant Directors are the most observably directive in their style of leadership. On the other hand, Interacting Socializers are the most naturally supportive in the way they go about their efforts to influence others and manage situations.

By contrast, the remaining two behavioral types are more introverted by nature and less easily identifiable in their leadership practices.You can still see, however, that *liking-motivated* Steady Relaters are more like supportive Interacting Socializers. But Steady Relaters are secondarily concerned with being supportive to provide the expected service or accomplish the identified result. And finally Cautious Thinkers are more similar to *self-determined* Dominant Directors. The difference is that Cautious Thinkers are concerned with achieving their own desired standards in a way that does not cause further problems by rubbing other people the wrong way.

The graphic entitled "Our Primary Natural Leadership Styles" will help you better understand the differing natures of these four leadership styles as well as those among the people you work with/for. You may want to note your own *strong suit* and *least developed approach* (as well as those of significant individuals in your work environment) before moving on to gain additional insights about both, which are provided in this chapter.

Unfortunately, when commonplace stresses and pressures accompany particular situations in the workplace, leaders often revert to their own instinctive state. If this happens, a less effective response is illustrated by "The Ineffective Expression of Our Natural Leadership Styles" graphic.

The Dominant Director Leaders

Move over and let them do their thing

They're like wild horses who don't like to run in rigid formation. But why hobble them if they're able to get blue ribbons in their own way? Or even start and develop their own herd? If you confine them, Dominant Directors may become harsh and stubborn; let them do their own thing and they may very well impress you. Agree on the goal and specify the boundaries of the playing field. Then get out of their way.

YOUR PRIMARY
NATURAL LEADERSHIP STYLES

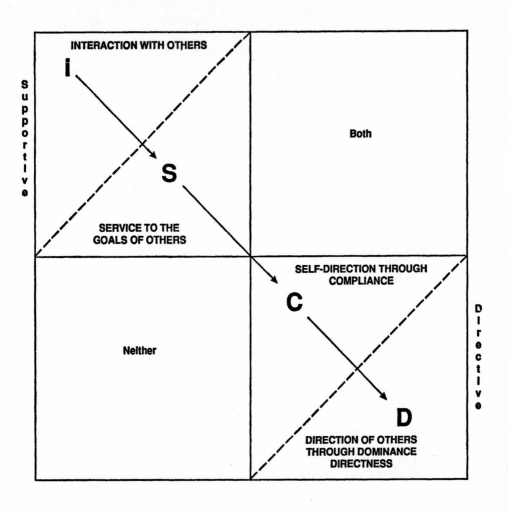

THE INEFFECTIVE EXPRESSION OF OUR NATURAL LEADERSHIP STYLES

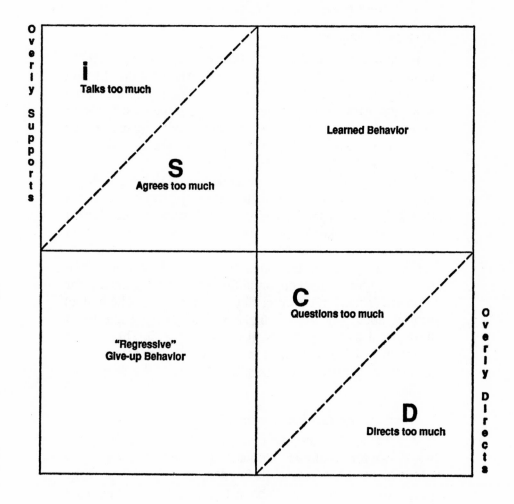

This requires other people to ignore some of the Dominant Director's natural competitive spirit and, instead, focus this energy on a common goal for bettering the organization. Dominant Directors seek this sort of encouragement and feedback to function most effectively within the general framework of shared expectations. But don't expect them to follow every procedure to the letter.

How to develop D's

When coaching a Dominant Director, he likes to learn the basic steps to quickly sift out what he wants. "I don't really plan to read this 200 page computer manual just to learn how to set up pages in three columns. Just teach me what I have to know so I can do that." In the interest of saving time, D's may try to find shortcuts, so show them the simplest, fastest route to get them to their stated destination.

The thought of reassuring someone or explaining something more than once smacks of frittering away precious moments that he'd rather spend on action and results. So he doesn't bother with details. Focus on the high points, please, like what is to be done by when. He wants to know only those details required to get a contraption to function so he can then turn to other important new opportunities—like making money, for instance. Instead of covering steps one through 24, he prefers hearing about key steps 1, 6, 12, and 24. Forcing him to sit through all 24 points seems like torture to a D. This lack of attention to details can result in his searching for new ways to streamline his routine jobs in getting his desired effects more readily.

Toward appropriate management

When Don Cipriano, the number one, all-time salesperson worldwide for Performax International, conducted a session on Motivational Management in London, he said, "We manage people the way they need to be managed, not the way we want to manage." One manager, John, commented that concept really hit home because his high D (Dominant Director) behavior was creating some problems with his S (Steady Relater) and C (Cautious Thinker) staff. For four months, John ran his office according to the way his staff needed to be managed, but when a new employee began working in his department, John didn't have the same success he had with the others. One day, she made an appointment with John and told him, "If you'd stop wasting time providing all those details, I could get my work done." John had made the common mistake of being so used to managing just S and C behaviors that he failed to recognize the high D behavior of his new employee. John later said to Don Cipriano, "I fell into the same trap, managing everyone the same way."

What's this company's philosophy?

Similarly, when Dr. John Lee, a renowned time management expert, conducts workshops, he often asks, "What is the operating philosophy of your company?" He says presidents of organizations seem floored when they notice the diversity of answers mentioned by their staff members. If a CEO doesn't verbalize, clarify, and gather input about what everyone is working toward, how can the company function smoothly? Like Dan's misguided idea of a dream company vacation, employees can benefit by a common, agreed-upon vision. Dan still made the ultimate decision, but with a little help from the group.

Who's managing whom?

Managing Dominant Directors is no easy task because they want to manage you! You can squelch them or you can encourage them to take control of certain arenas. Why not work with the D's strengths by allowing him to take the reins, where qualified, on particular projects? His preference for change and innovation makes him the natural choice for *new frontier* programs where he can implement his own ideas. Make sure the Dominant Director understands he needs to check with you at specific intervals, or he may demonstrate the renegade syndrome—doing his own thing, without answering to anyone but himself.

Getting D's to decide

Dominant Directors tend to make autonomous, no-nonsense decisions. If the decision will help them meet their goals, they go for it; if not, they'll typically say no. One of the few times this type will procrastinate in reaching a conclusion is when it will take too much time or effort to do the homework to determine the best alternative. You can prevent this procrastination by simply providing a brief analysis for each option you present to a D.

Motivating D's

Provide them with options and clearly describe the probabilities of success in achieving goals. "Ross, here are four possibilities for developing the Evans Estate. I've highlighted the key points for each suggestion, and included costs and time projections on the bottom of each one. The choice is yours."

Compared to the other types, Dominant Directors are more likely to thrive in pressure cooker situations. They naturally gravitate toward those power positions and career areas where they can take charge: executives, politicians, military officers, stockbrokers, and newspaper reporters. Think of win-at-any-cost tennis pro John McEnroe. When in doubt, he questions the decisions made by the referee. For better or worse, he deals directly with the source. It's not how you play the game—it's winning! And winning, more than anything else, motivates this type. Just think of Donald Trump, author of *The Art of the Deal* and *The Trump Game*, as one example of this leadership style.

Complimenting D's

Mention their achievements, upward mobility, and leadership potential. Omit personal comments and focus on their track record. "Jones, you've exceeded our company goals every month for the past year and have put in more hours than anybody but the top officials here. The CEO has his eye on you for an upcoming vice-presidential slot."

Counseling D's

Stick to the facts. Draw them out by talking about the desired results. Then discuss their concerns. Focus on tasks more than feelings. Ask them how they would solve the problem. "Anne, we've heard a few comments that need to be addressed. It seems that some of your employees don't feel appreciated for the extra hours they've been putting in for you on the Evans project. They say they've given up social engagements and worked 14-hour days to beat your deadline. How do you think we can bolster their morale?"

Correcting D's

Describe what results are desired. Show them the gap between actual and desired. Suggest clearly the improvement that is needed and establish a time when they will get back to you. "We need to streamline communication around here so that one hand knows what the other is doing. Last month, we had two separate divisions calling on the same CEO for corporate donations. I want you to work up a plan to keep everybody informed of who's working on what so we don't duplicate our efforts. Get back to me by the end of the week."

Communicating with D's

Be prepared to listen to their suggestions, the course of action they have in mind, and/or the general results they are considering. This enables you to begin on a positive note by indicating the areas in which you already agree. Then you can work backwards toward gaining agreement on the results you both want—and are willing to either mutually or independently allow the other to achieve. "Sarah, this format will give you the freedom to develop your branch your way and still allow Vern and Ellen to structure theirs another way . . . without sacrificing time or morale."

Making decisions and problem solving with D's

They will want to provide their own initial view of the decision to be made or problem to be solved and the process they prefer to follow in reaching a clear-cut, preferably quickly chosen solution. "As I see it, you have the most experience in organizing seminars like this, Charles, so why don't you throw out a few ideas!" You can anticipate, where possible, and be open to summarizing the achievements you've made (or, possibly in a case like this, your lack of achievements in this area). "Hal, you flatter me, but I've never undertaken an international convention like this before. As for ideas, why don't we decide who wants to perform which function and then we can all do what we feel comfortable doing!" With this approach, you're more likely to reach mutual agreement with the least hassle for everyone concerned . . . yourself included.

When suggesting a different idea, opinion, or action to them, be sure to point out you are trying to work in ways that are acceptable to them—and also yourself. Focus on your desire to identify solutions which will also meet their expectations. Stress that you don't want to cause difficulties for either them or you. "Phil, instead of writing this report as it occurs to you and me, I'd rather write an outline first and then the report. I know it takes longer initially, but it saves time in the long run because the writing will be better organized and make more sense to the readers."

When acknowledging D's

When it's appropriate to reward or reinforce their behaviors, focus on how pleased you are. Assume they are also pleased with achieving the desired outcome in that situation. Also mention how glad you are to be a part of that process working with them to make things better for both of you through cooperation. The bottom line? Each of you get better results by combining your energies on a common targeted goal: "Phil, this report turned out much better with your wonderful anecdotes and asides. Now we have something that's interesting, clear, and well organized!"

Delegating with D's

Give them the bottom line and then let them do their thing. So that they can be more efficient, give them parameters, guidelines, and deadlines. "We need to get that mall built a month sooner or we'll lose our shirts. Fourteen tenants are threatening to bail out of their contracts if we don't open in

Action Plan . . .

WHEN *YOU* ARE
THE DOMINANT DIRECTOR

- Allow others to do things without excessive or un-timely interference
- Participate in the group without expecting always to be in command
- Modify the tendency to give orders to others
- Enlist others' input and support through participa-tive, collaborative actions
- Give others credit when they deserve it
- Praise people for jobs well done
- Let colleagues and employees know that you real-ize it's only natural that you and others will make mistakes
- When delegating, give some authority along with the responsibility

WHEN OTHERS ARE DOMINANT DIRECTORS, HELP THEM LEARN TO:

- More realistically gauge risks
- Exercise more caution and deliberation before making decisions and coming to conclusions
- Follow pertinent rules, regulations, and expectations
- Recognize and solicit others' contributions, both as individuals and within a group
- Tell others the reasons for decisions
- Cultivate more attention/responsiveness to emotions

time for the holidays. Don't spend more than another $30,000, keep everything legal and out of the newspapers, and get back to me by Monday morning."

We know one Dominant Director who became visibly, though not consciously, agitated if anyone stayed in her office beyond 10 minutes. Her staff knew this, but anyone outside the office had no inkling until she began fidgeting and examining her stacks of paperwork, hoping the person would leave. One day, it dawned on her to delegate an *alarm clock* duty to her secretary. Then, whenever anyone stayed more than ten minutes, Mrs. Myers knocked on the door or buzzed her on the phone reminding her of the *next appointment.*

Catch people doing something right

If you happen to be a Dominant Director manager, use what you now know about behavioral types to make the workplace more productive. Try mentoring, training, or consulting as appropriate development practices, instead of criticizing or leaving them alone without guidance. Catch your employees doing things right and tell them about it. Ask employees for their feedback about policies, deadlines, and programs. Bouncing ideas off your co-workers can give you insights into how you can better motivate people to help you achieve your goals.

The Interacting Socializer Leader

Help them focus their abilities

With their energy and enthusiasm, Interacting Socializers can get so involved with so many different activities that they may accomplish goals with a flourish. Or, they may show flurries of activity, but not actually accomplish things in the most efficient way. Managers and co-workers can help channel that energy and enthusiasm with tactful reminders and hands-on assistance to help them prioritize and organize. Then, the entire office may function more smoothly. Since Interacting Socializers tend to be open books, the other types often can detect when Interacting Socializers are having off days and give them verbal boosts with a compliment and personal attention.

How to develop I's

When coaching Interacting Socializers, don't give them too much at once or they'll become overwhelmed. Skip as much of the detailed, boring stuff as possible. Get them involved. Interacting Socializers are typically kinesthetic, hands-on learners, so let them try by first getting a feel for what's involved, and then showing you what they understood so you can give them structured feedback. Frequently, this type wants to jump in and try before they're ready, or before they fully understand everything. Allow them to save face when they do something wrong, and heap on those compliments when they get it right!

Prioritizing with I's

Many Interacting Socializers find that sorting out priorities and solutions becomes very difficult when too many opportunities bombard them. When this happens, they may become uncharacteristically mute and immobilized . . . temporarily, of course. Other people can help by prioritizing items for Interacting Socializers to tackle. "This account needs attention sometime today, but I need your input on the Chase report in less than an hour." This approach enables him to separate his feelings from the facts at hand as well as other people's expectations. Ironically, when the Interacting Socializer's tasks become more organized, his anxiety level lessens—despite the fact that he bristles at the thought of organization. More importantly, since he can't be all things to all people, focusing and refocusing on what's most important, second-most, etc., is essential to his well-being.

Support I's dreams

Interacting Socializers operate predominantly from a multiple-focus, right brain perspective. They see mental pictures first, then convert those pictures to words. Preferring main ideas and generalities, not details, they base decisions on their impulses, gut feelings, and others' recommendations and testimonials. For this behavioral type, emotions rule. "Something tells me that I should buy this stock." This doesn't mean that they never use logic or facts, but that feelings and emotions come first, thinking processes being factors that are the servants to their feeling state.

Get ready to act more enthusiastic with an Interacting Socializer. Show you're interested in him by letting him talk and by using more animation in your own gestures and voice. Illustrate your ideas with stories or mental pictures that relate to him and his goals. He likes to interact with people, so try not to hurry your discussion. Include opportunities for small talk and getting personally acquainted.

Socializers like to envision the big picture. Generally less motivated by many facts and details, they respond better to short overviews or capsule summaries of what you plan to cover. Attempt to develop some stimulating, enjoyable ideas together while focusing on supporting their opinions and dreams. Interacting Socializers turn off to people who douse their dreams. Then support their ideas while showing them how they can transfer their talk into actions.

If you disagree, try not to argue because they dislike conflict. You might not win an argument with them anyway because their strong suit is feelings and intuition. If trapped, they can twist people around through very clever manipulation of feelings with their usage of words and emotions. Try to explore alternate solutions, instead. When you reach an agreement, iron out the specific details concerning what, when, who, and how. Then document the agreement with them, since they tend to naturally forget such details.

Motivating I's

They like special packages and a little something extra to inspire them to go the whole nine yards. "Hawkins, if you can clinch the Babbitt account, I'll give you an extra week's vacation and take you and Sharon to the fanciest restaurant in town." Or, show them how they can look good in the eyes of others. "When you close your next order, that will be your tenth major success story this year. You can all but clinch the

President's Productivity Award with your name engraved on a plaque next to the big boss himself."

Many businesses use yearly contests to motivate their employees. Interacting Socializers tend to sprint toward a quick win—for the first week or two. Then they may say to themselves, "Hey, I have a whole year to win this contest. Why am I working so hard now?" They may further get sidetracked by other things and do nothing more about it until a week before the contest ends. If they can get excited enough, they may win anyway, but the truth is they haven't worked toward the goal for 11 months. How can these types keep up their motivation? Since Interacting Socializers like constant rewards along the way, they may favor shorter contests with smaller payoffs, perhaps culminating in the *big one* when the year ends. One person even jokingly suggests, "How about an employee of the hour award?" Or, they may enlist other colleagues' assistance who are better at implementation than they are.

Complimenting I's

Pay direct personal compliments to them, as individuals when legitimately deserved. "You are a terrific person and a wonderful employee." Mention their charm, friendliness, creative ideas, persuasiveness, and/or appearance (or better yet, all of the above). While other types respond to more specific job-related comments, Interacting Socializers can mentally relive more global generalizations for weeks to come. "We are so lucky to have you with us, Dee. You're a real gem."

Counseling I's

Give them ample opportunity to talk about whatever may be bothering them. Pay attention to both facts and feelings, but put your primary emphasis on their feelings. Ask probing questions and involve them by asking how they could solve the challenge or difficulty. Sometimes, just airing their feelings and thoughts relieves tension for these individuals. Talking allows them to get something off their chests and can even become an end in itself, since their energy is largely influenced by the quality of their relationship with a person.

Correcting I's

When stress hits I's, they prefer looking the other way and searching for more positive, upbeat experiences. They avoid problems as long as they can. If the pressure persists, they tend to literally walk away from the problem. When this tactic fails, they may become emotionally candid in attempts to meet their needs. "I can't believe I let this happen, but I brought it all on myself." Sometimes stress manifests itself in animated panic. "I can't talk now, Hal. It's really hit the fan this time!"

Let these individuals know specifically what the challenge happens to be. Define the behavior that can eliminate it and confirm the mutually agreeable action plan in writing to prevent future misunderstandings. Since they prefer keeping the conversation light, avoid what they view as negative or distasteful approaches. Rather than, "Why did your sales drop off 50% last month?" use more optimistically stated questions like, "How'd you like to bolster your sales up to your normal range and beyond it?" They'd simply rather deal with things going right.

Communicating with them

Be prepared to listen to their personal feelings and experiences, since they have a need to be both expressive and able to share their emotions with others. Their style requires open and responsive interaction with others, preferably in a manner of congenial and unhurried conversation. It's much like that between long-time friends. "Just between you and me, Chris, I feel very uneasy about Jill and Howard handling this account by themselves."

Making decisions/solving problems with I's

They'll want to avoid a discussion of more complex, negative-sounding or otherwise messy problem situations. It's difficult for them to feel positive or agreeable with you or anyone else under these circumstances. In making decisions with them, they will be open to your suggestions—as long as these ideas will allow them to look and feel good—and not require a lot of difficult, follow-up, detail work or long-term commitments. "You know just about everybody who is anybody, George. Since we need to get $350 in pledges for the *Y* by the end of February, why not go ahead and wrap up all your calls by Friday. Then you can relax a lot more next week." When suggesting a different idea, opinion, or action to them, be sure to point out you are doing it that way if it's acceptable to them. Focus on your desire to identify solutions which will also meet their expectations. Stress that you don't want to cause difficulties for either them or you.

Above all, offer your suggestions as gifts which can make this situation (task or relationship) easier and more beneficial to them—as well as to other people who you feel are also likely to find this very acceptable and desirable. "You're lucky I'm on the Nominating Committee, Marilyn. So many people wanted the Hospitality position that I couldn't manage it for you this year, but I think I've got one that's even better than that—How about Junior High Dances?"

When acknowledging I's

When it's appropriate to reward or reinforce their behaviors, focus on how glad you are they have succeeded in finding a pleasant solution to their concern or objective. In addition, let them know how much you appreciate them for their openness and willingness to be responsive to you in a way that allows everyone to end up feeling good about the results afterwards. "George, I'm so glad we could reach a solution that both you and I feel good about. I appreciate your openness about only being able to call prospective donors on Friday night. That's fine with me. We'll work this out so that everyone is happy."

Delegating with I's

Again, make sure to receive clear agreement. Set up check points/times to avoid long stretches with no progress reports. Otherwise, I's may lapse into their natural way of doing things—spontaneously completing particulars which feel best while postponing less stimulating tasks, especially those that involve followup and checking.

By now, you realize that Interacting Socializers exhibit a natural talkativeness and ease with people. This makes them good choices for maintaining group morale and motivation.

They think out loud and enjoy participating in brainstorming sessions anyway, so why not get their opinions and assistance on recognition awards, entertainment, or fund-raising activities? They want to fill their natural need by striving for recognition, so activities which draw attention to themselves appeal to them.

I's are often concept people who come up with plenty of ideas, but not necessarily the means of carrying them out, so steer them toward ways of assuring the implementation of those ideas. "Olivia, this proposal for the King Company looks good so far, but how about including more direct benefits for each employee. Marian has surveys filled out by each employee. Get together with her, bounce some ideas around, and then include more essential information about the eight or so key people in your proposal. Add some extra *plus points* on the others . . . 12 pages in all. In this manner, you should do the job very well. And, Olivia, thanks for making the extra effort on this project. It's really important to all of us."

In this example, the manager praises the work done so far, tells Olivia where to go for more facts, encourages a participative exchange between Olivia and Marian, spells out the parameters (12 pages), and shows her the path for staying on track. He's utilizing this Interacting Socializer's natural strengths and allowing for her potential weaknesses. Instead of delegating someone to perform large tasks that are naturally stressful for them, why not structure the tasks to fit the natural work style of that person? As one bumper sticker we spotted on a passing car advised, "Never teach a duck to sing. It's a waste of time and it annoys the duck."

The Steady Relater Leader

Encourage them to update their methods

Steady Relaters contribute stability and perseverance to their workplace. Since they work toward harmony in the office, they usually fit comfortably into the work environment, but they may become used to using the same old methods again and again. Sometimes their procedures include steps that may have been needed when they learned the procedure, but can now be discarded. They may improve their work practices by utilizing shortcuts that eliminate extra steps. Dominant Directors and Interacting Socializers can often help them with this. And, when asked, Cautious Thinkers can generally demonstrate new ways to get things done.

How to develop S's

When he's in training for a job, he favors one-on-one, hands-on instruction with a real live human being, starting at the beginning and ending at the end. By learning each step, he generally is more comfortable with his functions. During training and in other newer situations, the S tends to observe others for a longer than average time. When he feels he can do a task, then and only then will he comfortably begin. This slower pace can frustrate Dominant Directors and Interacting Socializers, both of whom like to plunge right in with, "Oh, sure! I can do that," whether they've done it before or not! So understanding that Steady Relaters need to do things slowly can reassure the faster-paced types that the job will get done.

Get ready to be ready with the S. Have a step-by-step list of procedures or a working timetable/schedule at your disposal. Steady Relaters need to feel secure in their mastery of procedures until their actions become *second nature* and more routine. At the same time, they prefer a pleasant and patient approach while they learn what's expected of them.

Motivating S's

Besides thinking they can learn to master a series of procedures, S's like to also feel that their relationships with others can benefit from their follow-through. "If you can learn to use this computer by next week, you can send the whole Christmas mailing for Mr. Hawkins on Monday. Then he can go to Texas for his family reunion." Or show Steady Relaters how to strengthen their relationships with others. "When this office makes its 1000th sale, it can win the Outstanding Division Award for the year. And you, Arthur, can help that happen by getting Mr. Arens to look at this new demographic data."

Action Plan ...

WHEN *YOU* ARE
THE INTERACTING SOCIALIZER

- Attend to key details, when appropriate
- Improve your follow-through efforts
- Monitor socializing to keep it in balance with other aspects of life
- Write things down and work from a list, so you'll know what to do when
- Prioritize activities and focus on tasks in order of importance
- Become more organized and orderly in the way you do things
- Get the less appealing tasks of the day over with
- Pay more attention to time management of activities
- Check to make sure you're on course with known tasks or goals

WHEN OTHERS ARE INTERACTING
SOCIALIZERS, HELP THEM LEARN TO:

- Prioritize and organize
- See tasks through to completion
- View people and tasks more objectively
- Avoid overuse of giving and taking advice (which can result in lack of focus on task)
- Write things down
- Do the unpleasant, as well as the *fun things*
- Focus on what's important now
- Avoid procrastination and/or hoping others will do things for them
- Practice and perfect, when appropriate

Complimenting S's

Mention their teamwork and dependability. "Pam, besides plugging along on this project for two years, I really appreciate the fact you've encouraged everyone else to do their part. We couldn't have done it without you." Or remark about how others regard them, how well they get along with co-workers, and how important their relationship-building efforts have been to the company. "Limbrecht, you've been the glue holding this place together for the last 20 years." Effusiveness can arouse the suspicions of Steady Relaters, so stick to praising what they've done rather than more abstract, personal attributes. Otherwise, their modesty and your vagueness may cause them to dismiss your comments.

Counseling S's

Allow plenty of time to explore their thoughts and feelings so you can understand the emotional side of the situation. Steady Relaters usually express their feelings less directly, so draw them out through questioning and listening responses. Bear in mind this type tends to balk at sudden change, whether the change is good or bad. The key point is that their stability-motivated state is disrupted by the unknown. You can help reduce their fears by showing how specific changes will benefit them and their company. "Barbara, moving to Dallas will be an adjustment for all of us at first, but 80% of our staff has agreed to go. The company will move you and your family, sell your house, add more medical and dental benefits to your health plan, and give you a 10% bonus for loyal service. We like to take care of our own, and you are a valuable, trusted employee. And besides, you'll still be with many of the same friends, co-workers, and the company you've always been with day in and day out."

Correcting S's

Reassure them that you only want to correct a specific behavior. S's tend to take things personally, so remove the *something is wrong with you* barrier as quickly as possible. Don't blame or judge the person; keep the conversation focused on the behavior and its appropriateness. If the problem involves a procedure, help them learn how to improve it. Point out in a non-threatening way what they're already doing right while also emphasizing what needs changing. "Norma, I admire your persistence on this proposal, but we have to add more details to The Idea section before we send it out. For example,"

Communicating with S's

Be ready to do more talking than listening with them, since they don't naturally feel comfortable when the limelight is focused on them. You will want to clarify any key agenda item with them, working to stay organized and moving forward steadily but slowly as you check to make sure they both understand and accept what is being said: "Did you want me to stick around the office at a particular time each day in case you need to telephone me for emergency questions on this account, or do you want me to call you?"

Making decisions and solving problems with S's

In dealing with problems and decisions with this type, make sure to deal with only one subject or situation at a time, one step at a time. To gain clarity, before moving on to other items, make sure they are ready, willing, and able to do so. Recalling that they need stability, deal with matters calmly and in a more relaxed manner. Encourage them to share their suggestions as to how the decision might be made in a way that is likely to add even more stability to the current conditions than already, or previously, exist. "Would you mind writing down a schedule of your office's activities so I can get my proposal written up without missing anything? "

When suggesting a different possibility to S's, point out how you are trying to identify ways that you can help continue to make things pleasant for them. You simply have an idea or opinion in this respect which will also help stabilize your own relationship expectations with them and which is important to you, too. "I know that we initially agreed on 10 phone calls per day, but some of our volunteers are unable to make that commitment. Would you be comfortable making 15 calls a day if those calls included your personal friends and family?"

When acknowledging S's

When it's appropriate to reward or reinforce their behaviors, focus on how you genuinely and sincerely appreciate their willingness to work to make things good for you and others. Approach matters in a more systematic, low-keyed, and understandable manner. Also, point out how you have noticed they make important contributions when they take the initiative to share their own ideas, interests, and insights in helping make sure these results are achieved. "Just say anything about the impending merger that you want to share. We certainly don't want to use any high pressure tactics which is precisely why you meet our own expectations so well. John, thank you very much for your willingness to provide us with this desired input."

Delegating with S's

Steady Relaters may be reluctant to ask others to do their own share of the work. So you could make a personal appeal to their loyalty and sense of sportsmanship. "Al, you're an example for this company of genuine cooperative spirit. Your staff wants to please you, so by giving everyone in your department just 10 of those names to call, you can all reach the goal together by noon tomorrow. Otherwise, you'll probably have a lot more difficulty reaching all those people by the target date." Give them the task, state the deadlines that need to be met, and explain why it's important to do it that way. "I'll need 500 copies of these summaries typed and collated by 5 p.m. today. Mr. Jeffries is getting back from New York two days early and he wants them by tomorrow morning."

The Cautious Thinker Leader

Help them substitute quality for perfection

Since this type is characterized by the most complex thinking pattern, they base their decisions on proven information and track records. They want to make rational choices based on facts, not on other people's opinions or testimonials —unless those people are those Cautious Thinkers' personal heroes.

Action Plan . . .

WHEN *YOU* ARE
THE STEADY RELATER

- Stretch by taking on a bit more (or different) duties beyond your comfort level
- Increase verbalization of your thoughts and feelings
- Speed up your actions by getting into some projects more quickly
- Desensitize yourselves somewhat, so that you aren't negatively affected by your colleagues' feelings to the point of affecting your own performance
- Learn to adapt more quickly to either changes or refinements of existing practices
- Bolster your assertiveness techniques

WHEN OTHERS ARE STEADY RELATERS, HELP THEM:

- Utilize shortcuts and discard unnecessary steps
- Track their growth
- Avoid doing things the same way
- Focus on the goal without attending to other thoughts or feelings
- Realize there is more than one approach to tasks
- Become more open to some risks and changes
- To feel sincerely appreciated
- Speak up and voice their thoughts and feelings
- Modify the tendency to do what others tell them
- Get and accept credit and praise, when appropriate

Even then, they'll probably want to see it in writing. When a C says, "I need to think about it," she usually means it. You can help her make a decision by supplying the materials she requests and by allowing her the time to make the right decision for her. Focus on emphasizing deadlines and parameters so the Cautious Thinker can build those time frames into her procedures.

How to develop C's

When coaching a C, point out the most important things to remember first. Then demonstrate the procedure in an efficient, logical manner, stressing the purpose of each step. Proceed at a relatively slow pace, stopping at each key place in the process to check for his or her understanding. Ask for possible input, especially regarding desired refinements which may be appropriate. This approach ensures success with the task and minimization of stress for the Cautious Thinker.

Motivating C's

Appeal to their need for accuracy and logic. This type doesn't respond well to fancy verbal antics, so keep your approach clear, clean, and documentable. Better yet, provide illustration and documentation. Avoid exaggeration and vagueness. Show them how this is the best available current option. "Ms. Alberts, our office cleaning service should meet almost all your cleanliness needs. I think that a neat and sanitary environment is a key standard for more productivity. Do you agree or see it differently?"

If they decide to take part in a competitive situation, they'll probably do it as they do other tasks—bit by bit—until they do it right. Unlike their colleagues who may show enthusiasm at the beginning, C's often show the patience and follow-through to ultimately win—if they perceive the contest as worthwhile and don't become too preoccupied with details along the way. Whereas some people focus on winning shorter term battles, the Cautious Thinker is motivated by the ultimate sense of lasting personal glory derived from triumphing in the overall war.

Complimenting C's

Mention their efficiency, thought processes, organization, persistence, and accuracy. Don't mix personal and professional comments unless you know them very well. Even then, they prefer more privately communicated, plausible praise. "Jeffries, you were so thorough on this project that we had every shred of information we needed—and then some just in case we required a safety net. Thanks again for another good job!"

One C told us, "Compliments don't mean much to me. I really don't think about them. But I do like genuine, heartfelt appreciation once in awhile, like, "You did a fine job," or, "I've really benefited from your work and so have others who have told me about your contributions." In other words, keep praise simple and concise for a Cautious Thinker. He went on to say that what he thinks about some accomplishment is much more important to him. "I'm hard on myself."

Counseling C's

Elicit their thoughts about processes, procedures or problems, perhaps by asking something like, "If it were in your power, how would you change this to make things even better?" Like Steady Relaters, they often express their thoughts and opinions indirectly, so persist in your attempts to get them to talk. This type dislikes change because they typically view changes and the future as unknown variables where unforeseen mistakes might happen. They need to plan for change ahead of time so they can identify and bring under control any key considerations that have to be addressed in the process. When possible, allow them to investigate possible repercussions, especially at the beginning stages. That way they'll know more about the future and may be more comfortable with possible changes.

Correcting C's

Show C's the way to get a job done and they'll typically master the format, then modify it to suit their individual needs. They tend to start with what they have to work with, then personalize it, almost from the beginning, so that it works better as they see it. So they may avoid people whom they perceive might tell them to do things differently. This is one way Cautious Thinkers maintain control of their work. They tend to side-step authorities who they think are endeavoring to correct them. At the extreme, this behavior can appear sneaky to other types, especially if the C gets caught.

Specify the exact behavior that is indicated and outline how you would like to see it changed. Establish agreed-upon checkpoints and times. Allow them to save face, as they fear being wrong. "Nelson, your work here is typically done neat, on time, and right on the money. Now that we're switching the office to computers, you'll be able to turn out the same quality of work, only faster. I'd like you to take this computer class . . ."

Communicating with them

Be well organized and clear in your communications, since they are likely to ask lots of questions about a situation or subject in their search for a logical conclusion. You may want to have them clarify what their more pressing key concerns are. Ask your questions in a more discreet, non-judgmental manner to elicit the points, objectives, or assurances Cautious Thinkers want. "Lenny, I'm not trying to pressure you, but are you not interested in the auditor's position, or in any position?"

Making decisions and solving problems with C's

Set the stage by making sure they are open to discussing the problem or decision being considered at this time. If they aren't ready, either set a definite time that's better for both of you or explore their concern in even pursuing this subject. When the situation is being explored, review your impression of the entire process. "My understanding is this—you'd like to think it over for a week or so and figure out what kind of time commitment you'd be able to make to the group. When may I call you about your decision?" Decide on a logical approach for gaining common agreement about both the nature of the problem or decision involved and the most reasonable way of finding how to resolve it. Do so in a way that is likely to be most satisfactory to them, you, and any other key individuals involved.

When suggesting a different possibility to C's, point out how you would like to be able to identify those ideas, perspectives, or actions likely to allow you, them, and others to reach a more perfected solution or situation. Stress how less difficulties or confusion are likely to result. Ask them what insights and suggestions they, or individuals they know and value, could bring to this situation. "Carol, if we leave at 10 o'clock Friday morning and get to Palm Springs around 11:00, we can meet with Mr. Conkill and his V.P.'s for lunch to present our ideas for organizing their grand opening party. Do you know any wholesalers we can contact there so we can come up with a realistic estimate for making their party a bona fide hit?"

When acknowledging C's

Focus on your realization of how difficult it can be at times for them to attempt to meet the high personal standards they set for themselves. Also focus on how much you appreciate this personal characteristic for what it's done to make things better for you in your relationship with them. Cite a specific and appropriate example which proves this point. "Robert, you're a very good chef. That salmon was cooked perfectly— juicy and flavorful without a hint of dryness. I don't want to embarrass you, but I feel obliged to share with you how truly impressed I am. Thank you for your efforts." Then, notice his reaction. If it's discomfort, share with him that you did not mean to embarrass him, but just to let him know how much you value him. If his reaction is more positive, ask him to tell you more about the sense of satisfaction and enjoyment he derives from similar things. "I'll bet you like creating other recipes, too. Is that correct?"

Delegating with C's

Take time to answer their most critical questions about structure and/or guidance they require in a specific situation. The more they understand the details, the more likely they will be to complete the task properly. Be sure to establish deadlines. "Angela, the court date on the Mortimer case has been moved up to Monday, so we have to respond by speeding things up a bit. It will proceed almost as efficiently as if you researched everything by yourself if we enlist two associates to help you work, under your direction, on tasks you delegate to them and then review. Before getting started, do you have any preferences on the *who's* or *how to's* of this process that you think are essential to check with me at this time?"

The "best" leadership style

Remember, there is no such thing as one best, all-purpose leadership style. Instead, the best leaders are those who realize what a job, role, or specific situation requires for successful performance and then ensures those outcomes. At times, this may involve a clear-cut match between your own strengths and the required actions. At other times, behavior requirements may vary. The effective leader may adapt his own natural style by using new behavior methods he has learned. Or he might call upon other qualified individuals whose talents and energies can more productively handle the immediate problem. Or a good leader may take action to modify the environment. This could include shifting the work priorities to ensure the successful completion of the necessary task without sacrificing the well-being of other people. Productivity will be maximized by using these breakthrough leadership techniques and options.

Action Plan ...

WHEN *YOU* ARE THE CAUTIOUS THINKER

- Modify criticism (whether spoken or unspoken) of others' work
- Check less often, or only check the critical things (as opposed to everything), allowing the flow of the process to continue
- Ease up on controlling emotions; engage in more *water cooler interaction*
- Accept the fact that you can have high standards without expecting perfection
- Occasionally confront a colleague (or boss) with whom you disagree, instead of avoiding or ignoring them (and doing what you want to do, anyway)
- Tone down the tendency to OVER-prepare

WHEN OTHERS ARE CAUTIOUS THINKERS, GENTLY REMIND THEM TO:

- Share their knowledge and expertise with others
- Stand up for themselves with the people they prefer to avoid
- Shoot for realistic deadlines and parameters
- View people and tasks less seriously and critically
- Balance their lives with both interaction and tasks
- Keep on course with tasks, with less checking
- Maintain high expectations for high priority items, not necessarily everything

Chapter 7
Selling and Servicing With Style!

Every sales or service call has certain similarities; however, the techniques differentiate the professional salesperson from other salespeople. Professionals focus more on helping than selling, more on listening than talking, more on problem solving than persuading, more on creating long-term customers than one-shot sales.

The techniques used by professionals are simple, yet powerful. Salespeople who use this approach concentrate on a consultative process that allows both the customer and the salesperson to feel good about the sales/service exchange and each other. Professional sales and service staff go through five specific steps, though the approach may vary, depending on the personality style of their prospects.

You can apply the tips in this chapter to help you maximize your sales and service encounters, whether you fill the role of buyer or seller. Think of someone you know in a sales or service situation who sounds like the Dominant Director, Interacting Socializer, Steady Relater, and Cautious Thinker. How can you benefit with each one of them in a business relationship?

Step #1—making contact

The purpose of talking with your prospect is to begin building a business relationship by opening up lines of communication. Professional salespeople know that a solid business association goes beyond the immediate product or service being offered. The relationship, and therefore, the sale, requires the establishment of trust and the building of credibility. When prospects know you sincerely have their best interests in mind, the rest of the process can continue. Today's buyers are appreciative of professionals who show an interest in them, their businesses, and their lives.

Step #2—studying needs

Professional sales and service people spend a great deal of time studying their prospects' needs. They look not only for needs but for opportunities. Searching just for needs implies customers just have problems that must be solved. Looking for or creating opportunities puts the salesperson in the position of a consultant who can take someone's current conditions and improve upon them. They can encourage the prospect to become involved in this exploratory process. By asking well-structured questions, offering thought-provoking possibilities, and studying the many facets of the prospect's situation, you build cooperation—and a foundation for shared commitment.

Step #3—proposing solutions

After meeting with the potential customer and studying his or her situation, the next step is to propose a solution to the problem. The professional approach is one in which the presentation is custom tailored to the prospect's needs. Because of the comprehensive discussions the service or salesperson has had with the prospect, benefits naturally emerge as they relate to specific problems.

Step #4—gaining commitment

This is a logical conclusion to the ongoing communication and agreement that has been taking place with the prospect. Since the salesperson and prospect have worked together on a common goal since the beginning, there are few reasons why objections would be voiced at this point. There may be details to work out, but they won't get in the way. For professional sales and service people, the confirmation becomes a question of when, not if. If resistance occurs, it simply indicates there is a need for gathering more information or clarifying some details. Gaps in communication are not a problem because experienced salespeople are willing to spend time with the prospect until everything is understood and acceptable.

Step #5—assuring satisfaction

Professional sales and service people thrive on satisfied customers and see them for what they are—assets! These veterans begin assuring customer satisfaction after the sale by changing hats from salespeople to quality service providers. They make sure the customer receives the proper order on the right delivery date. They also help the customer track the results and analyze the effectiveness of the product or service for the specific problem(s) addressed. By assuring the satisfaction of each customer, professionals build a clientele guaranteeing future business that will become annuities for life.

How to Sell Your Product or Service to Dominant Directors

Dominant Directors want to know the bottom line. "What will this do for me?" and "By when?" Just give them enough information to satisfy their need to know about overall performance. They don't want you wasting their time reconstructing your product bolt by bolt, giving a laundry list of testimonials about your other satisfied clients, or getting too chummy with them. Even if you don't consider yourself a salesperson, remember that everyone sells something every day—whether ideas, integrity, credentials, image, or a less than palatable looking picnic lunch. Regardless of your work, you can probably apply to your everyday life a few sales tips that typically work with Dominant Directors.

#1—making contact with the D

When you write, call, or meet a Dominant Director, do it in a formal, businesslike manner. Get right to the point. Focus quickly on the task. Refer to bottom line results, increased efficiency, saved time, return on investment, profits, and so on. In other words, tell him what's in it for him.

If you plan to sell something or present a proposal to a Dominant Director, take care to be well-organized, time-conscious, efficient, and businesslike. As impatient as they are with a slower pace, Dominant Directors become especially wary if they question a person's competence Make sure they don't question yours. Remember, Dominant Directors don't want to make friends with you; they want to get something out of you if they think you have something to offer. And they're usually willing to pay for it.

As a sales or service person, it is your job to provide both sufficient information and enough incentive for the Dominant Director to meet with you. When you call, you might say, "Some of the ways I thought we would be able to work together are X, Y, and Z. Could we discuss those when I call you at a time of your choice?" By planting a seed, you may raise his interest level and the priority of your next call, unless, of course, he just isn't interested. Since individuals who fit this type pride themselves in being busy, they dislike granting several meetings. But if they think that time spent now will save time later, they're likely to initially explore matters with you now, rather than later.

#2—studying D's needs

To head off the Dominant Director's impatience before it surfaces, keep your queries interesting by alternately asking questions and giving additional information. Do this in a practical manner. Dominant Directors need to view the meeting as purposeful, so they want to understand where your questions ultimately lead. When asking a Dominant Director questions, it is essential to fine-tune and make them as practical and logical as possible. Aim questions at the heart of the issue and ask them in a straightforward manner. Only request information which is unavailable elsewhere.

When gathering information, ask questions showing you have done your homework about their desired results and current efforts. Know the Dominant Director's industry and company. Be sure to make queries that allow him to talk about his business goals. "Since your leadership has brought your company from 27th to 3rd in the country, what happens now?" Gear your studying toward saving the Dominant Director time.

#3—proposing solutions for D's

Your presentation, whether it is combined with studying or given on its own, must be geared toward the Dominant Director's priorities. He is concerned with saving time, generating money, and making life easier and more efficient. If you gear your presentation toward how he can become more successful, you'll no doubt get his attention. Zero in on the bottom line with quick benefit statements.

Because of their lack of time, Dominant Directors do not focus as much energy on contemplating and evaluating ideas. They want you to do the analysis and lay it out for them to approve or disapprove. Dominant Directors like rapid, concise analyses of their needs and your solutions.

So how can a salesperson get into a better business relationship with a Dominant Director? Act like a Boy Scout and *Be prepared.* In addition, demonstrate your competence and show him how your product will help him achieve his goals. Focus on results and highlight important specifics. Cut out intermediate steps when you make your presentation, eliminate the small talk, and stick to business. Professionalism counts with the Dominant Director.

During those times when it's appropriate to give historical data about your company or a more detailed presentation, write it out before you call. This allows you to highlight key points with a marking pen before you see him. Otherwise you're liable to bury him in a mass of paperwork. Skip over less important facts and show him the bottom line basics. Then leave a copy of the printout with him so he can refresh his memory later. Or he may want to delegate the fact checking to someone who really enjoys it—a Cautious Thinker or Steady Relater.

There's another good reason for reviewing your material, printing it out, and highlighting it. A Dominant Director may fire off questions at what seems to be a faster-than-the-speed-of-mouth rate. When he wants to hear about how your product ties into the bottom line, he wants to know now. Determine if he really needs the information immediately to make his decision or if he just wants to challenge you. In many cases, if he gets the information an hour from now, you can still meet his needs.

#4—gaining commitment with the D

With Dominant Directors, you can come right out and ask whether they're interested. You might say, "Based on what we've just discussed, are you interested in starting our service or carrying our product?" A Dominant Director will often tell you yes or no in no uncertain terms. At times, though, this type can put you off as if they can't make a decision, when, in fact, they aren't even thinking about it. They can become so preoccupied with other business that they literally do not have the time to evaluate your ideas, especially if they don't have enough information.

When you draw up a commitment letter, pay attention to how much time you spend on points the Dominant Director may not care about. Explain your commitment to attain both his bottom line results and your goals for a mutually acceptable agreement.

Consequently, the best way to deal with a Dominant Director is to give him options and probable outcomes. Bear in mind that the Dominant Director likes to balance quality with cost considerations, so include this information when you want him to make a decision. Then offer options with supporting evidence and leave the final decision to him. "The way I see it, you can go with Option A (tell pros and cons), Option B (more pros and cons), or Option C (still more pros and cons). I've outlined these three plans, costs of implementation, and approximate completion dates. Which one sounds best to you?" Dominant Directors seek control, so let them make the final decision. Brief and to the point, like the Dominant Director

SALES AND SERVICE STRATEGIES FOR DEALING WITH DOMINANT DIRECTORS:

- Plan to be prepared, organized, fast-paced, and always to the point
- Meet them in a professional and businesslike manner
- Learn and study their goals and objectives—what they want to accomplish, how they currently are motivated to do things, and what they'd like to change
- Suggest solutions with clearly defined and agreed upon consequences as well as rewards that relate specifically to their goals
- Get to the point
- Provide options and let them make the decision, when possible
- Let them know that you don't intend to waste their time

himself, this approach automatically fills his need to have the final word.

#5—assuring D satisfaction

Since Dominant Directors usually don't emphasize a personal relationship in business, if you sell to one, don't rely on past sales to ensure future purchases. Follow up with the Dominant Director to find if he has any complaints or problems with your product. If he does, fix them or his impatience may motivate him to seek help elsewhere, probably with another company. As Willy Loman found out in *Death of a Salesman*, contacts meant nothing in an age that emphasized change and product performance.

Impress upon your prospect that you intend to stand behind your product or service. Further, stress that you will follow up without taking a lot of his time. "You're buying this to save effort and time. I want to make sure it continues to work for you. I'll periodically check back to make sure everything is running smoothly, but I don't want to waste your time with unnecessary calls. When I telephone, if everything is fine, just say so and that will be it. If anything is less than what you expect, I want you to call me right away and I'll see to it the problem is fixed immediately." You may also want to offer a money back guarantee "If you aren't satisfied that you got your money's worth, I will personally take back the merchandise and write you a check."

How to Sell Your Product or Service to Interacting Socializers

As with the other types, apply your active listening skills, but be an especially empathic listener with Interacting Socializers. Give positive feedback to let them know that you understand and can relate to what they're feeling. When you talk about yourself, remember to use feeling words instead of thinking words. To paraphrase this concept, share your vision of the world in terms of your emotions, opinions, and intuitions. Tell stories about yourself, especially humorous or unusual ones, to win the heart (and sale) of an Interacting Socializer. Allow them to feel comfortable by also listening to their stories, even to the point of talking about topics that may stray from the subject.

#1—making contact with the I

When you write to or personally meet an Interacting Socializer, give the letter or meeting an upbeat, friendly feeling and faster pace. Don't talk about features, specifics, or performance data. In your initial benefits statement, stress those aspects of your product or service that will give them what they want—status, recognition, excitement, and being the first one on their block to have the newest, most dynamic product or service you can offer.

The first time you call an Interacting Socializer, use a more open-ended, friendly approach. Tell him who you are and say something like, "I'd like to come by and show you an exciting new product that will analyze and organize your accounts and help you become even more of a top performing salesperson."

When you meet an Interacting Socializer, think (or more specifically, feel) in terms of someone running for election. Shake hands firmly, introduce yourself with confidence, and immediately show interest in him personally. Let him set the pace and direction of the conversation. Since Interacting Socializers typically enjoy talking about themselves, ask questions about them. "How did you got into this business?" Prepare for lengthy answers, though. Plan to have as many meetings with an Interacting Socializer as necessary to build the relationship and gather information. After your first visit, you may want to meet for breakfast or lunch. Placing a time limit on those two meals is easier than putting a cap on dinner.

#2—studying I's needs

Interacting Socializers get bored quickly when they're not talking about themselves. That's why so much information gathering needs to revolve around them. But remember to strike a balance between listening to their life's stories and gathering the information you need to be an effective sales consultant. When asking business questions, keep them brief. If you can, work these exploratory questions in with the social questions. "You mentioned people as one of the keys to your success. How do you find (recruit) the people you work with? What kind of training do you give them?" The better your relationship with an Interacting Socializer, the more willing he'll be to cooperate and talk about the task at hand.

Interacting Socializers can be so open they may tell you their fondest hopes and aspirations. If you can demonstrate how your product or service can get them closer to their dreams, they may become so excited about your product—and you—that they're likely to sell themselves to you.

#3—proposing solutions for I's

Style is as important as substance, so sell the sizzle as well as the steak. The presentation should show an Interacting Socializer how your product or service will increase his prestige, image, or recognition. Talk about the favorable impact or consequences your suggestions will have in making their working relationships more enjoyable. Give them incentives for completing tasks by stressing how their contribution will benefit others and evoke positive responses from them. Presentations need impact for this type, so involve as many senses as possible. Interacting Socializers want both the presentation and the product to feel great. They also want to be reminded of who else has it; but spare them the details of other people's successes. Show them how you can save them effort and still make them look good.

Back up your claims with testimonials from well-known people or corporations. Interacting Socializers respond well to other people's positive experiences with your product or service—so tell them who else uses it. If one of their heroes tries something, they're likely to try it, too. Better yet, name some satisfied acquaintances that the Interacting Socializer knows and admires. He may even respond with, "Go no further. If it's good enough for Frederick Mullens, it's good enough for me. He probably spent weeks researching, comparing, and contrasting. He really knows what he's doing. You should put that guy on your payroll."

#4—gaining commitment with the I

Be open and ask, "Where do we go from here?" or, "What's our next step?" If your inventory is low, tell them. "I see you really are excited about this. I only have three left. Do you want one now?" Interacting Socializers are very spontaneous and respond well to the bandwagon approach "Everybody's doing it." If they like something, they buy it (all other things being equal). You may have to hold them back because they also tend to overbuy, a behavior that both you and your customer may live to regret.

Interacting Socializers don't like paperwork and details, so they're likely to hesitate, and even procrastinate, when it comes to spending the time required to create a commitment letter specifying who does what by when. "Do you really think I won't live up to my word?" While a handshake is usually good enough for them, you'd be wise to have a written understanding. Both of you may hear the same words, but Interacting Socializers tend to interpret those words in a positive light—and often to their advantage. For this reason, it may help to draw up a summary in advance and go over it with this type of prospect. Make absolutely sure that you agree on the specifics or, later on, you can almost bet on some degree of misunderstanding and disappointment.

When the Interacting Socializer tells you a written agreement isn't necessary, simply say that you need such a clear summary for your own benefit so as to help yourself and others remember what is expected. Also mention that you appreciate their show of faith in you. You might say something like, "I just want to make sure that we're in 100% agreement, Mark. I'll feel better about this if I keep a record for us to have if we ever need to refer to it in the future." When you put your concerns in terms of such desired positive feelings, how can the Interacting Socializer object?

"Okay, if it will make you feel better about it, but I'm already 100% sure," he may respond. Next, if required, change whatever details require changing and the job will be done, quickly and painlessly. Finally, go ahead and write up this agreement as a means of verification and send or, better yet, give him a copy in person. Then you'll have a much better shot at a more long-standing, productive business relationship.

#5—assuring I satisfaction

In business, as in love, Interacting Socializers frequently buy before they're sold. When they jump in too quickly, the probability that they may suffer buyers' remorse is higher than for the other personality types. Interacting Socializers need ongoing reminders that they've made the right purchase decision because they get bored quickly, even with new things. So make sure you reinforce their decision by giving them plenty of service and/or assistance immediately after the sale. Be certain they actually do use your product, or this type may get frustrated from incorrect usage and either put it away"never to be used again—or return it for a refund.

Think of yourself as an organizer for a basically less organized type to allow them to get the most out of your product. As a bonus for the extra effort, remember that they tend to *talk up* or *talk down* whatever pops into their minds. Since they mingle with so many people, you can even ask them if they would be willing to share with others their glowing testimonials about you and your product or service.

SALES and SERVICE STRATEGIES FOR DEALING WITH INTERACTING SOCIALIZERS:

- Show that you're interested in them, let them talk, and allow your animation and enthusiasm to emerge
- Take the initiative by introducing yourself in a friendly and informal manner and be open to new topics which seem to interest them
- Support their dreams and goals
- Illustrate your ideas with stories and emotional descriptions that they can relate to their goals or interests
- Clearly summarize details and direct these towards mutually agreeable objectives and action steps
- Provide incentives to encourage quicker decisions
- Give them testimonials

How to Sell Your Product or Service to Steady Relaters

Steady Relaters, concerned with maintaining stability for themselves, want to know step-by-step procedures that are likely to meet their need for details and logical follow-through action. Organize your presentation—list specifics, show sequences, and provide data. If possible, outline your proposals or materials. Satisfy their need to know the facts, but also elicit their personal feelings and emotions by asking for their input on "how to" aspects.

Listen patiently to Steady Relaters, projecting your true interest in them as individuals in their own right. Express your appreciation for their steadiness, dependability, and cooperative teamwork. Get to know Steady Relaters personally. Flex yourself to be non-threatening, pleasant, friendly, but still professional. Develop trust, credibility, and friendship at a relatively slow, informal pace. Then communicate with them in a consistent manner on as regular a basis as is required.

#1—making contact with the S

Contacts with to Steady Relaters are best when soft, pleasant, and specific. Include the human element as well as references to things. Mention the name of the person who referred you. "Hello, Mr. Newhouse, I'm Sheldon Doolittle with the Pinpoint Acupuncture Clinic. Mary Walsh said you would appreciate knowing about me and my clinic. Oh, she did call you? Good. If you'd like, I could come by, we could get to know each other, and I can tell you about the ways other people have relieved their allergies with our treatments." Remember, you may have the best product or service in the world, but if the Steady Relater doesn't like you, she'll settle for second, or even fourth best, from a salesperson she likes.

#2—studying S needs

Steady Relaters can be excellent interviewees. Talk warmly and informally and ask gentle, open questions that draw them out, especially around more sensitive areas. Show tact and sincerity in probing about their needs. "Mr. Harmon, I noticed that you've been here for 30 years. You must have seen a lot. Hypothetically speaking, how would you go about refining a few of the things that aren't working around here in the Information Systems Department?"

If they do not have a good feeling about your product, company, or even you, they will not take the chance of hurting your feelings by telling you so. They want to avoid confrontations, even minor ones. So Steady Relaters may tell you what they think you like to hear, rather than what they really think. This same reticence may apply to telling you about their dissatisfaction with your competitors. Even though this is exactly what you want to hear, the Steady Relater may think, "I know it hasn't been working well, but they're such nice people. I don't want to say anything negative about them."

#3—proposing solutions for S's

Show how your product/service will stabilize, simplify, or support their procedures and relationships. Clearly define their roles and goals in your suggestions, and include specific expectations of them in your plan. Present new ideas or variations from their current routines in a non-threatening way. Provide them with the time and opportunities to adjust to changes in operating procedures and relationships. When change becomes necessary, tell them why. Explain how long the changes will take and any interim alterations of the current conditions. Design your message to impart a sense of stability and security. "This plan will enable you to continue doing things the same basic way, with a few updates here and there. Don't worry about the updates because I'll be here to walk you through them each step of the way. And the real benefit, in the final analysis, is that this refinement will result in more stability than we now have."

Concentrate on security, harmony, steadiness, and concrete benefits. "This pension plan could help your entire staff save for their retirement with a minimum amount of worry. Even though Social Security may be tapped out by the time they retire, they'll be able to depend on this safety net." Answer their concerns about how and what as well as you can. Reassure them that you'll find out about the information they want to know; then do it. Stress that this isn't a big change, just a way to help them do what they already do . . . only better.

Steady Relaters like to be shown the appropriate steps to follow, so share those with them. "After you turn the equipment on, push the blue button to activate the computer. When you hear the motor, begin." Involve them by asking their opinions. "Is this an important concern for you, or are you looking for some other specific benefit, instead?"

#4—gaining commitment with the S

Steady Relaters are slow, deductive decision makers. They listen to the opinions of others and take the time to solicit those opinions before making up their minds. So make a specific action plan. Provide personal guidance, direction, or assurance as required for pursuing the safest, most logical course to follow. When you reach agreement, try to explore any potential areas of misunderstanding or dissatisfaction. Steady Relaters like guarantees that new actions will involve a minimum risk to their desired stable state, so offer assurances of support.

Try not to rush them, but do provide gentle, helpful nudges to help them decide, when needed. Otherwise, they may postpone their decisions. Involve them by personalizing the plan and showing how it will directly impact them and their co-workers. "Our system will identify which employees deserve immediate raises at a faster rate than our old method." When asking for a commitment, guide them toward a choice if they seem indecisive. "We've gone over all the possibilities for improving customer service, Seymour. I think this option is the best because it will generate the most customer interest. Why don't we go ahead and implement it now?"

Another approach is to lead Steady Relaters. Once you have determined which action is in their best interest, lead them to the confirmation with your recommendation. "Jean, we've talked about a lot of things and I firmly believe this is the best solution for you. I would not recommend it if I wasn't 100% convinced it will work for you." When you've gained agreement, you can gently lead the Steady Relater to the next step. "If you agree with everything we've just discussed, our next typical step with a customer is to fill out the agreement and then begin the process with a deposit."

There is nothing pushy or manipulative about this if you have studied your prospect's needs and are now recommending a solution that you honestly believe best satisfies their needs. Then it's a win-win situation. Anything less is actually a losing proposition for this prospect.

SALES AND SERVICE STRATEGIES FOR DEALING WITH STEADY RELATERS:

- Get to know them more personally and approach them in a non-threatening, pleasant, and friendly . . . but professional . . . way
- Develop trust, friendship, and credibility at a relatively slow pace
- Ask them to identify their own emotional needs as well as their task or business expectations
- Get them involved by focusing on the *human element* . . . that is, how something affects them and their relationships with others
- Avoid rushing them and give them personal, concrete assurances, when appropriate
- Communicate with them in a consistent manner on a regular basis

---

#5—assuring S's satisfaction

Practice consistent and predictable followup. Give them your personal guarantee that you will remain in touch, keep things running smoothly, and be available on an *as needed* basis. Steady Relaters like to think they have a special relationship with you, that you are more than just another business acquaintance. Remember they dislike one-shot deals, so follow up to maintain your relationship. Of all the types, they most prefer a continuing, predictable relationship. Impersonal, computerized follow-through is not as appealing to this type, so continue building your business relationship with your low-keyed attention and offers of assistance. "I'll call on you once each month to make sure you're satisfied with our product. If you have any problems or concerns at all, just phone me at my office and I'll get back to you as soon as I can. In fact, here's my home number."

How to Sell a Product or Service to Cautious Thinkers

Cautious Thinkers are precision people, efficiency experts who want to do their jobs as they want to do nearly everything else: the correct way. They also seek confirmation that they're right, but won't typically volunteer that need. Going about tasks slowly so they have enough time to check things out, they dislike rushing or being rushed. They operate on a level that prefers *thinking* words, not *feeling* ones, so build your credibility by remembering to think with your head, not with your emotions. Focus on their level of understanding about the *what's* and *why's* of your proposal.

#1—making contact with the C

Before meeting, tell them briefly what you'll cover so they know what to expect. This can be done when you make the appointment. Show them logical proof from reliable sources that accurately documents your quality, track record, and value. Once you've verified your credentials, preferably in writing or with tangible examples (make copies of a few), you can establish your product's or service's credentials, too.

Speak slowly. Economize on words. Explain why you are contacting them. This type doesn't care as much about social interaction, beyond courtesy and pleasantness, so get to the point. Avoid making small talk and speaking about yourself, except to initially establish your credibility. Cautious Thinkers tend to be somewhat humble and are naturally suspicious of those who *talk themselves up.*

#2—studying C needs

Cautious Thinkers often like to answer questions that reveal their expertise, so they can be very good interviewees. As long as you ask logical, fact-oriented, relevant questions, they tend to enjoy talking to you. Phrase your questions to help them give you the right information. "How many pages of completed copy do you typically write per week?" Ask open and closed questions that investigate their knowledge, systems, objectives, and objections. "When do you foresee finishing this project?" or "What possible problems do you think you might encounter?" Let them show you how much they know.

Make your own answers short and crisp. If you don't know the answer to something, don't fake it. Tell them you'll get the answer for them by a certain time, then do it.

#3—proposing solutions for C's

Emphasize logic, accuracy, value, quality, and reliability. Present obvious disadvantages. Make your points, then ask if they want further clarification. They dislike talk that isn't backed up with both supporting evidence and achievement-focused action. Describe the process that you plan to follow. Then outline how that process will produce the results they seek. Elicit specific feedback. "So far, what are your reactions? Do you have any reservations that you'd like to clear up?" (They probably do, so encourage communication.) "Specifically, how do you view the practicality of applying this computer program to satisfy your current requirements?"

Of all the types, this one is the most likely to see the drawbacks, so point out the negatives before they do. Such honesty will only enhance your credibility. If you don't draw attention to the disadvantages, this type may view your failure to do so as a cover-up. Instead, let them assess the relative costs versus benefits which are typical trade-offs when making realistic choices between available, competing, yet imperfect, products or services.

#4—gaining commitment with the C

Provide logical options with documentation. Give them enough time and data to analyze their options. Unlike Dominant Directors and Interacting Socializers, this type is uncomfortable with snap decisions. When they say they'll think about it, they're probably serious. On the other hand, when a Steady Relater says, "I'll think about it," he may be stalling, or may, in fact, not want your product.

Unless Cautious Thinkers have already researched the field and determined that your product is the best, they probably have your competitors calling on them. Know your competition so you can point out your advantages relative to what

---

SALES AND SERVICE STRATEGIES FOR DEALING WITH CAUTIOUS THINKERS:

- Prepare, so that you can answer as many of their questions as soon as possible
- Greet them cordially, but proceed quickly to the task; don't start with personal or social talk
- Hone your skills in practicality and logic
- Ask questions that reveal a clear direction and that fit into the overall scheme of things
- Document how and why something applies
- Give them time to think; avoid pushing them into a hasty decision
- Tell them both the pros and cons and the complete story
- Follow through and deliver what you promise

---

they offer. This type is the most likely to do their own comparative shopping, so mention your company's strengths as you suggest questions they may want to ask your competitors. "Ask them if they have an unconditional money-back guarantee," or, "How long have you been in business?" or, "Will they also train new employees at no additional cost?" In short, point out the things your company does as well or better than your competition. Do this in a factual, professional way that is based on allowing them to do a comparative *cost-benefit* analysis of the options.

#5—*assuring C customer satisfaction*

Set a specific timetable for when you'll measure success. Continue proving your reliability, quality, and value. Make yourself available for followup on customer satisfaction. "Mr. Quimby, I'll check back with you on Tuesday morning, if that's all right, to make sure that your new phone system is functioning correctly. Here's my card with the numbers of my office, home, and emergency 24-hour hotline if you experience any problems."

Part Three

Personal Applications

Chapter 8
The Social Scene

Accentuate the positive

Again, to get the most out of this material, picture real people you know who fit each of the basic four descriptions in a social setting. What are each one's more effective traits in a social encounter? The less effective ones? As you read, visualize how you can maximize your communication with each of them by appealing to their natural strengths.

Dominant Director Social Behaviors

A time and place for everything

By their nature, Dominant Directors are motivated to manage, lead, organize and rule. At times, however, this may be inappropriate; for instance, at someone's wedding, funeral or social lunch. For many Dominant Directors, respecting people's rights and opinions, allowing others to take charge, and just plain *letting go* are learned, acquired behaviors. Yet these are precisely the behaviors that can enable Dominant Directors to experience enhanced emotional satisfaction in their personal and social relationships.

The point must be clear

"Why are we doing this?" a Dominant Director might ask, especially if she has something better in mind. She doesn't like to participate in fun for fun's sake, but for a specific purpose. Regardless of how friendly the atmosphere or close her relationship to others involved, this type generally tries her hardest to be the best—and win—whether in the boardroom promoting an idea or the living room playing a party game. She tends to give 100% effort. She's not interested in a lot of details or in postponing her quest for victory with conversation, jokes, or other digressions.

Business and friendships often overlap for Dominant Directors. They like to mix their own business interests with pleasure, so they often pick friends from their work pool. When they find time for making friends, they do it by experimentation. If the experiment works, and it often hinges on how much potential friends agree with them and help them get desired results, great! If not, goodbye! Also, they don't like doing anything they don't want to do. For instance, they may very well bring their own cars to escape early, disappear to make a phone call, start reading the newspaper, or otherwise do something they enjoy.

The joke is often on you!

Dominant Directors favor humor that's to the point and pulls no punches, often with more than a bit of self-importance thrown in! They have been known to enjoy making fun of others. Don Rickles, Joan Rivers, and Roseanne Barr have all built careers from this type of perspective. Generally speaking, though, in many settings, Dominant Directors tend to take themselves too seriously. A well-placed joke can often help them and others benefit from laughing more and enjoying the humorous side of their own and others' actions.

Do You Really Want to Know?

If the Dominant Director just wants to kick back, that, too, is his decision. But he may prefer running an activity or pulling strings to get things done. Just ask and he'll generally tell you. As one astute observer noticed, "If you can't handle the answer, don't ask the question." Naturally blunt, Directors tend to tell it like it is—at least from their perspective.

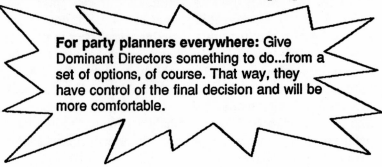

For party planners everywhere: Give Dominant Directors something to do...from a set of options, of course. That way, they have control of the final decision and will be more comfortable.

It's whether you win

Dominant Directors may engage in what they view as healthy competition with their more assertive friends. This can accelerate to a battlefield of keeping up with the Joneses if not monitored by all concerned. Who has the biggest, most expensive house? Who gives the best parties? Who has the most charming personality? And on and on. Dominant Director friends may even compete in catching each other in inconsistencies. "No one was supposed to start yet, Dom. I'm just repeating what you said, remember? Penalty, here!" Often Directors need to learn to cultivate tact and diplomacy, instead of telling others how they feel so bluntly that it yields counterproductive results for their social relationships.

Social niceties aside, Dominant Directors usually do not want to be saddled with the worst player(s) when they're working hard at winning. Knowing that Howard has virtually no know-how in *Trivial Pursuit* and that the hostess favors man versus woman teams, Dominant Director Marv may suggest, "Why don't we play with four teams instead of two? Carol, you and I can be partners." If he can avoid almost certain defeat with Howard, he'll do it.

Similarly, when this type works on an activity and strives to win, they keep score. "The men have beaten the women at Trivial Pursuit the last four times we've played. This time won't be any different." Then they may naturally immerse themselves in the game, sometimes provoking hurt feelings, and even heckling, along the way. "I can't believe you don't know the answer to that question. And you were an English major?" Downplaying their verbalizations of superiority can result in everyone having a better time. It is only a game!

They love taking the credit

One Dominant Director trait that can drive people up the proverbial wall is when they hear or read about a good idea and come to believe the concept really originated with themselves. "When the doctor told Rob to eat less and exercise more, I suggested that he join the Beach and Tennis Club and offered to sponsor him. Now he's claiming that the whole thing was his idea!" Maybe Rob actually believes it himself. Remember, Directors need to be in charge. When they think they're firmly in the driver's seat, their fear of relinquishing the controls to anyone else lessens. So creating ideas (or thinking they do) fits into that pattern of maintaining control. If you can live with that, fine. If not, jostle their memories in private in a joking way.

Lost without a task

For many Dominant Directors, learning what to do in situations that don't require "giving it their all" can be a difficult lesson. Director Melody says that when she was at a Super Bowl party, where everyone sat around and watched TV, she had no idea what to do. She usually tries to avoid situations like that because she literally doesn't know how to act. "When I'm not focused on a task, I'm very uncomfortable." Melody could benefit from letting go occasionally and allowing events and conversations to just happen, instead of looking for some heavy, underlying purpose.

Dealing with Dominant Directors

Remember they have a basic need to feel and be in personal control. They don't like thinking that you may be considering competing with, exploiting, or otherwise using them. As a result, try to convey your openness and acceptance of them as individuals through both your non-verbal and verbal responses. "Harry, you're still an unbelievable go-getter whether you win at this game of Monopoly or not."

Remember . . .

DOMINANT DIRECTOR:
TYPICAL SOCIAL BEHAVIOR

- Actively compete
- Play games to win
- Want to know the purpose of a function
- Like playing with toys and hobbies
- Play parallel to, but not necessarily with, others
- Prone to talk shop at gatherings
- Choose friends by experimentation

DOMINANT DIRECTOR:
PREFERRED SOCIAL SITUATIONS

- Want options from which to choose: Example: either swimming, dining out, or playing bridge
- Pay more attention to concrete things, less to emotions
- Resistant to doing anything they don't want to
- Favor direct humor with a touch of superiority
- Prefer groups subject to their control
- Like being in charge of something at social events and activities—score-keeping, judging, giving directions, cooking, chairing a fund-raiser

Action Plan ...

WHEN *YOU* ARE THE DOMINANT DIRECTOR

- Consciously concentrate on listening to others
- Respond positively to others' feelings
- Apologize or admit mistakes, when appropriate
- Slow down and take time to smell the roses
- Cultivate a less serious outlook
- Admit, and then laugh at, personal limitations
- View a game as a game and not life or death!
- Give sincere compliments
- Cultivate tact and diplomacy

WHEN OTHERS ARE DOMINANT DIRECTORS

- Convey openness and acceptance of them
- Listen to their suggestions
- Summarize your achievements/accomplishments
- Give them your time and undivided attention
- Appreciate and acknowledge them when possible
- Ensure all activities will be acceptable to them
- Meet their expectations when possible
- Focus on how pleased you are with their results
- Thank them for their contribution

Socializing with D's

They have a need to be considered important by others. Therefore, give them your time, undivided attention, and genuine appreciative acknowledgment when possible and appropriate. By watching their response, you'll probably know whether your actions are satisfying an important unfulfilled need for them. You'll also learn if some other need—in communication or decision making, for example—requires filling. "Hal, you're a take charge kind of guy. Why not see that we get these jobs done so we can hasten this party along."

Interacting Socializer Social Behavior

"People who love people"

Interacting Socializers specialize in just that—socializing. Most aspects of their lives are open books. They're likely to tolerate most subjects, no matter how close or remote your relationship. Showing and sharing their feelings come naturally to this personality type. Of the four groups, Interacting Socializers feel most comfortable talking about personal topics—marriage, finances, politics, aspirations, and problems—in the first 15 minutes of conversation, or, in more intense Interacting Socializers, even in the first five minutes. They also jump from one activity or topic to another. After a conversation with one, you may think, "Wow-ee! Uh, what did we just talk about?" Or "Their thoughts are like gumballs. They just fall to their tongues and roll out."

Did you hear the one about?

Events that may strike terror in the hearts of the other types often become positive experiences for Interacting Socializers. And, as adults, their hair-raising personal anecdotes make exciting, entertaining conversation pieces. So they delight in recreating their near-crash-en-route-to-London saga or their love-at-first-sight stories. The more unique the situation, the better. And of course, Interacting Socializers may embellish a story so it sounds better than what literally took place. They view this tendency toward stretching the truth as *spicing things up* for interested listeners. Since they love to talk, telling a story better and funnier than it happened comes naturally to them. Upon occasion, the more talkative Interacting Socializers have been known not to let facts get in the way of a good yarn.

Oh. Was that confidential?

This tendency may cause problems when friends tell secrets to Interacting Socializers. Unless they're expressly told not to tell anyone about confidential information, Interacting Socializers are not likely to realize the importance of remaining silent out of respect for others.

When you divulge your innermost fears to an Interacting Socializer, he's likely to encourage you with a pep talk. "I know you can do it, Harry! Whatever you decide, I know that decision will work out okay for you. Good luck, Buddy!" Interacting Socializers praise and support others en route to creating a positive environment where they can satisfy their own needs for social approval. They hate isolation, so they sometimes support others to prolong social interaction. Plus, compliments and encouragement make Interacting Socializers feel good, even when they're meant for somebody else. If no one praises him, he's likely to turn his attention to someone else's upbeat comments.

Life of the party!

This type also likes to wax poetic and exaggerate. We know one who, when attending her son's baseball games, cheered the batters on with personalized nicknames—Robert the Rocket, Slugger Seth, Go Johnny Go, Handy Andy, and so on. The other parents called her the resident poet laureate. They either enjoyed or tolerated her enthusiasm. Fortunately for her, no one told her to stop. Interacting Socializers seem to invite controversy, but the best approach in dealing with them is to behave non-judgmentally. If you express your disagreement, they love a good debate, as long as nobody else dominates it; they don't like too much head-to-head competition where they may lose face.

At parties, Interacting Socializers typically meet more people in the room than do the other types. They may stand with their arms around each other, hug, or show some other outward expression of their support for others. After all, it's a perfect setting for them to gain socially acceptable approval from many people in the same place and in a short period of time. They tend to be life of the party types who can make the transition to party animals relatively easily. We know one who makes extra money hiring himself out as a professional mingler and conversation starter at social functions.

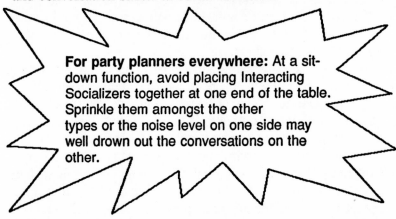

For party planners everywhere: At a sit-down function, avoid placing Interacting Socializers together at one end of the table. Sprinkle them amongst the other types or the noise level on one side may well drown out the conversations on the other.

They love the dynamics of relationships and talking; they despise feeling bored. People rally around them because they know how to create fun and find the action. Of the four types, the Interacting Socializers are the most like playful porpoises; they need to feel that many others enjoy their companionship.

That's the general idea

Interacting Socializers typically speak more vaguely when using facts and logic than do the other types. "I read about a case like this last year—in England, I think." Or, they may exaggerate and generalize facts and details they don't know. For example, they tend to round up: "Yeah, Andy made around $100,000 last year." (Actually, Andy only made $75,345.17.) Interacting Socializers feel more comfortable using "best guesstimates" than do the other types. Saki (H. H. Munro), a short story writer, succinctly described this Interacting Socializer tendency when he wrote: "A little inaccuracy sometimes saves tons of explanation." At the extreme, exaggerators like the ad character Joe Isuzu fit this description.

Interacting Socializers may even adopt quotes that strike a fond chord and then conveniently forget the source. As Buckaroo Banzai said, "Wherever you go, there you are." Next, it may change to, As someone once said, "Wherever you go . . ." Finally, extreme Interacting Socializers may say, "As I've always said, Wherever . . ." After a few usages, they may figure that it becomes theirs.

I's are sensitive

Of the four types, Interacting Socializers tend to exhibit the most emotionally sensitive qualities. They naturally scan people's body language, vocal inflections, and eye contact to determine how real the person's feelings seem to be. Their natural, emotional radar system leads them to quickly formulate their "intuitive" feelings about people. Besides feeling sensitivity for others, they also take perceived slights to heart, so their feelings get hurt rather easily. In fact, at the extreme, they can act so sensitive when it comes to their favorite subject—themselves—that others may perceive them as caring only about *me, me, me!* This habit of bringing their own names, achievements, experiences, and stories into conversations can give others the impression that they're less serious or concerned than they really are. As with any behavior, too much of a good thing can result in overkill.

Slapstick humor and belly laughs

When it comes to humor, Interacting Socializers prefer poking fun at themselves and others. They delight in slapstick humor and belly laughs that smack of high emotion. They look at the lighter side of serious subjects and our own idiosyncrasies and limitations. Rodney Dangerfield, Buddy Hackett, George Carlin, Norm Crosby, Carol Burnett, Gallagher, Dom Deluise, Goldie Hawn, Tracy Ullman, and Jackie Mason all deliver their lines along this self-deprecating (and sometimes other-deprecating), physical vein. These Interacting Socializer comedians involve their audience in characteristic *let loose* ways, leaving them with a lasting impression far beyond the influence of their non-stop talking act.

Lovers of gadgets, bells and whistles

Adult Interacting Socializers love gadgets, but they tend to prefer them most with the works—bells, whistles, and gongs! They also like to be the first ones on their block to own the new whatchamacallit nobody else has even heard of yet. This type may become captivated by calculators that double as video games or watches with alarms, radios, and TV screens. This gadget mentality reflects the need to seek out fun, as well as ways to simplify or lessen unavoidable types of work. Flurries of activity coupled with an opportunity for seeing and being seen constitute a nearly resistance-proof formula for attracting an Interacting Socializer.

I's enjoy making a grand entrance!

Showing up fashionably late is a technique appealing to many individuals of this type. The grander the entrance into a roomful of people, the greater the impact for Interacting Socializers. But sometimes they legitimately forget the details of their social obligations and then tend to fly by the seats of their pants. They may amble in an hour late to a dinner party, then feel embarrassed and say, "Gosh, I thought I was supposed to arrive any time between 7:00 and 9:00!" This type can avoid some of these minor tragedies by reading invitations thoroughly, putting them in a prominent, visible spot, and highlighting key points—such as when and where.

We know one Interacting Socializer who missed her best friend Amy's surprise bridal shower, given by Amy's law firm, because she misplaced the invitation. Ordinarily, Interacting Sheila would have relied on Amy as an optional strategy to keep the details straight. But Sheila didn't call the office to find out more because she didn't want to arouse Amy's suspicions. Two days after the shower, Sheila found the invitation and ended up apologizing profusely for unintentionally, yet somewhat predictably, standing up her friend.

Flight before fight

When stressful situations prevail, Interacting Socializers may say something like, "Boy, you could cut the tension in this room with a chain saw." They typically diffuse conflict with a joke or funny observation. Or they downplay the tension by trying to smooth things over. "C'mon, this isn't worth fighting over, is it?" They prefer to minimize stress by ignoring it. Under extreme pressure, Interacting Socializers bail out; to avoid a fight, they take flight. If stress continues to build, they tend to lead with their hearts, sacrificing logic to gut feelings. When they finally do fight, they do so emotionally. At their worst, they may name call or insult their adversary, sometimes saying things in anger which they regret later.

You can't please all the people all the time

It's difficult for the Interacting Socializer to accept that there are some folks out there who will not be charmed by his exciting personality and warmth. Some more controlled, precise behavioral types may even view more extreme Interacting Socializer behavior as flakiness or *form over substance*. The Interacting Socializer may worry about the disapproving person and attempt to win him over with his customary show of intimacy, perhaps divulging a deep personal secret which he feels may create a bond between the two of them. But this may only widen the rift; depending on the other person's behavioral type, he may expect the Interacting Socializer to behave more formally and seriously, with more facts and thoroughness.

Socializing with them

They want to be considered important and need recognition from others, both privately and publicly. You can demonstrate that you like and enjoy being with them by giving your attention, time, and physical presence in sharing common activities with them. "Let's share a position on the PTA Board next year so we can do more things together. We'll have a great time!"

Remember that they need to feel accepted and worry-free regarding others' approval of them. Therefore, focus on a positive, upbeat, and warm approach which conveys this

Remember . . .

INTERACTING SOCIALIZER:
TYPICAL SOCIAL BEHAVIOR

- Want to be liked and admired
- Fear public humiliation
- Will discuss most subjects, regardless of how distant or casual your relationship
- Are naturally warm, expressive and enthusiastic
- Enjoy bouncing ideas off others
- Are reluctant to fight or confront stressful people or situations
- Perceive life according to feelings
- Naturally discuss emotions with others
- Choose associates and friends by trial and error

INTERACTING SOCIALIZER:
PREFERRED SOCIAL SITUATIONS

- Prefer physical contact
- Like hosting or attending impromptu gatherings
- Prefer fun people with different interests
- Seek more positive people and settings
- Find it easy to laugh, joke and play games
- Seek higher visibility positions: host, emcee, etc.
- Prefer humor that pokes fun at their own and others' foibles
- Try to diffuse mild tension with jokes or funny observations
- Prefer to ignore stressors
  Like to share the moment with others

Action Plan . . .

IF YOU ARE
THE INTERACTING SOCIALIZER

- Speak less and listen more
- Focus on facts as well as feelings
- Stick to the subject!
- Realize you can't please everyone
- Fulfill social obligations responsibly and on time
- Work at following through to completion
- Balance socializing with tasks
- Avoid procrastination
- Focus more on substance, less on form

IF OTHERS ARE
INTERACTING SOCIALIZERS

- Focus on a positive, upbeat, warm approach
- Listen to their personal feelings and experiences
- Respond openly and congenially
- Avoid negative or messy problem discussions
- Make suggestions that allow them to look good
- Do not require a lot of difficult, followup, detail work or longer-term commitments from them
- Give them your attention, time and presence
- Publicly and privately acknowledge them
- Suggest different opinions, ideas, and actions by offering them as desirable *gifts*
- Focus on how glad you are when they succeed

attitude towards them. "Simon, we've been eagerly awaiting your arrival. Now the party has officially started!"

Steady Relater Social Behaviors

To find the answer, look within

Steady Relaters are actually quiet, evenly paced, and inwardly focused individuals. They recharge their batteries and renew their energy by looking for answers within themselves and a relatively small group of friends, family, and associates. As warm and open as they may appear, they have private thoughts they're unwilling to divulge to almost anyone. Their energy drains when called upon to tell all.

They're optimistic realists

Steady Relaters distrust the intangible. They dislike deviating from the established order and dealing with abstractions, preferring instead to follow a predetermined, sensible format. Like Sancho Panza in Don Quixote, their feet stay firmly planted on the ground in concrete reality.

They like routine, predictability, and stability. Consequently, they tend to anchor the other types with their patience, cooperation, and follow-through. They need a firm grip on the facts before feeling ready to proceed, so provide them with step-by-step information whenever possible. They enjoy team efforts and work willingly to bolster comfortable, efficient working conditions.

A pleasant time is the name of the game

People of this type often like to support and encourage everyone concerned, not just the kids on their own child's sports teams, for example. Priscilla usually roots for everyone on both soccer teams. "Nancy, your Cindy is such a conscientious goalie, she's caught every ball so far. Oh, my Laurie has the ball now. O-o-o-oh! Too bad, Laurie. Next time. But good catch, Cindy." We know one Steady Relater dad who had to leave a game early. As he walked away, he actually called out, "I hope the team that plays the best and acts the nicest wins.

And, remember, Carrie, enjoy yourself playing no matter what!"

Party time for S's

At parties, Steady Relaters like to seek out people they know quite well, or make advance arrangements to go to the event with someone else they know has been invited. Then they may end up conversing with that same person all night unless they remind themselves to mingle. They prefer having others approach them. In fact, they may project such a calm, accepting attitude that others often do seek them out. Sometimes, their peaceful demeanor can elicit unexpected responses. "Paul, this is only the second time I've talked with you, but I feel as though I could talk to you about almost anything." Paul may involuntarily blush, but after the fact, he may feel satisfied and appreciated by the compliment.

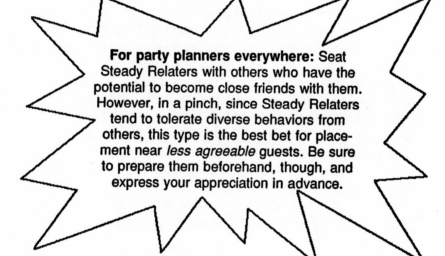

For party planners everywhere: Seat Steady Relaters with others who have the potential to become close friends with them. However, in a pinch, since Steady Relaters tend to tolerate diverse behaviors from others, this type is the best bet for placement near *less agreeable* guests. Be sure to prepare them beforehand, though, and express your appreciation in advance.

Low-keyed cheerleaders

Steady Relaters often spur on their group's effort in team board games: Pictionary, Scruples, or Trivial Pursuit, for instance. When it's their turn, though, they may inwardly cringe at the thought of all eyes being on them. They usually prefer to work behind the scenes and let others (often Dominant Directors and Interacting Socializers) accept the starring roles. They naturally tend to spread the credit around. "Joel is the one who came up with the answer. I just helped him a little."

Safe, stable relationships

They often choose friends by the test-of-time method. That is, if the relationships last, then they're the genuine article, safe and dependable. Like Interacting Socializers, they operate somewhat on a feeling level. However, for them, steady thinking comes first. They depend on ways of keeping their lives stable and secure. General conformity is one means used to satisfy their need to feel included by others. Steady Relaters like sincere attention from people and enjoy feeling well liked. They find it easy to listen and have a natural preference for participative communications. In fact, they can almost act so nice dogs seem to want to walk up and pet them!

Extreme niceness can equal gullibility

At times, the flip side of this niceness is that it can present real problems. For instance, they may respond too carefully to people so as not to hurt their feelings. Consequently, they find it hard to muster up an occasional no, often allowing more assertive types to take advantage of them. Steady Relater Michelle fits this modus operandi to a T. She's just a girl who can't say no. While driving from a San Diego shopping mall one drizzly afternoon, she stopped for a red light. After a second or two, she noticed a clicking sound on the passenger side of her car. Michelle turned to see a middle-aged woman with an armload of packages opening her door. Instinctively, Michelle moved her own bags from the passenger seat so the woman could sit down.

"Can you drive me to my mother's?" the stranger asked.

Michelle says she heard herself reply, "Sure. Do you need to make any other stops on the way?"

Luckily, the woman answered, "I just want to get there before it rains any harder."

So Michelle dutifully went out of her way to drive her new acquaintance to her mother's, without a hint that anything about their encounter seemed out of the ordinary. In fact, she says she drove all the way home before actually realizing that something unusual had happened.

Patient people may finish first

Steady Relaters are often naturals at eliciting others' feelings. When it comes to venting, they can be virtual shock absorbers. If a hotel or airplane becomes overbooked, for example, a Steady Relater may typically patiently wait his turn in line to confirm his reservation—despite the fact that a disgruntled person ahead of him has announced there is no more space available. Having listened to a barrage of complaints from the people ahead of him, the Steady Relater finally reaches the harried desk clerk. "It looks like you've been having a bad day." When the clerk nods her ascent, the Steady Relater says, "What happened? Would you like to tell me about it?"

The poor woman tells him her frustration about the bad weather and the overbooked conditions, then heaves a sigh of relief. Poof! Her burden is gone! (We call this the poof phenomenon.) She looks gratefully at this patient *sounding board*, now more calmly stating, "Even though all of our regular space is booked, we still have the Presidential Suite (or first class seating) open. Would you like to have it, at no extra charge?"

Lesson: Humble and patient people may inherit a hotel room (or other perks) just for displaying genuine concern and thinking of others first, rather than themselves.

An even keel

In the best of all Steady Relater social worlds, everyone would act friendly, pleasant, and cooperative. No one would strongly disagree, yell, participate in rowdy scenes, or talk anyone into anything against their will. Realistically, though"and this type does operate in a realistic mode—they generally prefer that people they associate with function without making a ruckus out of trivial matters. But they often accept others at face value. "Carl is really a nice guy. He's just rattled about a few things today." They tend to judge people by how they act with them, not according to other people's experiences with them. "I feel sad for Steve when I hear Jack and Bonnie tell those stories about how obnoxious he can be, but he hasn't done anything like that to me. Until he does, I still want to be friendly with him."

The present may be good, but the past is better

"Make new friends, but keep the old; one is silver and the other gold," lines from an old Girl Scout song, apply to Steady Relater types. Chances are they still keep in contact with childhood friends, or even teachers or now-retired doctors. Because familiarity feels so comfortable to them, they may prefer to live in the same neighborhood or area as they did during childhood. Their memorabilia tends to mean more to Steady Relaters than to the other types. It makes them feel more connected to the present, more secure. In this respect, they are possessive about things they own. Similarly, if something has worked in the past, they'll probably try it again. In most aspects of their lives, new or different things don't appeal to them as much as the *good ole* tried and true.

The same activities other types may perceive as monotonous often appeal to a Steady Relater's desire for repetition. Lunch at Leon's on Mondays from 12:00 to 1:00, Tuesday night movies with their best friends, and Friday night aerobics classes with the exercise gang from 6:00 to 7:00 at the Y perpetuate Steady Relaters' fondness for regularity. For them, familiarity doesn't breed contempt, but contentment!

Similarly, Steady Relaters exhibit a rather dry, straightforward, seemingly uncomplicated sense of humor. Henny Youngman's one liners or the perennial George Burns's wit and wisdom often employ just one humor technique, namely the use of reverse logic. They look at life from a slightly skewed, off-center perspective with predictable results in the punch line. Often, the listener can guess the outcome of the joke before it's ever completed.

They keep on keepin' on

Steady Relaters find it difficult to reach beyond their comfort zone and to take chances, so they may need a push to help them grow. They don't give up easily and can persevere for years. But this single-minded resolve has another, darker side, too—stubbornness! Although they might remain quiet about resisting change, they may secretly decide to passively revolt. They naturally let little annoyances slide, overlooking things that bother the other types more.

They may bail out

Although Steady Relaters exhibit more patience and long-suffering behaviors than many of their counterparts, they sometimes allow certain irritations to build up for so long that the burden becomes overwhelming. Because they don't like to rock the boat, they may give in rather than take issue with something. Steady Relaters also bruise easily. You may hurt their feelings without realizing it. When this happens, their attitude tends to be, "What did I do now to upset him that way? They have difficulty knowing whether or not they are responsible for another's emotional upset. As a result, they sometimes are rather easily confused or hurt by others and try even harder to improve matters.

What makes them seem so nice?

Steady types may appear almost saintly, simply because they usually don't say anything when something bothers them. They don't want anyone to dislike them. When the chips are down, they're likely to clam up, going into their own protective shell. They often think that if they say what's on their minds, they're less likely to remain friends. So they'll avoid confrontation—their biggest fear—at almost any cost. When confrontation becomes unavoidable, they'll typically submit so the relationship can get back to normal, ASAP.

So this desire for peace and stability can motivate Steady Relaters to succumb to compromise just to maintain favorable conditions or to avoid conflict. Ironically, instead of jeopardizing their position with others, speaking up and taking a stand can sometimes enhance their position—especially with people who may view Steady Relaters' tendency to give in as a weakness. Additionally, voicing their thoughts and feelings before they reach the end of their tolerance level can actually help Steady Relaters salvage some relationships before it's too late.

Dealing with Steady Relaters

Remember their primary need is to maintain stability in their own setting. On the other hand, they also fear and resist those changes which they feel are likely to result in more instability than presently exists. Your best approach is one that focuses on how you want to continue to make things as good as always for them, if not better—but on their terms, as they see it. To demonstrate your friendship, you might say, "Angela, I know your best friend's illness may mean you'll go back to Oklahoma for awhile, but you can count on me to keep an eye on things. I'll make sure Molly gets to school every day and that everything else goes along almost as though you were here."

Socializing with S's

They don't like being in a crowd. Instead, they're more comfortable in smaller groups, with people they've known for a longer time and had pleasant relationships with. They like to do things which are planned or at least known in advance. This provides them with a more predictable social experience with known dimensions—such as when things start and finish, when they will take place, who will be there, and how things will be done. To help them get mentally prepared, spell out the parameters and elicit their input. "John, your role in making telephone calls to organize our community Dance-a-Thon will begin about May 14 and end on the day of the event, October 31. If you make 10 phone calls a day, you'll more than meet our goal of 200 attendees; and, of course, you can invite anyone you choose, too. Are you comfortable with this plan, or would you like to modify it in some specific way?"

Remember . . .

STEADY RELATER:
TYPICAL SOCIAL BEHAVIOR

- Like to build ongoing relationships with a small group of people
- Want to be involved in and identified with their group
- Relate to others on a one-to-one basis . . . preferably with predictable role behavior by each person
- Prefer more casual, calming relationships
- Give and expect sincere attention
- Seek stability in their lives through practices such as conformity

STEADY RELATER:
PREFERRED SOCIAL SITUATIONS

- Like to participate in the group's communication and activities
- Enjoy performing regular activities the same way at the same time and place
- Prefer to communicate in a conflict-free gathering of associates or friends
- Want to know how to play games or complete activities through well-defined, step-by-step procedures
- Like to feel appreciated and well-liked by others, just for who they are and what they contribute

Action Plan

IF YOU ARE THE STEADY RELATER

- Stand up for yourself when others become insistent, or even belligerent
- Respond more favorably to required changes
- Occasionally vary your schedule and try new things
- Expand your circle of acquaintances by participating in activities with new people more frequently
- Respond somewhat less sensitively to others
- Occasionally confront others
- Consciously allow occasional disruption of your peace and stability

IF OTHERS ARE STEADY RELATERS

- Focus on a slower-paced, steady approach
- Avoid arguments and conflict
- Respond sensitively and sensibly
- Privately acknowledge them with specific, believable compliments
- Allow them to follow through on concrete tasks
- Show them step-by-step procedures
- Behave pleasantly and optimistically
- Give them stability and a minimum of change

Cautious Thinker Social Behaviors

Cautious Thinkers ponder

This type has the tendency to contemplate things until the opportunity may well slip away. They like to examine the pros and cons of a given situation, so they want to take everything into account. This need to weigh the possibilities and ramifications can create stress in the more impetuous behavioral types: Dominant Directors and Interacting Socializers. But conversely, Cautious Thinkers' innate caution can serve to modify the more impetuous tendencies of other types so that a workable solution may be reached.

C's are sensitized

If we were to say that Interacting Socializers show the most sensitive behavior, then Cautious Thinkers exhibit the most sensitized behaviors. Their internal antennae are primed to absorb virtually everything around them. As highly intuitive, astute observers of their surroundings, they are like electronic sponges, taking in and processing information about people and things. In fact, Cautious Thinker types often report having difficulty falling asleep and then getting back to sleep if they wake up during the night, saying, "I just can't turn off everything that keeps running through my mind." Additionally, since they are naturally comfortable accessing both the left and right sides of their brains, Cautious Thinkers tend to process many of the complexities of life that escape the other types.

Computerized thinking

Comparatively speaking, Cautious Thinkers operate much like the creator of a computerized program. Initially, they scan the occurrences transpiring through the course of a year. This includes special events or experiences that might require action on their part. An example would be sending cards or gifts to those who've done the same for them—based on their understanding of another's efforts in sending such items. And by the way, if they view such a relationship as lopsided, you may never hear from them again. Above all, they value privacy, individual space, and discretion in their relationships with others.

They act reserved and distant until they feel they know and can trust you well enough to let down their guard. They plan and select their relationships with others strategically and cautiously. Because they're such private people, they sometimes seem mysterious. Like the elusive Greta Garbo, the fabled film star of the '30s, they may want to be alone. Yet, in pursuit of their need for privacy, Cautious Thinkers are tactful, serious, and organized.

Non-verbal clues

When Cautious Thinker Raymond went to a beach party, the party-goers left their garbage wherever it happened to fall. Raymond's facial muscles tightened and he gritted his teeth. Without saying a word, he picked up everyone's litter and threw it in a trash can. But sometimes this precise behavior can embarrass others who may interpret it as, "He's so holier-than-thou." If the partiers had been given a chance to save face, maybe the outcome could have been different. Perhaps Raymond could have used humor instead of apparent disgust to motivate the others to action. For instance, (talking through a bullhorn made from a plastic cup), "This is the Shore Patrol speaking. Pick up your junk or proceed directly to jail. Do not pass GO, do not collect $200." Humor can be a great equalizer.

Since Cautious Thinkers do not readily discuss their feelings, or often even their thoughts, their initial responses can speak volumes about how they really think or feel. That first little smirk or quick, one-syllable laugh can tell you that they're pleased. Or the involuntary clenched fist or pursed lips may indicate disagreement. Watch Cautious Thinkers to detect these automatic, and often accurate, indicators of how they really react to someone or something.

In this respect, when they are upset, don't wait around for them to engage in a verbal boxing match. Instead, their attitude is most likely to be: "I'm not going to get angry; I'm going to get even." They retain a little black book in their minds and keep score. With memories akin to the size of an elephant, they seldom forget, especially when they think they've been wronged. So when you offend them, they mentally turn to the page with your name on it and put down another check mark. When the page fills up, which may take several years, watch out! Then, pow! The curtain descends on your relationship and they're gone, figuratively, and sometimes even literally.

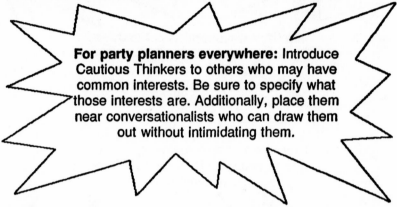

For party planners everywhere: Introduce Cautious Thinkers to others who may have common interests. Be sure to specify what those interests are. Additionally, place them near conversationalists who can draw them out without intimidating them.

Long on results

Cautious Thinkers aren't comfortable with stories or anecdotes about themselves or with sharing their feelings. When asked how they feel about an issue, they may respond with comments like, "I haven't made a final decision yet," or, "I like to keep my opinions to myself." If they really feel pressured by someone, they may tersely say, "That's my business." American cowboy movies often capture the essence of the Cautious Thinker. The Lone Ranger perhaps best symbolizes their short-on-words, no-nonsense, emphasis-on-results approach.

Unique, witty humor

Cautious Thinker humor typically shows a down-home, witty perspective, often from an unexpected third angle. It frequently seems to include a reactive, straight-man element, such as the Will Rogers *last sane man on the face of the earth*, ironic technique. Jack Benny, too, represents the Cautious Thinker comedian par excellence.

And what about Mark Twain or Dick Cavett? Like Woody Allen, their unique brand of humor typically emerges from thinking hard about human feelings and experiences. Then they capture them in timeless stories with penetrating insights of human nature—stories which have been clearly, simply, yet powerfully, communicated.

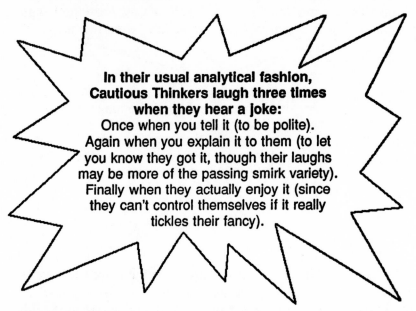

In their usual analytical fashion, Cautious Thinkers laugh three times when they hear a joke:
Once when you tell it (to be polite).
Again when you explain it to them (to let you know they got it, though their laughs may be more of the passing smirk variety).
Finally when they actually enjoy it (since they can't control themselves if it really tickles their fancy).

Who's on first?

Bob, a successful financial planner who enjoys coaching youth baseball, exhibits classic Cautious Thinker behaviors worth noting. He notices the details of the games and whether or not each player performs correctly. He naturally picks up on body positioning—how the boys swing the bats, anticipate catching balls, run and slide to the bases, and play according to specific patterns and rules.

Whereas people of other types may not quite put their fingers on what's amiss, Bob seems to see the problem with little effort. He enjoys discovering their latent talents, especially when he can point out that he was *right about Jeremy's pitching arm* to the other coaches. He even keeps charts to trace the height and weight patterns of the baseball playing adolescents in his neighborhood. From these, he projects each boy's anticipated growth spurts and eventual size.

At ease, but that takes time

Socially, Cautious Thinkers usually opt for small numbers of people with whom they are comfortable. It takes awhile for this type to reach a true comfort zone with others, allowing them to be at ease. In stressful situations, Cautious Thinkers may ask a single question, often confiding in a trusted colleague or friend they can count on for feedback. This confidante may even act as a spokesperson for them. Cautious Thinkers may not speak directly to the source, but instead prefer to work through a known, proven channel. This channel may be another person, a medium of communication, or a productive procedure or process.

Dealing with C's

Remember that they have a basic need for accuracy. Therefore, they are more fearful of mistakes or criticisms resulting from the natural state of human imperfection, which they find difficult to accept. So focus on your appreciation and realization of how hard they work to try to do things correctly and on how you, too, feel this is important, whether you have this same motivation or not. Let them know you value this attribute in them and the accurate results derived from it. "Lenny, when I want something done right, I know you're the one to ask. If you'll agree to fill the auditor's slot for our club, I will be very grateful to you, since we'll be able to rest easy that we won't have lots of problems with our books."

Socializing with C's

They are the most private of the four basic behavioral patterns, so they require more time and space in their dealings with people. They often think others complicate matters, so they prefer to keep involvement down to a few people. The more individuals, the more potential problems and the less independence and efficiency. "If we go away for the weekend with the Bergsons, that means their three children will come, too. That's not my idea of a relaxing weekend."

Remember . . .

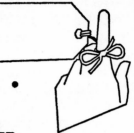

CAUTIOUS THINKER:
TYPICAL SOCIAL BEHAVIOR

- Quiet and observant; like to collect information before they enter relationships
- Socially cool and distant—wait for others to take the social initiative
- Discreet and tactful; usually won't tell secrets or *the naked truth*
- Serious—Naturally suspicious of others unless they've proven themselves in the past
- Guarded—Prefer small group of friends with whom they can let down their shield

CAUTIOUS THINKER:
PREFERRED SOCIAL SITUATIONS

- Attend a small gathering of close friends who have proven their value in the past
- Participate in organized activities where they can be right
- Converse logically about complete bodies of knowledge, adding key details to the conversation
- Can talk facts, not feelings
- Favor conflict-free environments

Action Plan ...

IF YOU ARE
THE CAUTIOUS THINKER

- Demonstrate more concern and appreciation to others with shared feedback: "I really appreciate your thoughtfulness."
- Deal more directly with difficult people and situations
- Adjust more quickly to changes, disorganization, and errors
- Avoid dwelling on someone else's mistakes
- Take more initiative by talking to someone else first
- Act somewhat less formal and more casual
- Accept and laugh at personal limitations
- Elaborate on a response instead of replying just yes or no

IF OTHERS ARE CAUTIOUS THINKERS

- Use a logical approach
- Listen to their concerns, reasoning, and suggestions
- Respond rather formally and politely
- Negative discussions are OK, so long as they aren't personally directed
- Privately acknowledge them about their thinking
- Focus on how pleased you are with their procedures
- Solicit their insights and suggestions
- Show them by what you do, not what you say

This type can be extremely diplomatic and accommodating to others (at least, on the surface) because they often mask their own inner thoughts and feelings. For a truer indication of where they stand, tune into their initial non-verbal reactions to situations, especially those which may require them to make a choice about their preferences. You may want to check out whether something which is being suggested is likely to be *the right thing for them at this time*. Or, ask what other ideas they have about what might be a better option, based on past experiences or interests you've shared with each other. "Gregg, your suggestion to ski at Killington after the Christmas rush was inspired. We skied all day on uncrowded slopes. What do you think about vacation spots this next year?"

Chapter 9
It's All in the Family

Try something extra

Someone once said, "You can pick your friends, but you can't pick your relatives." Families are a given entity, so it's inevitable that you may find somebody in yours who is more difficult for you to deal with than in those other groups where you have the luxury of selection. Think of someone in your family who typifies each behavioral style and envision how you can better communicate with him or her. What are their more compatible qualities with you? What behaviors do they exhibit which make the two of you less compatible? How can you modify your own behavior to make all four types of people more compatible with you?

Dominant Directors
and Their Family Interactions

Options . . . with concise supporting analysis

A variation on the theme of providing options for the Dominant Director still applies in a family setting. "Howard, I've narrowed down our vacation choices to four: Maui, St. Thomas, San Juan, or Acapulco, all warm places with modern conveniences, just what you said you wanted (reference to quality). Here are the costs and travel times for each one. Let me know your preference and I'll make arrangements with the travel agent."

Done that, been there

Dominant Directors specialize in taking charge and getting things done. They are masters and mistresses of delegation and like overseeing the final results. Even on vacations, they enjoy the bustle of performing many activities. For example, when the Brodericks visited Paris, Brian, the husband and father, wanted to see everything. He made sure they were all up by 6:30 a.m. so they could squeeze everything into five days. "Otherwise, what's the point of going to Paris if you don't see all the famous places?" And see the sights they did, whether they wanted to or not.

On the second day, they finally reached the Louvre at 4:00 p.m. That gave them exactly one hour to see the Mona Lisa, Venus de Milo, and thousands of other priceless treasures housed there. Unlike the other three, Brian was happy with literally seeing the sights, however quickly and haphazardly. "Done that, been there!" summed up his perspective on touring Paris. Brian, like other Dominant Directors, has a tendency to look over his family's shoulders to make sure they're conforming to his own expectations. He naturally expects the same breakneck pace from them that he does from himself.

What else can they find to manage?

He even orchestrated his own wedding—set a date (the day after his comprehensive exams in graduate school), secured a hall, planned the buffet menu, found a photographer, and generally managed the entire affair. "Don't worry about a thing," he told his fiancee. "I'll take care of it." And he came through.

Similarly, he planned a budget tour of Europe a year after their marriage. It was another *Hurry up, we've got another place to see* experience. Having visited eight countries in 28 days in their whirlwind travels, they literally fell into bed by 8 o'clock, too exhausted to walk another step.

Another Dominant Director we know assembled his son's crib in the living room. His wife observed, "How are you going to get it through the doorway? The crib is wider than the door."

"No, it isn't," he protested.

She came back with a measuring tape: "It's one inch wider than the door jamb. Start taking it apart and I'll help you haul the parts into Danny's room."

"Don't worry, I'll get it through," he said.

"This is ridiculous. Just admit it won't get through and start over."

"No way. It's going to fit, and that's that." And somehow he crammed that crib through the doorway. He won, but the door lost!

Work can become an obsession

Art, one Dominant Director we know, liked to work so much his career literally took over his life. When he and his wife Jean were invited to play bridge, he'd ask, "How long do we have to stay there? I want to be home by 9 o'clock so I can finish the Steinberg prospectus."

He thought he had to attend occasional formal dances for the business contacts and for the *ring kissing ceremonies*, as Jean described them. Since he disliked dancing, Jean learned to negotiate four dances per event. Finally, she said, "I'm sick and tired of your putting a ceiling on fun! Lighten up or I'll either be a rich widow in 10 years or a rich divorcee in six months." This, and subsequent marriage counseling, woke Art up to the realities of working on more things than his job. Working continued to be his greatest source of pleasure and pride, but he learned to add his wife, children, and friends to his list of priorities.

About D children

Dominant Director children typically busy themselves with things—puzzles, blocks, game shows, or sports—that keep them occupied for hours. They delight in showing Mom and Dad the fruits of their labors. Dominant Director toddlers exhibit telltale traits early in life. Dominant Director Justin seldom responded to strangers' overtures. In fact, his mother says, he usually ignored them or looked at them as though he was thinking, "Who is this person and what does she want?" He seemed to focus on his own preferred results soon after infancy. By age four, he demanded flash cards at bath time to the point where his parents contemplated burning them in protest!

If this Dominant Director child temporarily loses his parent in a public setting, his eyes may begin to brim with tears, but he'll usually hold his feelings inside instead of crying, as he actively searches for the missing person. Once taught to do so, you'll easily recognize older Dominant Director youngsters by the way they quickly seek clerks, security guards, or police if they want help locating an *errant parent*, other person, or things that interest them.

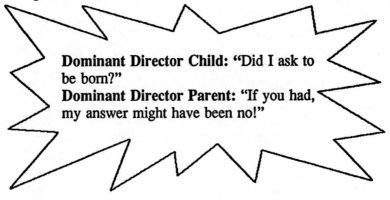

Dominant Director Child: "Did I ask to be born?"
Dominant Director Parent: "If you had, my answer might have been no!"

When they don't get their way, Dominant children often try to take charge of the situation. For instance, one child tried to gain control over the babysitter by holding his breath until he turned blue. Parents often describe Dominant Director children as headstrong or difficult, but understanding the child's need for near-complete control over his environment can yield surprising benefits. Allowing Director kids to have authority over pets, toys, their own rooms, or other personal activities can channel their natural need for control in a positive way. Otherwise, they may frustrate their siblings in an effort to parent them. Jessica usually pipes up, "Mom, he thinks he's the boss and he's not!"

When he was almost 13 years old, Jason pumped out one too many verbal abuses (from his mother's perspective). They had a discussion that resulted in a deal: He'd talk politely and civilly to her and she'd stop talking sarcastically to him. This seemed to work fine for two days. When she announced, "Dinner is ready," Jason hurried upstairs and said, "I'm ready." Then he waited. "Gee, Mom, I could have sworn you would have said, 'Yeah, you're ready all right'!"

"Not any more. We made a deal, remember? You're much more pleasant to be around now that you're watching your mouth, so I'm monitoring my sarcasm."

"I guess so, but you know what, Mom? I kind of miss it!"

Why? Because, whether they admit it to themselves or not, Dominant Director children (and adults) often enjoy confrontation. As one acquaintance told us, "This (dealing with a Dominant Director child) is definitely not the *E* ticket at Disneyland."

D's deal with tangibles

Since Dominant Directors often view themselves as *results specialists* working towards the realization of tangible goals, they may like to get the family together to elicit what everyone's doing. They can monitor subsequent progress and accomplishments. They typically like giving suggestions. "I'll bet you could do even better if you studied 15 minutes more every day." Or initiating games to develop particular skills. "We'll play this word game to help you build up your vocabulary," or, "We'll practice catching so you can become a better baseball player."

If their helpful hints are accepted as such without arousing anyone's negative emotions, Dominant Directors can maintain a rather high activity level with their families. Being concerned about everyone's feelings drains them of energy, so they prefer to direct conversations toward more tangible, less abstract topics.

Negotiation can become a way of life

Seldom can a family member ask a question of a Dominant Director without meeting with some sort of rebuttal. A simple,

"Would you like to go to the movies?" seldom receives a yes or no answer. "If we see Beaches sometime this afternoon, I'll go. Otherwise, I'm not interested." Or, "Okay, if we go to University Town Center. Then we can look at the wide screen TVs in The Television Shack." Dominant Directors often structure their responses in a controlling cause and effect mode. "If you (first) do so-and-so (something I want), then I'll do this (something you want)." Translation: "It needs to be this way, or I won't play." Why? They want to win, or at least have the final controlling say so.

Dominant Directors may favor parallel activities with their spouses and children. They may want everyone under the same roof, or in the same room. Other than that, they frequently have no further need for personal control and may be satisfied letting others do their own thing. One may build model airplanes, another read a book, someone else talk on the phone, and yet another study for an exam. So long as everyone is physically there, without necessarily overlapping or conversing, the Dominant Director is often content. This is because when positively motivated, the D need for control is more focused, limited only to the number one priority at that time, rather than wanting to control everything.

D's compliments have power

Dominant Directors have the dubious distinction of being the least natural listeners among the four types. Why? Partially because they've probably already arrived at an answer. Additionally, they are often too impatient to listen to long explanations or personal, emotional concerns. They also tend to find it easier to give criticism than to provide positive feedback to others. But all Dominant Directors have to do to make giant strides forward are to positively tip the scale in the direction of (1) giving more reinforcement, while also (2) listening more to increase their level of understanding and to communicate shared interest.

Health and relationship alert!

They also frequently report problems with two other areas of their lives—their relationships and their health. They often have high divorce rates and, as someone half-jokingly says, their children may call them *Uncle Daddy* or *Aunt Mommy*. Even when they're home, they may be there physically, but not always emotionally.

Regarding health, they may fall prey to heart attacks as part of their Type A behavior pattern. The good news is they usually don't get ulcers. Instead, they give them. They're carriers. Because of their self-imposed busy lifestyles, this type may figuratively have to pencil in *Romance the spouse tonight* on their to do lists. Then they can cross it off when they're done.

Dominant Director Marilyn's natural inclination was to manage her daughter and point out what she would do now, tomorrow, and next week. Then her husband observed that all day long, Molly was, in effect, being ordered around. Marilyn did find herself saying, "Molly, let's go swing," or, "Here. I'll help you onto the seesaw." So she consciously stepped back and allowed Molly an hour of personal choice. What better place than the relatively child-proof playground to give her daughter some emotional breathing space?

D's can find mutually acceptable solutions

Marilyn and her husband Joel also have four long-haired, indoor cats. One day, Joel fumed, "I can't stand those cats in the house any more. Their hair gets all over my suits, they have accidents on the stairs, and today I found a fur ball next to my shoes. They've got to go."

But Marilyn was determined to find an indoor solution. "They can't go outside because they're declawed. And I'm not getting rid of them. Let's find an answer where we both agree." They decided to convert their family room to a cat motel. They've already made arrangements to replace the carpet with tile (impervious to hair, accidents, and fur balls) and add doors to the family room to separate it from the rest of the house. They arrived at a workable compromise for each of them, where neither had anything to lose except the money invested to satisfy one another.

Remember . . .

DOMINANT DIRECTORS' FAMILY BEHAVIORS

- Favor the role of authority in the family system . . with them in charge
- Like doing activities on their terms
- Want the freedom to spend extra hours working
- Involve themselves in specific family activities that *mean something* in terms of concrete results

DOMINANT DIRECTORS' PREFERRED FAMILY SITUATIONS

- Being the undisputed head of the family
- Deciding what's what, when, and how
- Not having to deal with everyone's emotions
- Having the personal freedom to do what they're interested in doing
- Negotiating better deals, when possible
- Seeing family members stretch and grow
- Getting results that the whole family can feel good about

Action Plan . . .

HOW DOMINANT DIRECTORS CAN ADAPT THEIR BEHAVIOR WITH FAMILY/CHILDREN

- Allow the family to do things without being controlled by the Director's preferences
- Accept not being in charge all the time, moving toward a more democratic family system
- Verbalize positive emotions and encourage family members to do likewise . . . enjoying both in the process
- Learn to laugh at the lighter side of life
- Openly admit mistakes and say "I'm sorry"
- Unconditionally accept their family at face value

HOW YOU CAN HELP DOMINANT DIRECTORS MODIFY FAMILY BEHAVIORS

- Point out other family members' perspectives
- Trade off activities: "I'll do this if you'll do that"
- Voice your concerns gently, but firmly
- Politely refuse delegated duties, when appropriate
- Encourage them to verbalize praise and compliments to others
- Gently remind them to laugh and take life less seriously

And more mutually acceptable solutions

Because of Dominant Directors' focus on personal control, their family's suggestions may initially fall flat. "Why don't we all drive up to Alpine on Sunday?"

"No," the Dominant Director may respond from behind the newspaper.

"Why not?"

"I don't feel like it."

"It's only Wednesday. How do you know that on Sunday you're not going to feel like it?"

"Because I don't like going there. It's a waste of time and there's nothing to do when we get there. I'd rather stay home and relax."

"Well, we're all part of this family, too, and we want to do something together in the fresh air on Sunday. So why don't we all think about some suggestions and we'll talk about them in an hour, okay?" Under these kinds of circumstances when he realizes some outing seems inevitable, the Dominant Director may take the initiative to try something that is mutually acceptable. "Well, if you really want to get some fresh air, maybe we can go to Mission Bay Park and fly kites. Then I can bring my magazines."

Interacting Socializers and Their Family Interactions

Family fun

This type favors fun with family members. Even if he can't avoid his least favorite relative's annual Thanksgiving visit, he can usually find positive, diversionary activities to dull any unpleasant sensation he may feel. There are always group tours of the city, trips to the zoo or beach, or a group restaurant experience—all large enough arenas for separation within group activities.

I's live in the moment

Interacting Socializers enjoy sharing the moment, and projecting more shared moments into the future. They dislike most solitary activities and want to perform them with their family or friends. "Let's go for a swim!" or, "How about taking a walk with me?"

They like to feel that their family is close-knit and can solve most problems by verbalizing their feelings. When a family member hurts their feelings, they typically withdraw from them to recover, seeking solace in other family members or friends who can caringly listen to them vent their emotions. They tend to feel overburdened with secrets or with having to hold in their feelings. If they dislike a close relative's behavior, they usually verbalize it. But unless they are aware of the difference between hating the person and hating the act, they may say regretful things if they are deeply hurt.

"Can we talk?"

The Interacting Socializer likes to go with the flow, but in an impulsive, spontaneous manner. He wants to talk about anything and everything, from current events and how they affect him and others, to more personal subjects family members may not want to discuss. He likes enthusiastic greetings, hugs, squeezes, and outward displays of affection, especially if other people are around to see how much his family loves him. In fact, outside witnesses who tell others about his family's outpouring of emotion for him can make an Interacting Socializer's day. His status needs will be bolstered by these external factors (people testifying about his popularity).

Interacting Socializers, more than the other types, have that youthful quality of keeping in touch with the child within themselves. They often feel less inhibited than others about discussing both their triumphs and their warts (as they perceive them) with their families. "Yes, I did some stupid things in junior high school, Sam. I smoked cigarettes in Kathy's attic before her mom got home from work and once I even set fire to an overstuffed chair. Was I ever petrified! So I hope you won't act as dumb as I did and can learn from my mistakes."

About I children

Interacting Socializer children typically hear things like, "You don't have to tell anyone about the fight Daddy and I had last night." Otherwise, the entire neighborhood may know the family's life history. For this behavioral type, talking about any experience, good or bad, is almost as natural as breathing. As one observer pointed out, "Generally speaking, the Interacting Socializer may be *generally speaking.*"

Young Interacting Socializers may get reprimanded for talking with friends at school, often while the teacher competes with him or a Dominant Director child for the class' attention. Solitary activities bore them unless they learn to view them as games or socially related experiences. Of the four types, Interacting Socializer children respond the most spontaneously to treats and rewards when they've memorized their spelling words, or correctly played a musical piece. On the other hand, anything that smacks of potential stardom attracts these children like bees to flowers. Plays, recitals, pageants, or anything that draws special attention to themselves command their interest.

Unlike Dominant Directors, Interacting Socializers often respond positively to anyone's and everyone's attention almost from day one. Interacting Jessica gurgled and smiled at anybody within view, many of whom commented on her precocious flirting. According to Jessica, the world was populated by no strangers, only potential friends and allies.

People can help an Interacting Socializer deal with this need for universal approval by gently reminding him no one can please all the people all the time, not even him! For instance, the Interacting Socializer child who gets lost in a department store may continue wandering away without realizing it, enchanted with the unending array of toys or games, talking excitedly to anyone who'll listen.

"This will hurt me, too"

Although few parents enjoy dispensing discipline, Interacting Socializers often feel literally as badly as their children when they dole out punishments. "Barry, I hate to have to do this, but you ate candy after I told you not to. So no more sweets or TV for the rest of the day." Five minutes later he may return to Barry's room and ask, "How are you doing, Buddy? Do you want to go outside and practice soccer for awhile?" Or better yet (from the Interacting Socializer's point of view), he'll point out Barry's unacceptable behavior to his wife and ask her to take care of it.

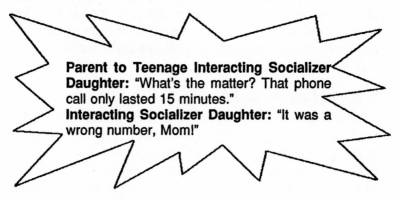

Peaks and valleys

This type tends to experience wide mood swings ranging from feelings of ecstasy to agony. There often doesn't seem to be much middle, smooth ground between the peaks and valleys. In this sense, they tend to live by their feelings. As a result, neutral feelings are equivalent to no feelings for Socializers. This perception fails to provide them with a needed gauge for determining what they want to do (that leads to increased good feelings) or avoid (because of the bad feelings which they experience). This stimulating, external orientation and sense of confusion results in overemotionality and a sense of confusion when they're under more intense pressure. "Can't you see I'm busy? Go away and leave me alone!" Or, under normal circumstances, they can be just plain emotional and sentimental. "Oh, Jamie, that's the most beautiful valentine I've ever seen!" In either case, I's seldom feel neutral about anything!

Enough is enough

We know one Interacting Socializer who told her preteen son more than he ever wanted to know about the opposite sex. This extended to off-color jokes, some of which were interpreted by her son as being personally directed. He felt embarrassed by his mother and thought she had acted inappropriately. Before friends came over, he began cautioning her, "Just say hello, okay, Mom? Joe doesn't know you that well yet, so please let him have enough time to get used to you." With her own feelings close to the surface, she felt hurt at first, but then cheered herself up by sharing her son's comments with her husband and sister. By viewing his request through the eyes of humor, she came to better understand her son's point of view.

"Oh, no! I didn't check!"

Of all the behavioral types, Interacting Socializers are the most likely to forget about things—ranging from class plays to PTA meetings, special dates, personal appointments, etc. Because of this natural tendency, they can benefit by coordinating their family, work, and social activities on one calendar or pocket organizer so they don't disappoint family members and themselves. Gentle reminders to Interacting Socializers can help them anticipate a family event. "Remember, Howard, Sarah's birthday party is this Saturday at noon. Let's make sure we get ready early so we get all the preparation out of the way, okay?"

Sometimes this type may respond to hearsay and, typically, not check before they reach a conclusion:

Socializer Linda: "Harry, I'm not happy that you told Martha I've gained weight!"

Husband Harry: "Linda, that's not correct. What I said was you thought it made you look heavier than you are. Isn't that exactly what you told me?"

They may leap before they look

Interacting Socializers often need to look before leaping. This extends to openly addressing their children with emotionally weighty questions. "Jimmy, I heard a very disturbing rumor. Is it true you've taken drugs?" This could be toned down to something like, "Jimmy, I heard a rumor that I think you want to know about. I'm not going to let myself get upset,

Remember . . .

INTERACTING SOCIALIZERS' FAMILY BEHAVIORS

- Shared activities with informal discussions..now and later
- Togetherness, which may include people outside the family in the fun
- Varied family activities in stimulating environments
- Spur of the moment decisions
- Focus on emotions and how family members feel about various matters which arise
- Tend to *talk up* or *talk down* others

INTERACTING SOCIALIZERS' PREFERRED FAMILY SITUATIONS

- Talking about their innermost joys and fears
- Sharing warm, emotional moments
- Laughing, joking, and acting silly together
- Feeling accepted by the family for being dynamic and fun-loving
- Relaxing and not having to deal with conflicts
- Feeling acknowledged as friends as well as spouses and children

Action Plan . . .

HOW INTERACTING SOCIALIZERS CAN ADAPT THEIR BEHAVIOR WITH FAMILY/CHILDREN

- Monitor their natural tendency to jump to conclusions and wait for all the facts to come in
- Discipline their children when appropriate, instead of succumbing to the fear that the children won't like them
- Understand that there are times when they can benefit by toning down their feelings of excitement
- Write down significant dates and events
- Better organize activities (or motivate someone else to do them)

HOW YOU CAN HELP INTERACTING SOCIALIZERS MODIFY FAMILY BEHAVIORS

- Express appreciation and compliments first, suggestions second
- Pitch in and help them rearrange (or get rid of) their clutter
- Show them how a little more efficiency can free them to do more fun things
- Temper spontaneity with some family planning
- Talk to this type privately about perceived challenges and areas which require improvement

so just talk to me and let me know what is going on with you, since we have always cared about each other enough to be open and honest about our feelings, right? Is there any reason for me to be concerned about drug use when you go out places with kids?" In this example, the parent asked open-ended questions while reassuring her son she was aware of her own tendency to get tense about situations and relationships that are important to her. The message was that she knows she has a problem to work on. Now she wants to know if they have a problem to work on—namely, drugs.

If the rumor is wrong, she will have both saved face and avoided accusing her son without justification. If her suspicions are confirmed, she can reassure Jimmy that she still loves him, but cannot accept the behavior. Then she can help him identify a course of action that will enable him to solve the problem without harming his self-esteem or jeopardizing their relationship.

Steady Relaters
and Their Family Interactions

"Like a bridge over troubled water"

Part of the Steady Relater appeal is that they tend to naturally accept and tolerate others, warts and all. Edith Bunker, a Steady Relater for all seasons, illustrates this type's tendencies to soothe the entire household. Even though Archie clashed with the Meathead, Edith got along beautifully with both of them. She occupied the role of *A Bridge Over Troubled Water*, the heart of the family unit. In her dealings with Archie, Michael, Gloria, and George Jefferson (the neighbor), she genuinely enjoyed their differing positive traits and also succeeded in overlooking the negatives. She personified the considerate, neighborly, and predictable behaviors of the Steady Relater: the *teddy bear* personality among the four types.

Today's events are tomorrow's memories

Steady Relaters are often collector types. They like to accumulate personal treasures, photographs, and souvenirs that aid them in reflecting about the way things were. They may balk at throwing any of these articles away because of the memories and sentimentality associated with them. "I know the image has faded on this photo, but it meant so much to my mother I just can't part with it." On the other hand, Dominant Directors may go through things once a year and throw out junk they haven't used. "We never look at these travel folders any more, so let's get rid of them." By contrast, Interacting Socializers count themselves lucky if they can find some of their old keepsakes. "I know my high school yearbook is here someplace."

Similarly, Steady Relaters often want to do things with family members in which they both share and have opportunities for reminiscing. "Remember the time we all went to Aunt Agnes and Uncle Joe's farm for a week? You milked a cow and rode the horses." At times, Steady Relaters can overdo their affiliation with family routine and become possessive. "But we always go to John and Mary's for the holidays. Why do we have to go somewhere else this year? After all, for me things just won't be the same—it'll be like missing out on these holidays altogether."

About S children

Steady Relater children often try to please almost everyone with their easy-going temperament. Their parents typically say, "That child never gave me a bit of trouble," or, "What a good baby!" Relater children tend to ask for permission before touching breakables, TV sets, or food in the refrigerator—filling their parents with pride when the family visits someone else's house.

This is very unlike Dominant Directors and Interacting Socializers who may make themselves right at home. By comparison, Steady Relater children seem quite easy to raise. They are more likely to take naps when told to, do their homework on time (but may avoid doing extra work), and seek peace and quiet. Their *Yes, Mom,* and *Yes, Dad,* responses have such an endearing ring.

Young Steady Relaters like to both participate in and watch the world go by. Even as infants, they enjoy going for walks in their strollers, whether or not their parents stop to look at things or talk to people. And they would stay in their cribs or playpens much longer than the other three types, without complaining. When admiring onlookers compliment your Steady Relater toddler, he may smile, but also blush and bury his head in Mother's rib cage. He likes attention, but he prefers occupying a seat in the audience to playing a starring role. Later, he may become a true team player, acknowledging everyone in his group for helping to reach the goal. A Steady Relater is not likely to accept, at least publicly, 100% of the credit.

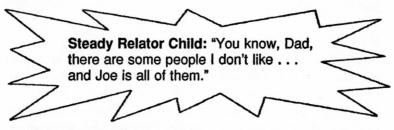

Steady Relator Child: "You know, Dad, there are some people I don't like . . . and Joe is all of them."

Let's keep things as they are

Moderation in all things tends to be another theme this type often lives by. Everyone could relax under the same roof, doing the things they like best, but following the accepted guidelines of family structure. In the best of all possible Steady Relater worlds, little would age or change. No dissension, anger, or even elation would enter their family's lives. Continuity from the past to the present, projected into the future, is important to them.

It's a family affair

For the Steady Relater, preparing and conducting outings and vacations is a family affair. They like input from everyone concerned and prefer to map out the details of the schedule ahead of time. If they are not required to follow more rigid guidelines, they'll want to include easily paced schedules and relaxation breaks. They generally want everyone to get involved in the planning stages of the actual event. If Susie can't take part in a group meeting, Steady Relaters try to represent her interests by including something special for her. "We'll be close to the Hopi Indian reservation. Susie would love to see the Kachina dolls."

Show Steady Relaters you care

They appreciate feedback on favors they've performed. "Oh, boy, Kachina dolls! That sounds great, Mom!" or "Dad, did you fill my car with gas? That was really nice of you." But, Steady Relaters prefer that significant others notice their thoughtfulness without prompting. So this type, especially, may not feel comfortable posting notes about impending birthdays or holidays. They prefer the family to remember on their own, just because they care.

A little bit of home

Steady Relaters may even begin their packing weeks in advance. They like to take extra things (such as home conveniences or emergency items) with them so they'll have what they may want at their fingertips. When Paula puts her suitcase together, she includes not only her clothing and accessories, but snacks, bandages, a small sewing kit, nail polish remover, cotton balls and swabs, plastic bags, large garbage disposal bags (in case it rains), vitamins, antiseptic, and anything else that she thinks her family may need.

"First I did this, then . . ."

Steady Relaters can sometimes be too set in their ways. Their literal mind-sets often think one step at a time. When a son, daughter, or spouse asks, "What did you do today?" the answer may become a chronology of the day's events: "I got up, exercised, showered, drove to work." Sometimes a simple, "I really didn't do anything out of the ordinary today," is sufficient. Additionally, they can learn to communicate in ways that aren't intended to elicit orderly recitations of similar blow-by-blow descriptions from other family members.

Unspoken needs

Communicating directly with loved ones about what may be bothering them can be a real problem for this type. Since they often make sacrifices and act as peacemakers in the family unit, they may inwardly expect acknowledgment and thanks, but fail to say anything about it. Taken to an extreme, this reticence about voicing their concerns, coupled with their modesty, sometimes places Steady Relaters in the tenuous position of martyrs or victims.

When they've had enough

For instance, Dominant Director Dick thought something was amiss in his relationship with his wife Sharon, a Steady Relater, but he never broached the subject. One morning Sharon cleaned out her drawers and began tossing her clothes into crates, cartons, and assorted luggage.

"Hey, what are you doing? We're not going on vacation," Dick said, in his Dominant Director way.

Since her Steady Relater's book was virtually brimming with check marks, she said, "We never go on vacations. That's one of our problems."

"What about three years ago when we had the quiet vacation at home?" countered Dick.

"You call that a vacation? You stayed home from the office and brought a briefcase full of work with you. That's all you did!" Sharon said. "I'm leaving you, Dick. I just can't stand it any more!"

"What are you talking about?" Dick pursued, wide-eyed in his disbelief.

"If you don't know by now, I'm not going to enlighten you," Sharon retaliated.

"I know!" Dick said angrily. "Sharon, tell me the truth. Is there another man?"

"There just has to be somewhere!" sighed Sharon, slamming her suitcase shut. With that, she left. When a Steady Relater closes the door, you may never get your foot in it again. Dick certainly never did.

Remember . . .

STEADY RELATERS' FAMILY BEHAVIORS

- Generally, tend to be naturally group-oriented
- Want to do things together for the personal satisfaction of being with others
- Enjoy customary family events: "Every Thanksgiving, we go to Grandma's house."
- Like regularly scheduled and planned participative activities—"On Wednesdays, we all go bowling."
- Want to be shown sincere appreciation for all they do

STEADY RELATERS' PREFERRED FAMILY SITUATIONS

- Their *ideal* families show how much they mean to them by expressions of warmth and displays of personal appreciation
- Like to help implement family decisions
- Home life is a well-structured and peaceful retreat where stresses seldom occur
- Live in the same, or similar, neighborhood all their lives
- Enjoy a lifestyle which is comfortably organized with predictable, routine schedules and activities
- No big surprises or changes disrupt them

Action Plan . . .

HOW STEADY RELATERS CAN ADAPT THEIR BEHAVIOR WITH FAMILY/CHILDREN

- Communicate more in abstract terms; i.e., accept less explicit, more generalized answers, when appropriate—such as exploring the big picture, new ideas, or the point of the matter
- Make decisions on their own, or take the initiative, when appropriate
- Recognize that change is inevitable
- Speak up when they're upset about something, rather than keeping silent until they've accumulated a list of grievances and pent-up frustrations

HOW YOU CAN HELP STEADY RELATERS MODIFY FAMILY BEHAVIOR

- Encourage a mutual dialogue on thoughts and feelings . . . good and bad
- Stress that not all situations/comments are personally directed
- Enlist their input in suggesting what tasks they can do and goals they can set on their own
- Tap their talents and encourage them to develop and grow, perhaps by seeking public recognition for them
- Help them assert themselves, when appropriate

S's Speak out

Like Sharon, Steady Relaters can benefit by realizing that those close to them may need reminders to thoroughly understand and be responsive to their needs, wants, and expectations. But if those needs and wants are only hinted at, not directly verbalized, spouses and children may not grasp the importance of meeting our personal expectations. Steady Relaters can learn to say, "Jim, Timmy is your son, too, and it bothers me when you don't take more of a part in spending time and taking care of him. For instance, when you're home from your business trips, I think you could give him a bath once in awhile and read him a bedtime story without my having to suggest it."

"The times of our lives"

When it's time for Junior to go to college, Steady Relaters like to become an integral part of the proceedings. For instance, they may want to share in studying or otherwise preparing for exams, filling out college applications, or assisting with composing essays. They tend to view these mutual moments and tasks as the stuff memories are made of. Participating in situations like these can also help Steady Relaters better adapt to impending changes. In this case, the son will leave home in September, so sharing the *times of our lives* can ease the transitional period for the Steady Relater parent between the more comfortable, known past experiences and the less comfortable future ones.

Cautious Thinkers and Their Family Interactions

Cautious Thinkers proceed carefully

At times, this type's concern can be overdone. For instance, Cautious Thinker Ed was so fire-conscious he bought fire extinguishers for his two-bedroom home—one for the hallway and one for the bathroom. He organized fire drills for his family so that everyone knew what to do in case of an emergency. "Remember to crawl on your hands and knees so there's less chance of being overcome by smoke inhalation." Ed's caution carried over to other aspects of family life. If anyone expected to drive more than five miles in the car, he'd throw up the hood and tinker around inside, making sure everything was safe before starting out.

Other types may detect faulty communications and deal with them directly. But Cautious Thinkers are often uncomfortable with interactions gone awry. As Raymond says, "If I can just put it out of my mind, then maybe it never was 'real' to begin with." They may just sweep those thoughts under the rug and try to forget about them. "Maybe it will go away," they may think. When Raymond experiences strong emotions, he tends to step back initially and analyze them. He likes to figure out what's wrong first, then express it. "I like to work out strategies before I act. When I get angry, it's difficult for me to confront somebody to express it. I do not express anger readily. The stronger the emotion, the less likely I am to deal with it directly."

Fix mistakes, downplay emotions

Although he strongly dislikes making mistakes, Raymond says now he's more likely to admit that he does make them. "I apologize more now and try to fix it, if necessary." He admits this behavior did not come naturally to him. He learned it during his 17-year marriage to Gail, an Interacting Socializer.

On one occasion, Gail commented on the tense, strained atmosphere when they visited Raymond's brother Len. She wanted to discuss it with Len. Raymond tried to dissuade her from making a big deal out of a little deal, but she insisted. "I don't like to jump to conclusions," Raymond says, "so I'm likely to give people the benefit of the doubt." He talked with Len, a Dominant Director, about Gail's concerns, but "I didn't enjoy it," Raymond said. "I prefer to let it fly with him. After all, it didn't turn out 'rosy' with him like it usually does when I talk things out with Gail. He let me know he didn't appreciate the fact that I brought those things up."

Different interests

Cautious Thinkers typically gravitate toward practical hobbies and interests. They often enjoy computers, novels or educational subjects, collections (stamps, art, music, etc.), and other pursuits that involve more private individual involvement. They may prefer that the family share their interests, but many will continue enjoying themselves alone, having learned that their hobbies lean toward the esoteric. Raymond admits that he tends to be a real individualist, so he's had to consciously work at getting more involved in shared family activities. He likes to go hiking with Gail and his two daughters, but he also truly welcomes chunks of time alone that enable him to rid himself of stress. "It helps me clear my thoughts just to have such quality thinking time," he says.

About C children

Cautious Thinker children often seem to be more serious than the other types, partially by showing signs of organization and order at an early age. They stack their toys, keep their puzzle pieces together, and generally favor places for everything and everything in those places. Like Steady Relaters, they like to watch and observe, but Cautious Thinker children hold their emotions within themselves. These are intense children who may lose themselves in activities and often are *seen, but not heard.* In fact, they can become so involved in what they're doing they may not even hear others speaking to them.

Individuals who fit this type often do well in school because of their many compliant-appearing traits. They may find it hard to accept behaviors they see, such as children failing to finish their assigned homework or refusing to study adequately for tests (which tend to make this type nervous). They like to know the expected structure, the emphasized information, and how to derive the correct answers. Often, Cautious Thinkers intuitively invent their own structure, method, or model for understanding and processing what they need to know or do. Of all the types, these kids *don't want to be caught dead in public* for not complying with commonly accepted standards of behavior, let alone those which they additionally expect of themselves!

Heidi, a 12-year-old Cautious Thinker, usually compiles a list before taking a family trip. She packs by laying her clothes out on the bed for her mother to check before putting them into the suitcase. This year, she made a two-sided list: one naming all the items, the other specifying color coding the day she plans to wear each outfit.

Cautious Thinker Child: "I had a really quiet evening alone reading a book last night."
Friend: "Wow, really? I'm afraid that's going to happen to me some night, too!"

Individual time with loved ones

Camille is not comfortable with large public or family gatherings. Rather than shun these events, she has learned how to associate with those few people who make her feel most comfortable. Of course, she politely and briefly touches base with others. But she'll go off by herself to just be with another person so they can talk privately without intrusions. Camille, like other Cautious Thinkers, usually keeps secrets quite well. Her uncanny memory helps her discreetly sort out what individuals may do with information—avoiding any possible complications that may result.

Need to be right

Cautious Peter carefully loaded his family's luggage on top of the station wagon by methodically placing it in what he viewed as the best areas for each suitcase. However, after a half hour of jostling around winding drives, a piece of luggage suddenly fell off the car and onto the side of the road.
"Let's put it inside this time," his wife Mary suggested. "There's plenty of room in the back."
"Well, the kids need quite a bit of room in back," Peter answered.

"But they have enough room. We'll get there quicker if the luggage goes inside," Mary persisted.

"I know these will fit on top if I just load them right," Peter pursued.

Irritated, Mary said, "Well, apparently you didn't tie them right before."

"Well, I'll make sure to this time," Peter said, resolute now in his decision to properly load every suitcase on the car roof. He'll show Mary who's right!

Like Peter, Cautious Thinkers have a need to be correct. In fact, more than any other fate, this type fears criticism of their work or efforts. Since they gauge their personal worth by their precision, accuracy and amount of activity, Cautious Thinkers pride themselves on their efficiency and perfectionism. But, if taken to its worst extreme, such perfectionism runs the risk of turning into nit-picking, faultfinding, or even thick-headedness.

"Read my mind"

Because they tend to be more comfortable thinking about their feelings than expressing them to others, Cautious Thinkers may expect people to know what they think, especially those who know them well. For 47 years, Cautious Thinker Helen agonized over the fact she had taken care of her mother-in-law since the beginning of her marriage. She expected her sister-in-law, Grace, to volunteer to house *Nana* for a few years. But Grace never offered. Helen's Interacting Socializer daughter finally asked her, "Well, did you ever discuss this with Aunt Grace?"

"Of course not!" Helen answered. "It was obvious what was going on. She just didn't want to take care of your grandmother."

"How do you know she felt that way if you never discussed it with her? Maybe she just assumed that was how you wanted it," the daughter pursued.

"She knew and didn't do anything about it," Helen said.

According to her, Grace had let her down. But Helen had never mentioned a word. Helen's *thinkings* got hurt. Sensitized Cautious Thinkers may sever relationships like this because, "Of course So-and-So must have known better! After all, I would!" But, the facts of human behavior tell us that unless So-and-So, too, was a Cautious Thinker, she may very well not have understood.

Self-discipline and logic

"I guess I'd like to be the boss because I like to have things my way, but it doesn't often work, so we usually have to compromise." By talking, however reluctantly, Raymond and Gail have arrived at common rules for disciplining the children. "I like self-discipline. I expect a lot from myself and those around me, but I've learned to be clear about my expectations. If they don't measure up, I tell them. "Look, I told you to clear the table and you didn't do it. You've started another task. First, finish clearing the table before creating another mess."

Cautious Thinkers sometimes are perceived by others as too picky. They ask lots of questions. "What about this, what about that?" One observer who married a Cautious Thinker says that sometimes their questions may even seem like an inquisition to others. She commented, "When something bothers them, count on at least 20 questions. Maybe they'll spread them out over the day, but they're still there."

Non-Cautious Thinker Wife: "Let's go to the movies tonight."

Cautious Thinker Husband: "What's playing?"

Non-Cautious Wife: "I think the new Robert DeNiro movie began Friday."

Thinker Husband: "Where is it?"

Wife: "I don't know, but almost anywhere is fine with me."

Thinker Husband: "Well, what time does it start?"

Wife: "I don't know what time it starts!"

Thinker Husband: "How can you expect to go somewhere when you don't have any kind of plan? Besides, what will we do with the kids?"

Wife: "I'll tell you what. I'll go to the movies and you can stay home with them."

A more productive dialogue

This malfunction in communication could have been prevented if the couple had been more responsive to each other's needs. The wife, recognizing the fact that her husband needs data, could have supplied him with some. "The movie begins at 7 p.m. at the Garde Theater. Maybe your sister can watch the children." Or she could have enlisted his help in figuring who could babysit or asked, "Do you have another option?"

The husband, observing his wife's stressful, emotional state could have acknowledged her feelings, "You seem emotionally drained. Do you want to talk about it?" or, "It does look like you might want to get out for awhile. Am I correct?"

Like Dominant Directors, Cautious Thinkers can become even more effective dealing with people by demonstrating greater concern and appreciation for others. A useful technique for accomplishing this would be sharing feedback, such as: I really appreciate that," or, "How thoughtful of you! Thanks!" Cautious Thinkers can also benefit by learning how to deal more directly with difficult people and situations. This includes quicker adjustments to disruptions, deviations, disorganization, or errors. They can concentrate on turning things around rather than dwelling on frustration responses like "I told you so," or "I knew it all along," or "What can you expect?"

Nobody's "perfekt"

Cautious Thinker adults can become more productive in interactions with their children by admitting to their youngsters it's natural and expected that people will make mistakes—even themselves. "Steven, I want you to look at this algebra problem I just did. The first time, I made an addition error. That's one of the reasons I'm more comfortable checking." Examples like this one can serve to help a child gain a more realistic perspective about the limits of all types of people. It also explains to the child why the Cautious Thinker parent behaves the way she does toward others.

Remember . . .

CAUTIOUS THINKERS' FAMILY BEHAVIORS

- Although they're naturally more stiff and formal with strangers, they can be quite demonstrative with their family
- They are most comfortable when family members exercise caution and look before they leap
- They carefully guard the safety of their family
- They keep mistakes at a minimum
- They practice self-discipline and the pursuit of quality
- Spontaneity and emotionalism take a back seat to caution and logic

CAUTIOUS THINKERS' PREFERRED FAMILY SITUATIONS

- Their home environment is organized, neat, and efficient
- Their family behaves logically
- Other people in the home adhere to their (Cautious Thinker) standards
- They can choose to interact or not, and their family will understand
- They want to be right; when mistakes happen, they prefer to 'fix' them
- They prefer individual time with loved ones

Action Plan . . .

HOW CAUTIOUS THINKERS CAN ADAPT THEIR BEHAVIOR WITH FAMILY/CHILDREN

- Accept the fact that no one is right all the time . . . not even them
- Vocalize their feelings more often (or what they *think* about their feelings)
- Occasionally behave spontaneously
- Voice their disapproval or criticism in a caring way
- Lighten up and not act and think so seriously at home

HOW YOU CAN HELP CAUTIOUS THINKERS MODIFY FAMILY BEHAVIORS

- Encourage them to verbalize positive thoughts and feelings about family members
- Help them lower their perfectionistic standards for some things
- Calmly explain that caution can sometimes be overdone
- Gently prod them into seeing the humor in their own foibles and those of others
- Mix occasional spontaneity with planning and organization
- Help them view life less critically and more optimistically

As natural critical observers, Cautious Thinkers may also practice easing up a little on what their children may perceive as *raining on their parade*. When the neighborhood kids go roller skating, perhaps it isn't necessary to analyze their skates for near-perfect wheel alignment and performance capabilities. Children need to experience some aspects of life spontaneously, otherwise their capacity for just plain having fun may be snuffed out.

People Smart Principle #10—The Principle of Acceptance-Resistance: "When you treat people only your own way, it increases the tension-resistance level between you."

Chapter 10
Romance, Romance!

One person's attraction is another's distraction

Just as each behavioral type has different needs and fears in other life settings, they may also have different general patterns and relating preferences in a romantic relationship. Visualize a Dominant Director, Interacting Socializer, Steady Relater, and Cautious Thinker you've dated, known, or would like to know more intimately. Then apply these general romance enhancers to maximize your next encounters with people of each personal style, based on your newly found insights about their wants and needs.

Dominant Directors and Romance

D's usually know who they want

When Dominant Director Rory sees someone he's enamored with, he goes after her. After meeting Jane, he decided he wanted to win her love. Since he's going to graduate school and, consequently, studies for hours in the library, he often asks Jane to come along so he can spend more time with her. Then he assigns her chores: searching the subject and authors' indexes for books, locating newspaper articles on microfiche, and running out to pick up sandwiches for lunch. Even in romance, Rory uses his Dominant Director tendency to delegate. Unless he's specifically told otherwise, Rory assumes it's okay to take the initiative. From his perspective, Jane can say no if she wants to, so if she doesn't object, he assumes she wants to do various things he requests.

And what they want

His assumptive behavior extends beyond delegating duties to Jane. For example, if he's double dating with Jane and another couple and feels like getting a back rub, he'll just directly ask for one. If Jane refuses, he'll ask his friend's date. Once while eating in a restaurant, Rory even startled people when he complained, "My toes have cramps in them. Will you crack them for me, Jane?"

Embarrassed, Jane replied, "Here? Now? You've got to be kidding!"

"Why? Is it disgusting? They really hurt, Jane." His room-mate's date Sylvia made eye contact with Rory, so he pursued, "Sylvia, can you please just pull my toes a bit for me?" Not knowing what to say or do, Sylvia, a Steady Relater type, reluctantly submitted to his insistent request.

Rory's roommate Walt, another Dominant Director, uses a somewhat similar approach. He and Rory routinely inquire all around their apartment house for someone to type their college projects—free, of course. "If they don't want to do it, they can always say no," Walt and Rory contend.

If a man calls Dominant Director Holli to say, "I'd like you to come with me to La Jolla Shores on Saturday. I'll pick you up at 11:00," she understandably wants some input regarding time and place. She says that in these situations, she's tempted to say, "Hey, wait a minute. Why La Jolla Shores? I'd rather go up to Del Mar. And another thing, how about picking me up at a time that's convenient for me, too, rather than just you?"

When D's make up their minds

Dominant Director Melody chased Stan until she caught him. When she met him, she decided, "This is it." Even when Stan told her the relationship would never work, Melody was determined to convince him they were a good match. For months she fielded his objections, saying she had a clear picture in her head of the two of them together. Finally, he too began to see what she had seen all along. Melody describes her iron will like this: "When I make up my mind, I'm like a little terrier dog chewing on a slipper. You can shake me and try to grab that slipper away, but I hold on no matter what. And do you know what? I've always gotten what I wanted that way."

But sometimes the Dominant Director's will doesn't square with the logic of a situation. For example, when John went skiing for the first time with Maureen, he thought skiing looked easy. A self-professed natural athlete, John just knew he'd be good at it. Far be it for him to allow a little thing like never having done it before to keep him off the advanced slopes. Besides, if Maureen could do it, surely he could. So down he went, shooting out of his chair lift full speed ahead. Multiple bruises later, John learned the hard way that some things do require more than the self-proclaimed attitude, "Of course I can do that."

Love Me, love my alma mater

When Don took Ann to visit his old college alma mater, he expected her to mirror his enthusiasm about the place, even though the temperature was 35 degrees, the wind whipped through the campus, and rain pelted them as they walked around the football stadium. "I scored the winning touchdown here in my first game," he told her. "What a welcome that was!"

"Don, I'm soaking wet. Can we go someplace indoors now?" Don made hard eye contact, then withdrew, hardly speaking a word the rest of the afternoon. "Are you angry with me because I didn't want to go outside while it was thundering and lightning?" Ann finally asked.

"I can't believe you don't share my thoughts and feelings about this campus, Ann. I'm really disappointed."

Ann, perceiving this as the beginning of the end of their romance, asked, "Are you trying to tell me that we won't be seeing each other any more?"

"No, I just wanted to tell you how much this means to me, that's all," Don answered. "I'd like you to get excited about it tomorrow."

In this example, Don succeeded in saying exactly what he was thinking, communicating the information to Ann, and verbalizing the importance of her sharing his enthusiasm about the campus. Dominant Directors may blow off steam, feel better, then want to pick up where they left off as though nothing happened.

D's can learn to relinquish control . . . once in awhile

Dominant Director Holli says she can benefit by learning to allow her date to take control some of the time. Since she typically likes to call the shots in her relationships, she could profit from permitting more mutual give and take. She admits that when she sees evidence of her date wanting control, at first she tends to view that trait as a negative.

She also says more benefit could be derived from trusting her dates more. Since Holli was and is an independent woman, she's used to doing things the way she wants. Consequently, she often has to consciously force herself to do things according to someone else's perspective. Since this type is generally very comfortable making unilateral decisions, they may unwittingly leave out the other person's point of view altogether. They may naturally continue this behavior in the dating world, unless someone gently enlightens them about this personal blind spot.

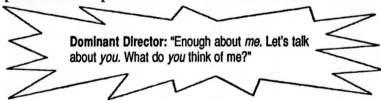

Dominant Director: "Enough about *me*. Let's talk about *you*. What do *you* think of me?"

They let others know

This type tends to make strong requests. "Requests?" Al said to Mary. "You don't make requests, you make demands. You say it like it's an order!"

"Well, how do you want me to say it?" Mary asked.

"Like I have some choice. It seems clear that when you make up your mind, there is little or no choice."

"Give me an example," she said.

"All right. I'd like to go to the beach this weekend, but I'm open to suggestions. That still leaves me an option."

"That sounds reasonable. I'll try it this time," Mary responded.

Dominant Directors may want to tell love interests some things 'for their own good'. But the recipients of these words of wisdom may not respond in kind. Al says, "Mary has learned not to put her fingers in the gears."

This means she now asks first. "Do you really want me to tell you the bottom line?"

"If he says yes, then he has to deal with it. So now we're both more tuned in to the results both of us want," she says.

They tell it bluntly

So brace yourself for direct comments from a Dominant Director. If the answers to certain sensitive questions may result in hurt feelings, it may be advisable to ask less blunt ones, instead. Even when they try to be tactful, Dominant Directors waste no time in telling their opinions. So when Veronica asks, "Mark, do you like my new outfit?" Mark may say, "Are you sure you want to know?"

"You don't like it?" Veronica inquires.

Naturally blunt, he may say, "No, not at all."

"Why not?" she asks.

"It looks cheap. You look like you just stumbled out of a thrift store." Of course, his lack of tact may be unwelcome, but most significant others know just where they stand with a Dominant Director. If the Dominant Director gets his or her way—and of course, they're more than likely to try—their dates will at least seriously consider their advice.

An enjoyable evening?

Dominant Director Matthew may initially find it difficult to yield to his dates' visions of a pleasant evening. When he asks her to a specific restaurant, he may automatically balk if she suggests dinner at an alternate place. "Boy, that must be a half-hour drive. I'm on the road all day, so I'm really not looking forward to driving again," he may protest. But if she offers to drive, he may capitulate. Why? They're natural negotiators. If Dominant Directors contemplate giving in, they typically want something in return. That way, they still get that key result they want.

In pursuit of the bottom line

Ryan, another Dominant Director, has to force himself not to complete his dates' sentences and thoughts. He interrupts to get to the bottom line quicker. "Why waste time searching for the words when I'm right there to supply them?" Others may interpret this behavior as his version of filling in the blanks. But who wants to think of herself as a blank? Besides appearing rude, Ryan risks not really knowing how his dates think or feel about matters. He could learn to count to 10 (at least) and let others say what they want at their own pace, in their own way.

"I'm the manager"

Dominant Director Christine's latest love interest lived 12 miles away, so she decided to find another apartment for him that was within walking distance. "Guess what? I've found an apartment for you and Gil just two blocks from mine."
"But we don't need another apartment. We like it here," Chad protested.
"You know how you hate getting up early, right? Well, this summer you're going to have to get up an hour and a half earlier to commute for your internship. If you live here, you can take the train and leave a whole half-hour later. Plus, you'll be closer to me," Christine explained in her most charismatic voice. (Dominant Directors can be quite forceful and charming, if they want to be.)
On moving day, Christine choreographed the traffic flow, duties, and pace for both Chad and Gil. If they wanted to sit down, she chided them, "You'll get done quicker if you save your break until the first load is hauled off."
"Christine, you're really beginning to bug me. What exactly are you doing, anyway? Besides giving orders, I mean," Chad asked.

Remember . . .

DOMINANT DIRECTOR
DATING/ROMANCE CHARACTERISTICS

- Seek results-oriented relationships—"What's in it for me?".
- Like to assume the role of pursuers
- Want to set the unwritten rules for the relationship
- Like winning over the other person and reaching their relationship goals
- Are likely to ask for whatever they want
- Want to take control of the relationship
- Often delegate duties and concerns

DOMINANT DIRECTORS'
PREFERRED DATING BEHAVIORS

- Special arrangements by the date to be available for them
- A lot of control in deciding where to go and what to do
- To say what's on their minds
- Not being asked questions whose answers may harm their chances of meeting their needs (desired results)
- To negotiate—"I'll concede this if you'll do that"

Action Plan

HOW DOMINANT DIRECTORS CAN LEARN TO ADAPT IN DATING SITUATIONS

- Compromise occasionally, instead of insisting on doing things their way
- Accept other viewpoints as valid, too
- Participate more, delegate less
- See themselves in a more light-hearted way
- Avoid interrupting
- Make requests instead of demands

HOW YOU CAN HELP DOMINANT DIRECTORS MODIFY THEIR DATING BEHAVIOR

- Gently remind them when less desirable behavior surfaces
- Use shared humor to help them laugh at their own imperfections
- Calmly tell them how their behavior makes you feel
- Speak non-judgmentally and stick to the facts
- Try negotiating, yourself—"Next time I get to choose"
- Repeat, when necessary: "I'm not comfortable with that situation."
- Explain that you want a voice in decision making, too
- Let them know that you appreciate it when they listen patiently

"Why, I'm managing this entire project, of course," Christine said.

"Well, stop managing and start lifting," Gil and Chad laughed, handing her one of the heaviest cardboard boxes. "How does it feel to be one of the slaves, instead of their overseer?" Gil smiled.

Christine smiled, too. But Gil's analogy flashed into her brain as a new, heightened glimmer of self-awareness. "I guess I can come on strong sometimes, but at least I've cultivated a sense of humor about it," she said.

Romance and Interacting Socializers

There's a party going on

The Interacting Socializer's favorite dating, and date prospecting, spots tend to include places with party atmospheres. If he doesn't go to an actual party, then comedy clubs, dances, concerts, galas—almost anywhere where he can see and be seen—will do. Joyce and Joe are two such party animals. Although not romantically involved, they often drive to a *happening* together, then mingle with the rest of the singles, working the crowd as they explore interesting possibilities. Each has perfected the process of zooming through the room for prospects, scanning from a distance, and then finally emoting up close and personal when they get that magic feeling. They even jokingly refer to themselves as *Spuds* and *Studs*.

Putting on a show

Flirting by an Interacting Socializer is likely to appear quite obvious. Other types may almost imperceptibly crinkle up the sides of their mouths and consider that flirtatious behavior. Not so for Interacting Socializers. They may grin, wave, wink, hold hands, or otherwise leave no doubt that they're interested when they make up their hearts, rather than their minds, about pursuing someone.

The idea of meeting a new potential love interest fuels them for putting on a good show. This type of person, more than any other, can act his perceived part and then project himself into the audience to sense the impact of his own theatrics. Tuning into other people's positive reactions to him serves to reinforce notions of his own desirability. Think of Bruce Willis of TV's MOONLIGHTING or Bette Midler—both larger than life, and *on* at a moment's notice. They exude and often captivate their audience with outspoken charisma. Whether the performance consists of dancing, telling jokes, sharing anecdotes, or posing in an eye-catching outfit, observing their Interacting Socializer behavior while on the prowl is an entertaining experience.

They may play the field

As a group, Interacting Socializers are likely to enjoy dating lots of different people. To paraphrase a quote from the classic movie *The King and I*, Interacting Socializers can behave like bees—flitting from flower to flower to flower. They tend to feel comfortable with a rather active, or even hectic, dating schedule. "Let's see, I'm going to a play with Ralph Friday night, then off to the beach with Scott on Saturday afternoon, miniature golfing with Ted Saturday night, and then a cocktail party with Ralph again on Sunday."

Falling in and out of love

Of all the types, Interacting Socializers report succumbing more to falling in and out of love (or, at least, fascination with others) than their counterparts. They may become quickly smitten, then almost as suddenly transfer their affections elsewhere. Since they are comfortable with newness and change, it's rather natural for them to keep their options, and their eyes, wide open. Yet they're impulsive. "Yes, let's get engaged!" At the extreme, this practice can lead to later regrets and fanciful thoughts of what might have been; and possibly a roving eye. But when someone really very special comes along, they're also likely to fall faster, harder, and more passionately than others.

Flattery may get you far

Flattery may carry you a long way with Interacting Socializers. They enjoy glittery compliments more than the other types, even when they perceive them as sounding a bit much. Similarly, they may freely compliment others. "John, I wish I had a shirt like that. It's so soft and it makes your body look great." At times this rather uninhibited behavior may be interpreted by more restrained people as a come-on, whether the Interacting Socializer intended it that way or not. Interacting Socializers may view these comments merely as part of socially acceptable behavior between two people of the opposite sex, especially if they share a repartee filled with humor and wit. Interacting Socializers tend to admire quick, witty minds and enjoy verbal jousting, as long as the other person avoids sarcasm at their expense—something they're guaranteed with long-time friends.

I's may have telephonitis

Since they tend to be natural conversationalists, they usually like social telephone interactions, too. Their calls can stretch into hours. We even know one who liked to play Golden Oldies via the phone while he filled the role of deejay. "Wait till you hear this one. It's a classic," he'd voice into the mouthpiece. Then he'd spin the record (or play a tape) for about 30 seconds while his girlfriend played the role of a contestant on NAME THAT TUNE.

The burden of boredom

When George asked Interacting Socializer Jean to accompany him on some errands at the Motor Vehicle Department, bank, and hardware store, she said, "Gee, George, those things are boring, boring, boring! How about if I go shopping while you run around to get your duties done. Then we can meet for lunch." This tendency to want to escape from confining, uneventful circumstances is typical of this type. She apparently wants to see George, but not necessarily under just any circumstance.

Interacting Socializers are likely to want time off from the potentially smothering one-on-one pairing to go out with friends or otherwise participate in some activities without their *main squeeze*. Sometimes, just the thought that they have the option to go out with the girls or guys, if they want to, is sufficient to satisfy their need to freely flap their own wings.

I's like excitement and surprises

Non-Interacting Mel: "Eileen, about our date Saturday night. There might be a problem."

Interacting Socializer Eileen: "Uh oh, what kind of problem?"

Mel: "My cousin just flew in from Jacksonville and will only be here through Sunday afternoon."

Eileen: "And the problem is?"

Mel: "Well, he's already seen the movie we wanted to go to. I haven't seen him in so long, maybe we can postpone our date till later in the week."

Socializer Eileen: "We can go to the movies any time. If you'd like, I'd love it if your cousin came along with us. I could fix him up with Cheryl, or we could go sightseeing. I don't care. It would be an adventure to play tourist guide. I'm sure I could help him have an even better time than usual."

While some types tend to look forward to a particular event, Interacting Socializers like Eileen often welcome less ordinary activities. Whatever their reaction, their emotions generally come through loud and clear for their dates to read. In fact, parents may caution grown Interacting Socializer sons and daughters, "You wear your heart on your sleeve. Why don't you first consider whether keeping some of your reactions to yourself may be more appropriate, at times?"

Naturally flirtatious

While on dates with Steady Relater Corinne, Interacting Socializer Ken continually flirted with other women. He'd smile and say hello to perfect strangers—all female, of course —and make approving guttural sounds when a good-looking woman passed by. Noticing that Corinne was uncharacteristically quiet, he said, "Aw, Corinne, you're not mad at me for having a little fun, are you? C'mon now, where's your sense of humor? I'm just trying to have a little harmless fun."

"A sense of humor!" Corinne snapped. "This has nothing to do with a sense of humor. This has to do with being rude and hurting my feelings. I don't behave that way when I'm with you, and I think at least you could have the decency to reciprocate."

"Wow, Corinne! You sure are touchy tonight!" Ken mumbled.

"Look, you're the one who asked me out, Ken. It's really insulting to me when you flirt with other women right in front of me. If you've got to do it, reserve it for sometime when you're with the guys, okay?"

Since other dates had also displayed negative body language when he acted friendly and had even said they were busy the next time he called, he later reconsidered what Corinne had said. He realized her observations may have been, unfortunately, right on target. Later he called her, saying, "Thanks for straightening me out last night, Corinne. Of course, I really didn't mean to hurt your feelings. I don't particularly like negative feedback, but I guess you're right after all. I'll try to be more considerate from now on, all right?"

Notice that Corinne expressed her concerns in terms which Ken could clearly understand—her feelings—and how his behavior affected them. If Interacting Socializers perceive that they've made someone feel badly, they'll usually prefer to know about it, if it will allow them to smooth things over and make their relationship *right* again.

Romance and the Steady Relater

They aim to please

When Steady Relater Sid attended a hockey game with his date Shelley, he brought fresh snacks galore, offering Shelley cantaloupe wedges, bananas, grapes, and orange slices. "Is there any more cantaloupe left?" she asked.

"Oh, no," Sid said, "I'm sorry, but I just ate the last slice. If I'd known, I would have given it to you. Would you like my orange instead?"

"No, thanks. My taste buds were set for cantaloupe, but it's no big deal."

"I know you must be hungry. How about half the orange?"

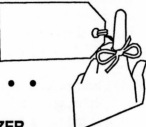

Remember . . .

INTERACTING SOCIALIZER
DATING/ROMANCE CHARACTERISTICS

- Seek approval and admiration from the date
- Like excitement, variety, and light-hearted fun
- Enjoy the thrill of the chase (romance)
- Tend to look for a socially acceptable match that may provide the bonus of favorable attention
- May want to date many people simultaneously or play the field
- May become rather easily infatuated, experiencing love at first (or at least second) sight

INTERACTING SOCIALIZERS'
PREFERRED DATING BEHAVIORS

- Unexpected situations and surprises tend to energize them
- Their dates pay obvious attention to them, in private and in public
- Like to share fun activities with their companions, but will go to extremes to avoid duller, routine tasks
- Prefer a date who lets them know how much he or she is admired
- Like to laugh and maintain a light-hearted tone
- May want universal approval from past and present dates; they like to remain on friendly terms
- May want *space* in their relationships to satisfy needs to socialize with those who are important parts of their lives

Action Plan . . .

HOW INTERACTING SOCIALIZERS CAN ADAPT IN DATING SITUATIONS

- Downplay their openness and, at the extreme, their flirting or showing off
- Focus more attention on their date and less on themselves (or the impact they're making)
- Tone down their tendency toward gushiness, a trait that can cost them some credibility
- Censor their words, rather than say whatever pops into their heads at a moment's notice
- Commit, when appropriate, without accompanying feelings of confinement

HOW YOU CAN HELP INTERACTING SOCIALIZERS MODIFY THEIR DATING BEHAVIORS

- Warmly explain that quiet moments are sometimes appropriate
- Offer to assist them in getting more organized
- Pitch in and help them finish one thing at a time
- Share in making small changes instead of bigger, more impulsive ones
- Plan some things, proceed spontaneously with others
- Don't trample their dreams, but mentally divide their ideas in half
- Specify secret information

"No, thank you, really," Shelley answered.

"What if I peel it for you?" Sid persisted. To a Steady Relater, service is his business. He literally aims to please as a way of satisfying his own need for amiable relationships with others.

After a positive first encounter, Sid will pursue from there, trading off preferences. "This first time let's do what you want, then next time maybe what I want, okay?" He likes a reciprocal dating situation, even though you can see that it's a lot harder for him to assert himself in developing one.

But will this last?

After the relationship has endured for a year or so, this type slowly begins to think that it may last. Steady Relater Cecelia actually dated her boyfriend for 11 years, thinking he'd eventually feel ready for marriage if she just waited long enough. However the time for the big decision never did arrive.

S's tend to stick with their dates

At a party, Steady Relater Polly felt as though she would devote most of her attention to her date. Unless he knows people there, Polly's inclined to stay with him, even if her close friends happen to be there, too. She wants to make sure her date has a good time.

Polly says that if she decides to flirt, she does it subtly by smiling gently, telling stories (perhaps even about herself, but never about him), while acting helpful and pleasant. Even if she thinks wonderful things about him, she doesn't tell him so until later in the relationship. Her brother Ken, another Steady Relater, concurs.

Less is more

Steady Relaters often shy away from anything that smacks of being too overdone. They're basically more middle-of-the-road people who like things on a steady, even keel—No extreme hairstyles, obviously overdone makeup, ultra-flashy clothes, or embarrassing dating prospects for them.

Price consciousness

Steady Relaters tend to view dating behavior as located between extremes. Consistent with this relative reservedness and comfort with moderation, they are typically more price-conscious. Consequently, Steady Relaters may be very aware of what a date will cost. At a restaurant, they may think twice before ordering the most expensive thing on the menu, even if they might be really tempted to risk this splurge. When invited to a school dance, they almost immediately think in terms of the finances of each step toward the big night: formal attire, $_?_; hair styling, $_?_; accessories, $_?_; transportation, $_?_. Then they add up all these prices ($-?) and weigh them against how much they want to attend with that person ($+?).

S's take things personally

As with other areas of the Steady Relater's life, he prefers that others discover him. Taking most things personally, he may particularly fear rejection in the dating market. He doesn't bounce back as quickly as some of the other types, so he prefers to hold, "Would you like to go to out for a drink or bite to eat?" until he's more assured of getting a yes answer.

If their friends say so

Many Steady Relaters entrust their friends with looking out for their romantic interests. If Ray and Sally say that Jack or Jill is great, then they're apt to go by their friends' recommendations. They prefer to meet the person with the friend who recommended them. An informal introduction at their house, a party, or a movie makes the Steady Relater most comfortable. Collective dates with friends allows them the security of knowing they're likely to have a more pleasant time, whether they hit it off with the date or not.

"Chase me"

Steady Relater Ken says he often likes the woman to make the first move. He also appreciates her setting the pace for an intimate relationship, as long as she doesn't come on too strong or too soon. If he perceives he's being overpursued, he may become uncomfortable and deal with the situation by avoiding her. When she calls, he may not be there, or at least create the illusion he is gone. He'll arrange to have already made other plans or be busy on a project whenever she wants to get together with him. In typical Steady Relater fashion, he likes to avoid confrontation and wounded emotions, hoping she'll get the hint he isn't interested by his avoidance behaviors. As Ken says, "If I'm not ready, I'm not ready—and pushing me isn't going to get me ready any sooner, whether people think so, or not!"

S's like their dates sunny side up

Steady Relaters like their dating partners to exhibit a good sense of humor and a mild, easygoing disposition. Their ideal date generally is a person with a sunny disposition who laughs readily, smiles easily, perhaps knows a few good jokes or stories, and just enjoys spending time with them. This type wants to be sure their romantic interests think they're special and worth another person's time. Toward this end, they may choose to go along for the ride if the date just wants their company, sit in a doctor's office while the other gets some treatment, or even wait in the car while the loved one does some errands. Togetherness in this way appeals to them more than any of the four types.

Hum-drum for some, but fun for S's

They like constancy, those things they can count on doing week after week. In this respect, Steady Relaters tend to be creatures of habit. For example, Saturday night may be reserved for going out, Tuesday, for dinner at home. And Thursday is probably for double dating at the movies with close friends. As with other aspects of their lives, they favor relatively smooth progressions in their dating routines. Although this type naturally prefers a minimum amount of stress, when they commit to someone, they want to make things work out. They often are willing to lend support and help their loved one weather the hard times by showing evidence of their loyalty and concern.

"You choose;" "no, you choose"

Since Steady Relaters often tend to accommodate their date's wishes, they may give in to the date's preferences without voicing their own. "Oh, any restaurant you like will do. You pick, okay?" At the extreme, when Steady Relaters allow their dates to make decisions for them, they may unknowingly set themselves up for victimization. Too much acquiescing can make them appear wishy-washy or opinionless, as well as contribute to their own feeling of being trapped. They can benefit by learning to speak up occasionally, saying what they'd really like to do instead of allowing someone else to dictate until it gets out of hand. By doing this, the problem often can be avoided in the first place.

S's hesitate to hurt people's feelings

By the end of a date, even though many Steady Relaters may decide that the person was not for them, they might go to the date's place anyway. When Steady Relaters are invited home, they typically don't like to appear too rude or brash. But if one thing leads to another, then the situation may accelerate to the point of becoming difficult to escape from the date's apartment, all to spare the other person's feelings.

"No, maybe, all right"

The same holds true for declining dates. Steady Relater Cindy says that even if she had a miserable time on the first date, she'd say yes to subsequent ones. Why? She didn't want to make him feel bad. Back in the days when *going parking* was a common practice, she found it difficult to say no, even to the boys she hoped she'd never see again. Since then, Cindy says, "I've wised up and learned to be more assertive, to escape my *doormat* mentality." Yet another Steady Relater, Mary Agnes, says that except for a horrible first-time date, she usually will go out with someone who doesn't really appeal to her another time, just to confirm that her initial impression was right. After that, she'll avoid him by saying she's busy or by postponing telling him about the decision she's already made.

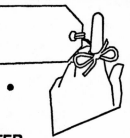

Remember . . .

STEADY RELATER
DATING/ROMANCE CHARACTERISTICS

- Tend to cooperate and accommodate
- Like identification with the significant other
- Give and like to receive sincere attention
- Naturally operate on a one-to-one basis
- Want to familiarize themselves with the unwritten rules regarding the relationship
- Tend to view dating in a more conservative, progressive, stepwise manner

STEADY RELATERS' PREFERRED
DATING BEHAVIORS

- Seek approval and some sincere, steady pursuit by the other person
- The dating process proceeds in a relatively routine, expected, uneventful way . . . with few unpleasant surprises
- Prefer to participate in the different facets of the loved one's life
- Generally want to share time according to a regular, slower-paced schedule
- May prefer to avoid a stressful relationship in favor of a calm, predictable one

Action Plan . . .

HOW STEADY RELATERS CAN LEARN TO ADAPT IN DATING SITUATIONS

- Voice their opinions and thoughts, instead of deferring to their dates
- Say no, when appropriate
- Somewhat reduce their servicing tendencies to limit other person's dependence on them
- Accept some changes in relationships as natural
- Attend more to their own thoughts and feelings
- Act more assertive, when appropriate
- Understand and deal with other types' natural behaviors

HOW YOU CAN HELP STEADY RELATERS MODIFY THEIR DATING BEHAVIOR

- Encourage them to aim higher
- Support them in verbalizing their thoughts and feelings
- Share in developing more assertiveness skills
- Help them plan for some disorganization in their lives
- Show them that disagreement does not necessarily equal an argument
- Assist them in speeding up, at times

"Check with me next week or so and we'll talk about it, okay?" If her avoidance is successful, he won't call again and she'll be reprieved from putting him off yet another time.

Why trade the known for the unknown?

Steady Relater Randy has been a widower for 13 years. He confesses that he misses a real family, but he isn't sure he's yet found the person he wants to settle down with for the rest of his life. He's been seeing his receptionist Wanda steadily for six years, but doesn't feel he's actually in love with her, so he's still on the lookout for Miss Happily Ever After. Yet he can't seem to break off his existing relationship for a potentially more productive one. His attitude amounts to, "Why disrupt a sure thing?" Meanwhile, Wanda persists in the possibility that he'll make her the final offer.

Cautious Thinkers and Romance

C's prefer long-term statistics

The way to Cautious Thinkers' hearts is through their logic. Even with love, they tend to use a rational approach. "Before I let myself go, how realistic is it to be infatuated with this person?" They look at the long-term probabilities for a possible match. Forget about what his date says; what does she actually do to indicate what she's really like? Cautious Thinkers are the most naturally reticent and doubting of the four types, as well as the least verbal. *Show me* is their motto. Like Steady Relaters, Cautious Thinkers need time to establish a relationship. But they may also want to check your track record to predict the odds.

When Cautious Thinker Kathleen meets a romantic prospect, she likes to verify that they have common interests—job, movie, book, or vacation preferences, for instance. To Kathleen, someone interesting means a man who is low-key, quiet, conversational, and doesn't talk a lot about himself. She dislikes game playing and wants everything clearly spelled out. "If he says he'll call and doesn't, I'll give him one more chance and that's it." Compliments don't impress her. She wants to hear a sincere, "I'd really like to spend more time with you." "Wooing is not for me," she adds. Cautious Thinkers' logic can extend to gift giving. Often, they may give practical presents that fit the known, personal interests of the recipient—a small set of tools, a local road map, or a how-to book—instead of more romantic, personal items. Those are reserved until a much deeper, long-standing relationship has evolved.

C's use diplomacy

Cautious Thinker Ralph says dating is hard work. All that energy poured into pursuing a potential date drains him. He likes women to go after him, but, like his Steady Relater counterpart, turns off to women who are too aggressive. "I try to be diplomatic. If a woman I'm not interested in keeps going after me, I'll be roundabout in telling her I don't want to see her any more. Maybe I'll make an excuse, like—I'm going to a wedding." Cautious Thinker Paul used this ploy and became trapped when his erstwhile date discovered he had told her a white lie. So Paul wound up going out with her one more time. This turn of events triggered enough assertiveness to tell her, "No more, please."

Hard to get back in their good graces

When the Cautious Thinker makes up his mind to break up with the significant other, it may take awhile before he can build up to it. The essence of the message is usually akin to, "I've given this adequate time and opportunity and this is just not going to work." When pressed, they're probably able to tell you why, but not likely to do so unless assured it won't add fuel to the fire that keeps things burning, or even smoldering. Remember, they like dealing with specifics. And if forced into telling their former dates what's on their minds, they may beat around the bush anyway. Finally, when this type closes the door, they usually padlock it. So once they've made their decision, it's very difficult to get back in.

Do they care what you think?

One difference between the Cautious Thinker and Steady Relater is that the S type cares what you think; the C isn't generally as concerned about this. So Cautious Thinkers may not make an effort to get along with someone they dislike. They'll simply keep away from them or become even more quiet and reserved. Withdrawing is their way of coping when they're not having a good time. Here's a lesson: When dating a Cautious Thinker, keep your word. If you want to keep the relationship moving forward, be where you're supposed to be when you're supposed to be there and seek their feedback on how you're doing.

Does the world seem absurd?

Ralph says, "I think Woody Allen is funny. Groucho Marx had a perverse quality that I like. And Monty Python has a keen sense of the absurd. I guess I like people who see the ridiculous. Ultimately, the world is a ridiculous place." John Lennon, another Cautious Thinker, seemed to share a similar tongue-in-cheek view of life. Whether true or not, from their viewpoint life is seen from a quite different and comparatively unique perspective. Of the four types, they are the ones who most often truly march to the beat of a different drummer.

C's are likely to know quality places

Often, the Cautious Thinker can contribute helpful suggestions regarding where to go and what to do. This is an area where his emphasis on quality can really shine. "Soderman's Restaurant in Old Lyme has good seafood and reasonable prices. Or Jake's is good for chicken fried steak, Yankee pot roast, and grape nut custard pudding." Like Steady Relaters, they often opt for a proven favorite over a new place that may not meet their known standards.

And, of course, the proverbial icing on the cake is when the date acknowledges, "Andrew, you were absolutely right about this restaurant. The gravy on that chicken fried steak alone was worth the drive. What a well-kept secret! How did you discover it?"

They want to do things right

En route to the destination, the Cautious Thinker typically will have already found or called for exact directions, possibly writing them down while consulting a map. Cautious Thinkers usually become nervous and worried when they're with a person who wings it and isn't sure of where they're going:

Cautious Thinker: "Why don't we stop at that gas station and ask how close we are to Laurel Street?"

Non-Cautious Thinker: "There's no need for that. I know it's somewhere around Poplar and Elm."

Cautious Thinker: "But we only have two minutes to get there. Our reservations are for seven o'clock."

Non-Cautious Thinker: "Do I look worried? Don't fret, we'll be there soon."

But to a Cautious Thinker, getting there at the right time is important. This type often is very precise with exacting standards. Therefore, a Cautious Thinker may view a seven o'clock dinner reservation as a seven o'clock sharp deadline. Left to her own more self-disciplined preferences, she would have shown up on the dot, if not even sooner.

The sound of silence

When Cautious Thinker Darren and his long-time date Celia go to their favorite diner, conversation between them may sound like this:

Celia: "Well, Darren, what are you going to order tonight?"

Cautious Darren: "The usual." (Silence)

Celia: "Did you read about the air crash today?"

Cautious Darren: "Yes."

Celia: "Isn't it horrible? All those innocent people!"

Cautious Darren: "Yes, it is." (More silence)

Celia: "Would you prefer being alone?"

Cautious Darren: "No. Why do you ask?"

Celia: "Because I feel like I'm talking to myself. Pulling one-word answers out of you isn't much fun."

Cautious Darren: "My answers have been more than one word."

Celia: "That's not the point. The point is I feel like I'm cross-examining you. Try keeping up your end of the conversation, okay?"

Cautious Darren: "You know that I'm a quiet person of few words."

Celia: "Quiet is one thing; uncommunicative is another. I need you to talk with me, not just respond to my talking, all right?"

Cautious Darren: "All right, Celia. I'll try to do better. Am I talking more now?"

Celia (laughing): "That *IS* better, Darren. At least you're asking me something now."

To Celia, talking is an important part of togetherness. To Darren, sharing the same activity may be enough. In this example, Celia tells Darren her specific needs. Darren, in turn, responds to those needs by talking more and asking her a question. By behaving uncritically, both can more easily see the positive side of their natural differences and learn to appreciate one another and develop a deeper, more mutually satisfying relationship.

Excited on the inside

Because Cautious Thinkers are, by nature, difficult for others to read, it's helpful if they say what is truly on their minds. Typically, they may throw in a quiet suggestion that can become overridden by more boisterous dates or small groups who may literally not hear the Cautious Thinker's comments. Since this type seldom discloses their real feelings and thoughts—except to a trusted, long-term friend or date, they sometimes hesitate to protest what the group decides. Sometimes they may think, "My opinion probably won't change the outcome anyway," so they hesitate to share their views. Then they may remain quiet because they resent their own compliance. Mustering up enough assertiveness to make sure their opinion is heard can contribute to a more successful group experience.

As in other aspects of their lives, they firmly control their emotions, so once romance has been offered and accepted, it's doubly important that they express their feelings. Otherwise, the date may wonder if the Cautious Thinker still feels and thinks the same way about him. "Audrey, remember what we talked about last night? You seem so quiet, I'm just wondering if something's wrong."

"No, really, everything is fine," Audrey assures him.

"Well, you don't seem very excited about being in love."

"Of course I am," Audrey elaborates. "I just don't show my excitement as much as you do. But I'm actually excited on the inside, even if it's not apparent to you."

Like Audrey, Cautious Thinkers tend to get inwardly enthusiastic. This can be frustrating for more talkative types, but is more easily tolerated when the feeling of excitement (or anger, happiness, warmth, etc.) is verbally communicated. Picture Clint Eastwood or John Wayne in their typical movie roles. When they're interested in *getting the girl*, they usually pursue her in a less verbal, more emotionally controlled, and painstaking way. They leave a lot to the woman's imagination. "Does he or doesn't he care for me?"

Their feelings for the loved one are usually shown by what they do for the heroine, not by what they say or promise. They seem to live by the axiom: "Talk is cheap. Let's see what you do." Even when they appear emotionally hooked, they sometimes don't realize it until late into the film. Emotions, after all, are an area of less familiarity than things for Cautious Thinkers. And getting their emotions right can prove to be a greater task than they at first envisioned.

Once committed, though, Cautious Thinkers often become intensely involved in the relationship. They may even reach the point of overprotection of the time, the activities, or even the relationships of their mate with others.

Birds of a feather . . . or opposites attract?

So which type is best suited for which? Which axiom applies: Birds of a feather or opposites attract? Actually, any type can be well suited to another if both make an effort to learn what is important to the other—and if they acknowledge their own, as well as the loved one's, natural strengths and weaknesses. If the two appreciate and accept each other, despite their respective natural limitations, they'll be on the

Remember . . .

CAUTIOUS THINKER
DATING/ROMANCE CHARACTERISTICS

- Seek acknowledgment that they are right
- Want to share quality time
- Usually prefer to date only one person at a time
- Think about the possibilities for the relationship before falling for someone
- Look objectively at the loved one
- Proceed in a cautious, rational manner
- Look at probabilities and variables to determine if a relationship will last

CAUTIOUS THINKERS' PREFERRED
DATING BEHAVIORS

- Dislike unexpected situations and surprises
- May want close to exclusivity in their relationship, doing most social things as a twosome
- Prefer a date with substance and depth
- Want some freedom in their relationship for *alone* time
- Observe and mentally collect 'date data' to help them make decisions

Action Plan

HOW CAUTIOUS THINKERS CAN LEARN TO ADAPT IN DATING SITUATIONS

- Accept the other behavioral types for themselves, without expecting them to become more like them
- Reveal more about themselves and their feelings
- Give and receive sincere compliments
- Participate more, go off by themselves less
- Behave less critically and more light-heartedly

HOW YOU CAN HELP CAUTIOUS THINKERS MODIFY THEIR BEHAVIOR

- Gently remind them that human errors can be reduced, not eliminated
- Help them tap their sense of humor by pointing out funny observations
- Encourage them to let their guard down occasionally
- Support them in developing more direct behaviors
- Help them verbalize their feelings
- Calmly point out that life consists of gray areas . . . not just black or white ones
- Demonstrate by your actions that you care about them—right or wrong

way to a successful love relationship founded on mutual understanding and respect. The important thing to remember is that each behavioral type has needs which they strive to fill. But when both people in a romantic relationship put themselves in the other's shoes, then the potential for a more productive, mutually beneficial match increases significantly.

Dominant Director plus Dominant Director

Two Dominant Directors can try to dominate each other and become stubborn, impatient, and tough. "I'm the boss." "No, I'm the boss." At worst, this basic tug of war over the need to be the top dog can ruin a budding relationship before it ever really begins. A sense of humor, verbal expressions of each other's admiration, and win-win usage of those natural negotiating skills in an accepting, understanding atmosphere can go a long way toward cultivating a romance between a Dominant Director duo. Like Stan and Melody, they can learn to listen to each other and come up with mutually acceptable solutions that allow them both to win.

Dominant Director and Steady Relater

Negatively, a Dominant Director and a Steady Relater can also result in a persecutor/victim type of unfortunate relationship in which each person becomes trapped in a nightmare of pace and priority differences. More positively, they can share a complementary pairing in which each one accepts and appreciates the different strengths which the partner possesses. This blend of types also gets a possible vote as the match made closest to heaven if adaptability exists. That is, the Dominant Director needs to compassionately listen to and draw out the Steady Relater and learn more about the Steady Relater's feelings and opinions. Similarly, the Steady Relater has to understand the Dominant Director's need to get up off the couch and do things in the process. They can also benefit by learning to accept, versus stand up to, the Dominant Director's take charge positions.

Dominant Director plus Interacting Socializer

A Dominant Director/Interacting Socializer match may result in an activity-filled, risk-taking, dynamic duet. Or it can be a combustible battle of the century pitting will against ego. In its workable form, this combination can become a fast-paced balance between business and pleasure, with each type enhanced by the other. For this to happen, the Interacting Socializer has to learn to accept the other's discomfort with discussing feelings at the expense of actual facts. The Dominant Director can learn to recognize the Interacting Socializer's natural priority for personal and shared feelings which may otherwise cause them to filter out problems and complexities. Dominant Directors can use their negotiation and delegation resources. Interacting Socializers can use their seemingly unending supply of enthusiastic ideas and positive energy to help both of them find common solutions to challenges that come along. Otherwise, each type may engage in a frenzied competition for *what I want* that leads in two different or opposing directions.

Dominant Director and Cautious Thinker

When Dominant Director meets Cautious Thinker, their mutual task orientations and inclinations for not verbalizing feelings can bond them. But their conflicting paces, quantity versus quality preferences and Direct/Controlling versus Indirect/Controlling lifestyles, can clash like an atomic blast. The fast-moving Dominant Directors can slow down their pace and learn to tolerate the Cautious Thinker's natural need for caution. On the other hand, Cautious Thinkers can recognize that Dominant Directors may become impatient and blunt, at times, and learn to verbalize their discomfort with those traits. Both want different types of control, but Dominant Directors go about getting it directly, while Cautious Thinkers do it indirectly. A move toward redefining their shared expectations and concerns assures them their desired results will be achieved. It can be the foundation for a powerful and unique type of bonding relationship between these two self-determined types.

Interacting Socializer plus Interacting Socializer

When two Interacting Socializers get together, they have been known to try making life a perpetual party. Or they may engage in a bitter rivalry, each trying to outdo the other. They may even attempt to foist work onto each other. Since both prefer to deal in the realm of their feelings and the big picture, who will deal with the nitty-gritty details? The one who feels more comfortable with them may write tasks down for the other and help the loved one to get more organized. "Where there's a will, there's a way."

Whatever the creative solution, chances are these two will want to entertain each other and have fun along the way, not to mention talk about virtually everything that pops into their minds. However, for this relationship to flourish, they have to first explore together and then agree about *TCB*—how they'll take care of the business that must be achieved for them to keep feeling good about each other.

Interacting Socializer plus Steady Relater

A Steady Relater/Interacting Socializer duo often provides a warm, emotive, mutually supportive combination. But it has also been reported to end with the Steady Relater's resenting the partner's search for center stage, universal approval, and flurries of activity—often in the absence of the Steady Relater. In this scenario of conflict in natural chemistry, the Interacting Socializer may feel squelched by too much routine, steadiness, and boredom with staying put. Their relationship could result in a more flexible set of optional routines for fun and games (including wild card options), thereby better meeting the needs of both.

The Interacting Socializer has to realize that the Steady Relater is more private, safety-seeking, and organized. Those traits could have a stabilizing effect on the Interacting Socializer if the Interacting Socializer agrees to meet the Steady Relater halfway. Similarly, the Steady Relater has to learn to accept the Interacting Socializer's natural spontaneity, persuasiveness, and sociability. While both enjoy people—including their own companionship—the issues to resolve primarily focus on who, how often, when, and for what mutually derived purpose?

Interacting Socializer plus Cautious Thinker

An Interacting Socializer and a Cautious Thinker are another set of intriguing individualists with quite different tendencies. This can result in a complementary relationship where each partner makes up and compensates for the less developed strengths of the other (which can certainly simplify matters, since they have such obviously different preferences). However, it can also intensify each other's stress levels with the suppression of their differing paces, priorities, and approaches. The pairing of these two results in two intuitive types combining in a potentially creative, innovative relationship.

The Interacting Socializer needs to understand the Cautious Thinker's private lifestyle and desire for a deeply private relationship, including their discomfort with having to socialize. The Cautious Thinker has to learn to accept the Interacting Socializer's need to be with people and their disinterest in dealing with messy details or complications. They must also understand the Socializer's desire for varied recreational activities—whether watching TV, going out to eat, calling on friends, or going to movies or sporting events. By working out and appreciating their individual differences and providing each other the space and time for these to co-exist, they can become a productive combination—with each compensating for what the other naturally lacks.

When Steady Relater meets Steady Relater

With another Steady Relater, this relationship tends to become a paragon of consideration and stability. However, sometimes it also decays into stagnancy and over-predictability, with neither party taking any risks or doing much out of the ordinary. As with any match of the same types, they might share a lot in common, but each may also tend to view life in such a similar way that they have to stretch beyond themselves to attain growth and balance. Since both parties generally are pleasant and tolerant, problematical issues may remain hidden, with neither one wanting to initiate a possible confrontation.

But someone ultimately has to take charge of the harsher realities and assume more control. Given Steady Relaters' natural propensity for perseverance, they, more than the other types, may stick it out, hoping they can make it work. The real challenge for this couple involves how they will successfully manage adverse situations—with significant differences in their personal values systems being the most threatening of all to the stability of their relationship.

Steady Relater plus Cautious Thinker

A Steady Relater and a Cautious Thinker share a slower pace, but Steady Relaters are somewhat more people- and feeling-oriented than Cautious Thinkers. Steady Relaters support others; the Cautious Thinkers subtly control people and situations. Steady Relaters prefer a more casual, relaxed atmosphere of involvement with people; Cautious Thinkers prefer a more formal one with the option of being left alone to do their own thing. Both strive for peace, calmness, and tranquility. Both typically take an organized, though indirect approach. If they can agree to discuss important, but uncomfortable, issues and feelings, they can encourage each other's further growth and development. Neither one is naturally assertive. The Cautious Thinker might find greater success initiating tasks, while the Steady Relater can perform the social activities, personal discussions, and follow-up implementation required.

Cautious Thinker plus Cautious Thinker

Two Cautious Thinkers have been known to harmonize beautifully; however, the two have also been reported to become so task-oriented and detached from common objectives that their relationship suffers dramatically. Again, a match of the same type can result in a wonderful sharing of similar thoughts and actions, but it may also stymie those areas where a bit of stretching is required—assertiveness, directness, socializing, and expression of feelings. If two Cautious Thinkers choose each other, they'll typically want to make the relationship right and may proceed with extreme caution. They share perfectionism, thoroughness, creativeness, and an intellectual approach to life. Their relationship could be organized and workable for them. However, it could also become rigid, with both being convinced that their priority or their way is the only way to go—leading to a cataclysmic, or even irreversible, battle of unspoken differences.

How to make any and all combinations work

Each combination of types can make or break their own relationship according to how accepting and adaptable they're willing to be in their dealings with each other's natural needs, fears, strengths, and limitations. The crucial difference in a relationship is in tolerating and shrugging off each other's irritating traits and recognizing when it is appropriate to modify one's own natural behavior. Then, increasingly more acceptable solutions can be reached which result in the mutual satisfaction of their individual needs. The issue here is not so much compatibility as it is commitment. Commitment calls for mutual respect and trust of another person, despite individual differences and weaknesses. People who stay together communicate and reciprocate with each other in the context of shared commitment. They affirm strengths and appreciate the partner's individual uniqueness as they adapt their style to meet the other person's needs. Understanding and applying these *People Smart* principles can make the difference for the individuals they and you want to love.

Afterword

After reading *People Smart,* we hope that you will apply what you've learned to enrich all aspects of your life from your workplace to the social arena, including family experiences and romantic encounters.

You now have the tools to create more positive relationships for yourself and others.

Mutual respect and commitment are the keys to understanding and getting along with people. Of course, degrees of respect and commitment vary from relationship to relationship. You probably don't feel as committed to your grocer or butcher as you do to your spouse, significant other, or best friend. But using what you now know about *People Smart* concepts, you can learn to accept and even appreciate the differences in others. Remember, people's strengths can be carried to the extreme at times. You can actually encourage them to act in more positive ways by consulting the appropriate charts and graphics in Chapters 5-10. Identify the person's behavioral style by using the inventory in Chapter 2, identify the environment, then use the visuals to help you enhance your relationship with that person.

Additional Learning Materials

Alessandra On . . . The Platinum Rule

How to get what you want . . . by giving others what they want. This highly entertaining program includes "live" footage from Dr. Alessandra's dynamic keynote speech, in addition to studio footage. He reveals his innovative techniques for interactingwith others more successfully by getting on their wavelength. Learn how to understand each style, easily identify one from another and specific techniques to successfullyrelate to all four styles. The program includes a 55-minute video, a 64-page workbook and two audio tapes. It's perfect for a training workshop or for individual use. **Order #2105—($89.00; (1) Video, 64-page Workbook)**

The NEW Relationship Strategies Audio Tape Set

The single trait that is most often shared by outstanding successful people is the ability to build rapport quickly and easily. In this highly entertaining program Tony reveals his innovative techniques for interacting with others more successfully. Behavioral styles and behavioral adaptability are the central concepts of Relationship Straategies. Topics covered include: communicating with others; identifying different behavioral styles; and relating effectively with Directors, Socializers, Relaters and Thinkers. A must for supervisors, managers and sales representatives. **Order #2003—($59.95; 6 Cassettes and Reminder Card)**

The Platinum Rule Workbook Set

Would you like to substantially increase your compatibility with other people? This workbook assembles a number of simple tools that can be easily applied to improve both business and interpersonal relationships. It offers guidelines for understanding and adjusting to the differences in people. Topics covered include: behavioral characteristics, how to identify the four styles, verbal-vocal-visual clues, relationship stress and behavioral flexbility. A laminated, pocket-sized summary card is included. **Order #1010—($24.95; 64-page Workbook, 45 minute Audio Tape, and Reminder Card)**

To oder call Alessandra & Associates • (800) 222-4383
or write to P.O. Box 2767, La Jolla, CA 92038
www.alessandra.com

Training Resources

Life Associates

In the late 1960's, Dr. Michael O'Connor founded Life Associates. Its services emphasize both public and in-company train-the-trainer and management consultancy projects to further increase both personal and organizational performance and productivity.

LIFE's training resources consist of more than 100 off-the-shelf pre-packaged training workshops, seminars and related materials. It also provides custom-designed provgrams and their unique application in an organization's own setting.

LIFE's consulting resources involve high level personal consulting services, focusing especially on CEO/COO and key management staff, and application of PEOPLE SMART concepts to further enhance business success. It is a pioneer in the field of computer-based personnel and organizational assessment, management, and targeted development systems. For futher information about LIFE's services contact: Life Associates, (941) 947-1111.

Dr. Tony Alessandra

A marketing strategist and behavioral scientist, Dr. Tony Alessandra is a leading authority on high-leverage strategies for increasing customer loyalty. Recognized by Meetings & Conventions Magazine as "one of America's most electrifying speakers," Tony combines an endearing charisma and a unique command of his craft that consistently captivates his audiences.

Tony's credentials include 30 years of exceptional business success plus an extensive academic background. He worked his way through college as a salesman, earning his B.B.A., M.B.A., and Ph.D., in Marketing.

In addition to profitably running his own training and consulting firm, Tony is Chairman of Mentor University, an Internet company providing online courses, coaching, and a virtual community for help sales and marketing professionals.

As a professional speaker, Tony Alessandra holds the CPAE (Professional Speakers Hall of Fame Award) and CSP (Certified Speaking Professional) accreditations from the National Speakers Association. He has delivered more than 2,000 presentations since 1976 to corporate groups and associations worldwide, consistently earning rave reviews as the top rated speaker.

Dr. Alessandra has authored 13 books including Charisma, The Platinum Rule, Collaborative Selling, and Communicating at Work. He is featured in over 50 audio/video programs and films, including Relationship Strategies, The Dynamics of Effective Listening; and Non-Manipulative Selling. Tony also hosts the TPN/Primestar network talk show, Strictly Business.

Tony's polished style, powerful message and proven ability as a consummate business professional assure a top-notch program every time.

If you would like more information about Dr. Alessandra's books, audio tapesets and video programs, or about Dr. Alessandra as a keynote speaker, call his office at 1-800-222-4383 or visit his website at http://www.alessandra.com

Index

Give the Gift of "People Smart" to Your Friends and Colleagues!

ORDER FORM

YES, I want _____ copies of People Smart at $24.95 each, plus $3 shipping per book. Canadian orders must be accompanied by a postal money order in U.S. funds. Allow 15 days for delivery.

☐ Check or Money order enclosed.

Charge my ☐Visa ☐MasterCard ☐AmEx

Name_____

Organization_____

Address_____

City/State/Zip_____

Phone_____

Card # _____Exp. Date_____

Signature_____

Check your leading bookstore or call your credit card order to: (800) 222-4383 or (760) 603-8110

Holli@alessandra.com

Url: www.alessandra.com

Please make your check payable and return to:
Alessandra & Associates, Inc.
P. O. Box 2767
La Jolla, CA 92038

Printed in the United States
42580LVS00004B/112-129